WITTGENSTEIN AND SCIENTIFIC KNOWLEDGE

By the same author
STUDIES IN AMERICAN SOCIETY: I *(editor)*
STUDIES IN AMERICAN SOCIETY: II *(editor)*
KNOWLEDGE FROM WHAT?
ABANDONING METHOD

WITTGENSTEIN AND SCIENTIFIC KNOWLEDGE
A Sociological Perspective

DEREK L. PHILLIPS
Professor of Sociology
University of Amsterdam, The Netherlands

First edition 1977
Reprinted 1979

Published by
THE MACMILLAN PRESS LTD
London and Basingstoke
Associated companies in Delhi
Dublin Hong Kong Johannesburg Lagos
Melbourne New York Singapore Tokyo

ISBN 0 333 21314 9

Printed and bound in Great Britain by
Redwood Burn Limited
Trowbridge & Esher

954380

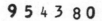

For my father and in memory of my mother

Contents

Preface

In the natural and social sciences alike, there exists a rather rigid separation between those thinkers concerned with the *practice* of knowledge and those concerned with questions about the *theory* of knowledge. This is in contrast to the situation for the early Greeks and, much later, for such seventeenth-century thinkers as Descartes and Locke, where there clearly existed an explicit concern with the connection between the theory and practice of knowledge. Just as clearly, the twentieth century has witnessed an obvious separation between the interests and practices of scientists and philosophers, and consequently between 'science' and 'epistemology'.

This distinction between the theory and practice of knowledge is heightened at present by the gulfs dividing different intellectual disciplines. Such a separation has been especially pronounced in sociology, where an emphasis on imitating certain methodological practices of the natural sciences seems to have reproduced the latter's indifference to what are regarded as 'philosophical' problems. It is perhaps partially because of their collective insecurity about the 'genuine' scientific status of their discipline that sociologists have reacted with either indifference or antagonism to questions about the status of their knowledge.

There is nonetheless one branch of sociology where problems of knowing and knowledge have been an explicit focus of attention: the sociology of knowledge. Here, as well as in the sociology of science which forms one of its subparts, there has been some interest in certain aspects of knowledge, including epistemological questions. As these fields have developed in recent years, however, their practitioners have tended to ignore epistemological questions in favour of questions concerning such matters as the origin of scientific ideas, their communication to other scientists, scientific productivity, the reward systems in science, and related matters. Indeed the direction of these fields is, I believe, very much at odds with many of the earlier formulations of the sociology of knowledge and science.

Many sociologists of knowledge and science have been concerned with the origin of scientific ideas, and with the relation of these 'discoveries' to social and cultural factors and contexts. Robert K. Merton, for example, systematically reviews a number of questions pertaining to the social origins of knowledge, while generally omitting questions about the validity or justification of the knowledge-claims involved.[1] This distinction between the genesis of scientific ideas and their evaluation is ignored by most sociologists. Indeed, the division of labour between philosophy and sociology, authorised by sociologists, is maintained in the practice of sociology. This of course leaves epistemological matters to the philosopher and (more recently) to the historian of science.

By ignoring epistemological issues, sociologists have put themselves in the position of having very little to say about two problems of concern to many contemporary thinkers: first, the problem of the theoretical and empirical foundations upon which *authority* rests in Western society and, more specifically, in contemporary science; and second, and closely related, the problem of *relativism*.

The former problem has been dealt with at length by John Schaar, who argues that legitimate authority is declining in the modern state, and that 'the crisis of legitimacy is a function of some of the basic, defining orientations of modernity itself: specifically, rationality, the cult of efficiency and power, ethical relativism, and equalitarianism'.[2] Sociologists, I believe, by generally neglecting questions regarding their status as knowers and the status of their knowledge, have effectively cut themselves off from a concern with this issue of legitimate authority. Questions about what it is to 'know' something, and about who is to establish the criteria or standards for showing that one does know or that one group knows better than another, are simply ignored by most sociologists. If one shares with Schaar, as I do, the belief that the modern condition is characterised by the shattering of authority, then one longs for 'an account of reality, an explanation of why some acts are preferable to others, and a vision of a worthwhile future towards which men can aspire'.[3] Sociologists have had very little to say about such matters.

An awareness of the absence of moral absolutes and certainties is of course widespread in contemporary society. In ethics, the notions of 'right' and 'wrong' have come to be recognised as culturally dependent, as *relative* to particular societies and groups. But now there is a growing conviction that *science*—which has been viewed by many, including sociologists, as the source of absolutes and certainty—is a fully human enterprise, where truth is not something lying 'out there' but, rather, a construction of scientific communities. This can be seen, for example, in recent controversies in the philosophy and history of science, involving among others Popper, Kuhn, Feyerabend, Lakatos and Toulmin, controversies which will be considered at length in the following chapters. Despite the enormous attention given these problems today, they are almost totally ignored in the sociological literature. This is somewhat surprising in that Mannheim and other sociologists of knowledge were concerned with similar issues.

Both of the problems mentioned above—authority and relativism—are clearly major problems of our time. On the one hand, by accepting that each separate culture or group should decide by its own standards what properly counts as 'scientific understanding' or 'knowledge' (or 'equality' or 'justice') we opt for relativism. On the other hand, by accepting the existence of universal, abstract definitions of 'knowledge', 'equality' and the like from outside, we land ourselves in absolutism. The question is whether we must choose between these, or whether there exists a middle way which allows us to steer a course between the relativist and absolutist extremes. Further, there is the question of who the 'we' are that are involved in such a choice.

In addition to the problems of relativism and authority, we have a specific problem in contemporary sociology: what Gouldner has referred to as a 'crisis' within our discipline.[4] As Wittgenstein would say, we do not know our way about. To understand and untangle our problems we need another platform, another vantage point from which to view the activities of science and, more particularly, sociology. In my view, philosophy, and specifically the ideas of Ludwig Wittgenstein, represent the alternative platform from which we can get a different slant on our activities and concerns.

This book has two central goals. First of all, I want to bring the work of Ludwig Wittgenstein to the attention of sociologists and other students of social life. Especially in the United States, Wittgenstein and his writings are generally unknown among social scientists. In those cases where social scientific inquiry is influenced by his work, there is little more than passing reference to Wittgenstein's ideas. I am thinking here of the interesting work by some ethnomethodologists (such as Cicourel), by sociologists such as Alan Blum and Peter McHugh, and by Tracy Strong among the political scientists. A notable exception is the very excellent book *Wittgenstein and Justice* by the political scientist Hannah Pitkin—a book concerned mainly with political theory, and with considerably different objectives from the present volume.[5]

Even in England, where Peter Winch's *The Idea of a Social Science*[6] has created widespread controversy and where a growing number of mostly younger social scientists are paying more explicit attention to Wittgenstein's work, there is seldom an attempt to confront fully the implications for scientific inquiry and practice. And in none of these books, including Winch's and Pitkin's which link Wittgenstein with sociology and social science, is there anything more than a cursory reference to the life of this complex and fascinating man. It is my belief that we need to consider both Wittgenstein's work and Wittgenstein the man to benefit fully from his wisdom and ideas.

My second goal is to utilise a perspective informed by Wittgenstein's work in order to confront the problems of relativism and authority which are today a matter of debate and controversy among philosophers and historians of science and, to a far lesser extent, among some sociologists. I say that my perspective is 'informed' by Wittgenstein rather than claim that I am conducting a Wittgensteinian analysis, that I hold a Wittgensteinian viewpoint, or something of the like. That is, I do not claim to be fully faithful to a Wittgensteinian 'world-view' (whatever that might mean), nor do I claim to have consistently incorporated Wittgenstein's ideas into all of the work presented here. Rather, I *use* certain notions, ideas, viewpoints, and so on, which are derived from Wittgenstein's writings. And I use them specifically in order to advance certain theses and ideas which may shed light on current debates surrounding scientific practice and knowledge, debates which, I believe, are concerned essentially with issues of relativism and authority. These debates involve Kuhn, Popper, Lakatos, Toulmin, Polanyi and Feyerabend. Although the debates raise important questions about the very foundations of scientific knowledge, they are, as I observed earlier, generally ignored or unrecognised by most sociologists. This is ironic in that men like Kuhn are paradoxically more 'sociological' than are many persons who claim membership in the sociological community. My second goal, then, is to bring these debates to the attention of practising social scientists, and to do so from a perspective that is informed by the work of Ludwig Wittgenstein.

I must acknowledge, however, that Wittgenstein himself gave far less attention to issues surrounding scientific knowledge and understanding than I do in this volume. Science seemed to occupy a privileged position for Wittgenstein, so that scientific practice was largely exempted from the penetrating analyses which he gave to philosophy and mathematics. Perhaps that is not surprising, in that his work is the product of an era in which confidence in natural science was at a high point. In recent years, however, the adequacy of positivistic science has been called into question, particularly in regard to its epistemological status. It is now increasingly recognised that scientific knowledge is not the only mode of knowledge and that, furthermore, it is a *product* of scientific inquiry rather than something lying out there to be discovered. Given the enormous controversies in contemporary philosophy and history of science concerning the foundations and status of the natural sciences, it is ironic that most social scientists continue to imitate what they (mistakenly) consider the dominant practices and modes of inquiry in the natural sciences. I hope that the present volume will help to contribute to an awareness of the fully *social* nature of scientific practice and, most especially, of the crucial place of *language* in the natural and social sciences alike.

Although the central focus of this volume is on utilising the ideas of Ludwig Wittgenstein in order to shed light on the problems of relativism and authority in science, a number of different topics and issues are considered in the following pages. It is therefore useful to discuss briefly the general structure of the book.

I begin by examining Wittgenstein's life, a necessary prelude to confronting his ideas and their relevance for current controversies about science in later chapters. Then, in the second chapter, I turn directly to a short discussion of Wittgenstein's early work and to a much more lengthy consideration of his development and thought in the later stages of his life, where he dealt with issues and problems more directly relevant to the concerns of this volume. The third chapter introduces and discusses two images of science: the 'dominant image', associated with positivism; and the 'new image', represented by the work of Hanson, Feyerabend, Toulmin and, most especially, Thomas Kuhn. Certain similarities in the work of Kuhn and of two sociologists of knowledge—Karl Mannheim and C. Wright Mills— are considered, and it is argued that both Kuhn's work and the writings of these two sociologists have the consequence of leading directly to relativism. Chapters 4, 5 and 6 all deal, in somewhat different ways, with this general problem of relativism. In chapter 4, 'Relativism and Wittgenstein', I pursue the relativistic implications of the work of Kuhn, Mannheim and Mills somewhat further, and then show how Wittgenstein provides a middle ground between the relativist and absolutist extremes. I also consider the relativism issue in chapter 5, specifically as it concerns Kuhn's argument about the 'incommensurability' of paradigms. Here I develop Wittgenstein's ideas in such a way as to lead us away from the enormous difficulties ensuing from acceptance of the incommensurability thesis, and towards the formulation of a position less deterministic than the Kuhnian standpoint. In chapter 6, 'The social nature of mathematics', I show that mathematics, like science more generally, and in common with other human practices, is a fully social activity. Contrary to the views of some sociologists, there is no reason to exclude science and mathematics from sociological inquiry. In this chapter I draw heavily on Wittgenstein's philosophy of mathematics, which represents an attempt to find a middle way between Platonism and conventionalism. Also in this chapter I discuss the relevance of Peter Winch's work for questions about scientific practice.

Then, in the last three chapters, I move to a consideration of the general problem of 'authority' in science. In chapter 7, 'The demarcation problem in science', I deal with two questions that are a source of debate in contemporary science: first, what criteria distinguish science from non- or pseudo-science; and second, who should have the responsibility for establishing such criteria? Chapter 8 focuses on the relationship between the individual scientist and the scientific community to which he directs his truth- and knowledge-claims. Following Wittgenstein, a heavy emphasis is laid on the notions of 'possibilities' and persuasion, and the crucial place of language in scientific communication and in the process of persuasion is discussed at length. Finally, in chapter 9, I confront the issue as to what validates the view of science and scientific practice set forth in this volume and, further, the issue of whether the viewpoints presented here do not call into question *all* conceptions of truth and knowledge. Again the position of the individual scientist is considered, not as someone standing alone but as part of a tradition with a history and a collective set of practices. Especially important here is an understanding of the extent to which our ideas, including those of science, are rooted in how we choose to live our lives. The intimate relationship between an individual's life and his work will begin to emerge in the following pages where we turn to a consideration of 'Wittgenstein the man'.

Chapter 5 has appeared previously in *Theory and Society*, and chapter 6 was published in somewhat different form in the *Kölner Zeitschrift*. Permission to use these materials is gratefully acknowledged. For whatever merits this volume may possess, I am indebted to several persons for their useful comments and criticisms. Louis Boon's objections to some of my assertions have helped me to sharpen (and sometimes alter) my views. Nil Disco and I have argued through much of the manuscript, and I have learned much from our discussions. Tracy

Strong provided detailed and extremely useful comments on an earlier version of the manuscript. I have also benefited from the presence of Alvin Gouldner—alas, now back on the other side of the Atlantic—as my colleague and companion for three years here in Amsterdam. While it is customary to thank one's friends and colleagues for their help, I cheerfully hold them responsible for the book's flaws and errors as well. Finally I would like to thank J. H. H. Hasenack for his assistance to me personally and for labouring to make the Sociological Institute a place where one could do serious intellectual work.

Amsterdam   D.L.P.
1976

1 Wittgenstein the Man

Bach put at the head of his *Orgelbüchlein*, 'To the glory of the most high God, and that my neighbour may be benefited thereby'. I would have liked to be able to say this of my work.

LUDWIG WITTGENSTEIN[1]

This is not a book about Ludwig Wittgenstein, although he is a central figure throughout the volume. It is, rather, a book concerned with bringing certain controversies in the philosophy of science to the attention of social scientists and with using some of Wittgenstein's ideas to shed light upon these controversies. Nevertheless, it is instructive to turn our attention to Wittgenstein's life before we move on to consider his philosophical views and their relevance for the practice of sociology and science more generally. Not only can we better understand the thought of Ludwig Wittgenstein by examining the social and intellectual milieu in which it developed, but we can also see the intimate link between his life and his work.

As Alvin Gouldner has repeatedly emphasised, many of a man's intellectual and scientific concerns are prompted by the desire to know things that are personally important to him.[2] This was most certainly the case with Ludwig Wittgenstein. Throughout his life, he wrestled with the kinds of questions that have long been of deep concern not only to philosophers but also to many others who wish to unravel life's mysteries: the nature of the good, of truth, of knowledge, the meaning of life. Like others concerned with the good, Wittgenstein sought after certainty. Even in his time, moral certainty had begun to disappear. Whereas God had once vouched for designations of good and evil, He seemed to disappear with the Modern Age and the appearance of science and a new method of arriving at certainty: the so-called scientific method. But now science itself, as we shall see in later chapters, has been called into question. No longer do many of us believe that

1

science can provide the certainties which men and women everywhere seem to seek and require. To recognise this is not to be thrown into despair, but rather to realise fully the freedom to choose and the responsibility of choice. Without the freedom of choosing one's actions, there is no responsibility. Without human responsibility, there is no morality. This is as true in the practice of science as it is in the practice of moral philosophy. Wittgenstein's life serves as a clear example of one man's willingness to take responsibility for his actions and for the quality and nature of his work. It also reflects the moral character of philosophical inquiry and of the practice of academic philosophy.

More importantly, many of the problems which Wittgenstein encountered in his life and work are the same problems faced by those who today live for, and all too frequently off, ideas. But far more than in Wittgenstein's time, the edifice of science is today being subjected to intense criticism. It is attacked from outside its ranks by those who have come to see the dark side of the scientific enterprise. And it is increasingly being called into question by its practitioners as well. Witness the heavy criticisms of sociology by Gouldner, Habermas and Cicourel,[3] and of the history and philosophy of science by Kuhn, Polanyi, Feyerabend and Toulmin.[4] These writers direct their arguments to the very practitioners at whom their criticisms are aimed. That is to say, they remain within the very scientific communities against whom their onslaughts are directed. Other critics, of course, are so disenchanted with the state of their craft that they opt out entirely. Still others continue the practice of science in the 'same old way', paying no attention to what they regard as essentially an irrelevant philosophers' debate, and focusing instead on building careers and making a good living. Many of them seem to be quite willing to ignore those criticisms that call into question the very foundation of science, so long as they themselves are handsomely rewarded for their scientific activities. For them, Wittgenstein's life will have little relevance for their own. Nor will they find the contents of this volume to be other than a source of annoyance, for they are willing to accept science as it is (or purports to be) and have no wish to be bothered by questions which might tend to undermine the privileged position of the scientific establishment. But for those men and women who are aware of, and perhaps preoccupied with, the deep controversies found today in all sciences and, most especially, with the ways in which these controversies touch upon their everyday lives as well as upon their scientific activities, an examination of Wittgenstein's life is illuminating.

My intention in reviewing, albeit briefly, Wittgenstein's life here is threefold. First, I want to point, as I noted earlier, to the complex relationship between his life and his intellectual work. Obviously I believe that this relationship is not peculiar to Ludwig Wittgenstein, but is an almost inevitable element in the lives of all men and women who are engaged in the practice of science and philosophy. Second, the moral concerns of Wittgenstein, i.e. how we *choose* to live our lives are, as I will try to show more fully in the last chapter, concerns which none of us can avoid. And finally, an examination of Wittgenstein's life will help highlight his conception of the specifically therapeutic nature of philosophy. Let us, then, turn to a consideration of Wittgenstein's life.

The life of Ludwig Wittgenstein had a dramatic quality that did not rest exclusively on his contributions to philosophy. For not only was he responsible for influencing the two schools of thought which have dominated twentieth-century Anglo-American philosophy (logical positivism or logical empiricism, and what is generally referred to as analytical philosophy), but he was a man of rare genius and personal integrity whose unconventional behaviour and magnetic appeal made an enormous impression on all who knew him. He was, as I will try to indicate, an extraordinary man, a man of many qualities.

Ludwig Josef Johann Wittgenstein was born in Vienna in 1889, the youngest of the eight children of Karl and Leopoldine Wittgenstein.[5] His father, a millionaire engineer and industrialist, was famous for having introduced innovations that transformed many failing factories into productive enterprises which came to dominate the steel industry of the Hapsburg Empire. But Karl Wittgenstein was more than a rich industrialist; he and his wife exercised a strong artistic and musical influence on their children. Karl Wittgenstein was a patron of the musical arts, and the Wittgenstein home was visited by such musicians as Gustav Mahler, Bruno Walter and Johannes Brahms. All of the Wittgenstein children were talented in one or another of the arts: music, painting, literature and the theatre. Aside from Ludwig, the best known of the Wittgenstein children was his brother Paul. Although he lost his right arm in the First World War, he became a well-known concert pianist. In fact he commissioned piano works for one hand from Ravel and Strauss, among others. Ludwig, too, was very musical. His friend von Wright states:

He played the clarinet, and for a time he wished to become a conductor. He had a rare talent for whistling. It was a great pleasure to hear him whistle through a whole concert, interrupting himself only to draw the listener's attention to some detail of the musical texture.[6]

Until he was fourteen, Wittgenstein was educated at home by private tutors. The next three years he attended the Linz *Realschule* in upper Austria. From there he proceeded to the Technische Hogeschule in Berlin–Charlottenburgh where he studied engineering and occupied himself extensively with experiments in aerodynamics. Whereas in the United States and Britain engineering has always emphasised practical considerations, in Berlin (and in continental Europe in general) engineering required a thorough intellectual grasp of theoretical physics and mathematics. Furthermore, as part of his education, Wittgenstein read philosophy at school. In 1908 he left Austria for England, where he registered as a research student in the department of engineering at the University of Manchester. He continued as a student there until the autumn of 1911. During his time at Manchester, he was occupied with research in aeronautics as well as being interested in pure mathematics and the philosophy of mathematics. It became increasingly clear to him, however, that he was not really at home in the practical sciences.[7]

Apparently at this time Wittgenstein asked someone for advice as to what he should read concerning the foundation of mathematics. He was told of Bertand Russell's *Principles of Mathematics* which had appeared a few years earlier. Russell held that any statement could be broken into its atomic facts, and that each part would have a meaning or reference. Russell's goal was to build a formal logical system. Wittgenstein's enthusiasm and high regard for Russell's book led him to study the work of Gottlob Frege, a famous analytic philosopher. Reading Russell and Frege convinced him that he should give up his studies of engineering and enter philosophy.

He visited Frege in Germany and was advised to go to Cambridge to study with Russell. While it is often assumed that Russell and Frege introduced Wittgenstein to the problems that were to capture his attention in future years, a recent analysis suggests that Wittgenstein was already preoccupied with the philosophical problems that were to concern him, prior to encountering the logical positivism of Russell and Frege.[8] Be that as it may, Wittgenstein entered Cambridge in 1912 and remained there through part of 1913. Hermine Wittgenstein visited Ludwig in Cambridge in 1912, and was invited to join her brother and Bertrand Russell for tea in Russell's room. She reports that Russell suddenly turned to her and said: 'We expect the next big step in philosophy to be taken by your brother.'[9] Russell's views were apparently shared by others at Cambridge. Russell describes once asking G. E. Moore, his Cambridge colleague, who his best pupil was. Moore replied: 'Wittgenstein.' When Russell asked him why, he answered, 'Because, Bertrand, he is my only pupil who always looks puzzled'. Wittgenstein, says Russell, *was* always puzzled.[10] Wittgenstein spent five terms at Cambridge, then visited Norway with a friend in the autumn of 1913. After returning briefly to England, he returned alone to Norway to work on a book in total solitude. He built himself a log cabin on a rocky point of land jutting into a fiord. He lived there in isolation until the outbreak of the war in 1914.

Though exempt on medical grounds, Wittgenstein entered the Austrian army as a volunteer, eventually being taken prisoner by the Italians in 1918. He had received several medals for bravery and had been slightly wounded in an explosion. When captured, his rucksack contained the manuscript of what was eventually to be known as the *Tractatus Logico-Philosophicus*, the first of his two major works. During the nine months he spent in a prison camp in southern Italy, he corresponded with Russell and sent him the manuscript. Russell remarks that: 'It appeared that he had written a book in the trenches, and wished me to read it. He was the kind of man who would never have noticed such small matters as bursting shells when he was thinking about logic.'[11] Russell helped him find a publisher for the book and, after many rejections and delays, it was eventually published in 1922. Upon completion of the *Tractatus* in 1918–19, Wittgenstein felt that he had solved all philosophical problems. So he gave up philosophy.

A 'career' in philosophy was not important to Ludwig Wittgenstein. This is not to say, however, that he had no interest in philosophy in a deeper sense. While I doubt that Wittgenstein was acquainted with Thoreau's *Walden*, he would surely have agreed with the sentiments expressed in the following words:

> There are nowadays professors of philosophy, but not philosophers. Yet is admirable to profess because it was once admirable to live. To be a philosopher is not merely to have subtle thoughts, nor even to found a school, but so to love wisdom as to live according to its dictates, a life of simplicity, independence, magnamimity, and trust. It is to solve some of the problems of life, not only theoretically, but practically.[12]

Wittgenstein, as I noted, gave up philosophy. But in the deeper sense, expressed by Thoreau, he never ceased being a philosopher.

In this connection, it is useful to offer some preliminary remarks about the *Tractatus*. These remarks are made here rather than in the following chapter because they are, for the most part, irrelevant to my central concerns there. They are not, however, irrelevant to an understanding of Wittgenstein the man. In the *Tractatus*, Wittgenstein set out to present a comprehensive philosophical picture of the world. He did this using the tool of logic to elaborate his world picture. But it was not logic that mattered to him, but philosophy. And beyond what philosophy could *say*, there lies what he considered really important. In contrast to the positivists, who did find much to admire in the *Tractatus*, Wittgenstein held that we must be silent about all that really matters in human life. This is made clear in a letter to Ludwig Ficker, where Wittgenstein describes the *Tractatus* as follows:

> *The book's point is an ethical one.* I once meant to include in the preface a sentence which is not in fact there now, but which I will write out for you here, because it will perhaps be a key to the work for you. What I meant to write, then, was this: My work consists of two parts: the one presented here plus all that I have *not* written. And *it is precisely this second part that is the important one.* My book draws limits to the sphere of the ethical from the inside as it were, and I am convinced that this is the ONLY rigorous way of drawing those limits.[13]

For Wittgenstein, there were important things which, while they cannot be said, can be *shown*. If the form of language is laid bare in a proper conceptual notation—as Wittgenstein tried to do in the *Tractatus*—then the essence of the world will be open to full view. Things which are unutterable, which cannot be stated in propositions, are nonetheless manifest in meaningful propositions, that is, they show themselves. Further, there are things about which we cannot speak and which we must consign to silence. But this does not mean, Wittgenstein held, that they do not exist. Rather it is what is felt—the mystical—and this is not spoken in language. That which is really important cannot be said by natural science, but it can be shown by literature, religion, music, art and poetry. In giving up philosophy, then, Wittgenstein was attempting to put into practice the ethical portion of his philosophy as it was developed in the *Tractatus*. 'What is the use of studying philosophy,' Wittgenstein once asked, 'if all that it does for you is to enable you to talk with some plausibility about some abstruse questions of logic, etc., & it does not improve your thinking about the important questions of everyday life?'[14]

Wittgenstein decided to become a schoolteacher, and spent the academic year 1919–20 at the Vienna Teachers' Training College. From 1920 to 1926 he taught in various villages in Lower Austria. Until very recently, little was known of this phase of his life, but Bartley's book, based on research and interviews in the villages where Wittgenstein had taught, provides rich insight into his life during this period.[15] Whereas other commentators have ignored the six years that Wittgenstein spent as an elementary schoolteacher, Bartley has recognised the importance of this experience for Wittgenstein's development and later work.

Wittgenstein's decision to become a schoolteacher, says Bartley, was consistent with the Wittgenstein family's tradition of social work and public service. His eldest sister, Mining, had opened a day school for poor Viennese boys, and his sister Margarethe Stonborough had been appointed Herbert Hoover's personal representative for the American Food Relief Commission in Austria. Ludwig himself had made a gift of 100,000 Kronen to aid poets and writers, a gift made, he explained, according to the custom of the family. Nevertheless, Wittgenstein's decision to become a country schoolmaster was at first incomprehensible to his family.[16] His becoming a schoolteacher was apparently associated with his general sympathy for the school reform movement that was then beginning in Austria. This movement was a reaction to the highly structured, generally authoritarian and regimented systems of instruction then existing in Austria. The intention of the school reform movement, with their 'working schools', was to encourage active participation by students in their lessons, thus bringing about a greater degree of independence and original thinking on the part of students.

Especially in the small villages of Austria, these new teaching methods were viewed as a programme for encouraging revolution and dissent; the new modes of instruction were highly threatening to the villagers' way of life. Wittgenstein's first teaching position was in Trattenbach, a small, isolated village with some 800 inhabitants. It seems likely that Wittgenstein entered into his new job with a kind of naive romanticism based partly on his reading of Tolstoy's *A Confession*, a book for which he had great enthusiasm. Tolstoy had established and taught in peasant schools, and reported great success with his endeavours. Whatever Wittgenstein's expectations, he was soon disappointed. While many of the children adored Wittgenstein and responded positively to his interest and his intensity for ideas, the adults in the village reacted negatively to his ruthless and impassioned honesty. He was able to show affection and tenderness to the three dozen children whom he taught, but had difficulty in getting along with their parents and other adults in Trattenbach. Part of this was probably due to his general inability to relax when outside the circle of his family and a few close friends. In addition, however, there were the enormous differences in the values of Wittgenstein and most of the village's residents. They aspired to respectability, order, and escaping the poverty in which so many of them lived. Wittgenstein, on the other hand, showed a contempt for monetary things, for standards of proper dress, and the like. Furthermore, the willingness of many of the children to remain at school with Wittgenstein long after normal school hours, rather than to return home to their parents and to certain chores which they were expected to perform, undoubtedly served as an additional source of bewilderment and resentment for many parents.

As mentioned above, the school reform movement was intended to encourage self-activity as an alternative to the usual force-feeding and rote memorisation that were customary in Austrian schools. Part of the new way of teaching involved helping children to discover the rules of grammar and spelling for themselves. Towards that end, Wittgenstein asked his students to compile word lists containing the words they had used in their own essays. At the same time, Wittgenstein compiled a corrected master list of all the different words used by the children in their essays. This became the children's classroom 'dictionary', a dictionary containing the words the children had chosen for inclusion in their essays. Only after the children had written essays, in which there was no requirement that they pay any particular attention to correct grammar or spelling, did Wittgenstein turn their attention to the rules of grammar and usage. He believed that the children should learn the principles first by doing what was interesting for them. One result of the children's self-activity in compiling their word lists, and an eventual dictionary, was their gaining an awareness of the ambiguities of their own usage of the language. Wittgenstein apparently was highly successful in this mode of teaching, and had similar success in teaching other subjects.[17]

During the years that Wittgenstein taught at Trattenbach, and later at Puchberg am Schneeberg and at Otterthal, he continued to work to awaken the minds of his young charges. And at all three places he encountered resistance and resentment from their parents and other adults in the villages. Finally, at Otterthal in 1926, Wittgenstein was accused of slapping a child and legal proceedings were launched against him. This was apparently the opportunity that some had

waited for as an 'excuse' for getting rid of Wittgenstein, in that cor-
poral punishment was a rather common practice in those schools.
Bartley comments that:

> According to the villagers, a genuine 'conspiracy' against Wittgen-
> stein had formed by this time. The leader, or at any rate, the chief
> agitator, was a man named Piribauer, who is said to have spent
> months 'waiting in ambush' for an opportunity to 'get Wittgenstein
> into trouble'. His opportunity came at last when Wittgenstein
> slapped on the cheeks a child whose foster mother dwelt in Piri-
> bauer's house.[18]

In any case, Wittgenstein resigned on the spot. Although he was
later acquitted, he never taught school again.

This recent account of Bartley's concerning the years between Wittgenstein's two stays at Cambridge is interesting not only for what it tells
us about Wittgenstein's life during that time. It also suggests that he
must have learned a great deal from these children, both with regard to
teaching and, most especially, with regard to his later philosophy.
And, as Bartley suggests, Wittgenstein's exposure to writers concerned
with child psychology and education undoubtedly influenced his subsequent work in philosophy.[19] Especially influential here were the
Gestalt psychologists and the Viennese psychologist Karl Bühler. We
will see the full effects of these influences in the following chapter
where the early and later Wittgenstein are compared.

Although Wittgenstein had enjoyed some aspects of his life as an
elementary schoolteacher, and is remembered today, Bartley found,
as a 'great' teacher by many of his former pupils, this was a generally
unhappy period for him. His letters to Engelmann reveal that he
several times contemplated suicide. 'I had the task,' he wrote, 'did not
do it, and now the failure is wrecking my life. . . . My life has really
become meaningless and so it consists of futile episodes.'[20]

I have already mentioned Wittgenstein's great respect and enthusiasm
for Tolstoy's *A Confession*. Reading this book one can see why he should
have been so drawn to it, for some of the questions which apparently
tormented him also bedevilled the great Russian novelist. 'What will
come of what I am doing today or shall do to-morrow?' asked Tolstoy.
'What will come of my whole life? Why should I live, why wish for
anything, or do anything?'[21] Tolstoy expresses his condition in words
very much like those later used by Wittgenstein in writing to his
friends: 'I felt that what I had been standing on had collapsed and
that I had nothing left under my feet. What I had lived on no longer

existed, and there was nothing left.'[22] And, again like Wittgenstein, Tolstoy's thoughts often turned to suicide:

> It had come to this, that I, a healthy, fortunate man, felt I could no longer live: some irresistible power impelled me to rid myself one way or other of life. I cannot say I *wished* to kill myself. The power which drew me away from life was stronger, fuller, and more widespread than a mere wish. It was a force similar to the farmer striving to live, only in a contrary direction. All my strength drew me away from life. The thought of self-destruction now came to me as naturally as thoughts of how to improve my life had come formerly.[23]

Wittgenstein must have noted the great similarities in the feelings expressed by Tolstoy and his own psychological state during the years as a teacher of small children in Austria.

After resigning his position as a schoolteacher, Wittgenstein took a job as a gardener's assistant with some monks at Hütteldorf, near Vienna. Bartley found that those who remember Wittgenstein there report that he was 'a very good and highly industrious gardener—and a left-winger!'[24] During that time Wittgenstein considered entering a monastery, but never did so. In the autumn of 1926, Wittgenstein accepted an invitation from his sister Margarethe Stonborough to design her a house in Vienna. At the beginning of this venture he collaborated with a friend, the architect Paul Engelmann. Before long, however, he took responsibility for the job himself. Engelmann, Wittgenstein's sister reports, 'had to give way to the much stronger personality, and the house was then built down to the smallest detail according to Ludwig's plans and under his supervision'.[25] During this same period, Wittgenstein did a sculpture of the head of a young woman in the studio of his friend, the sculptor Drobil, whom he had met in prison camp. As with the house he had designed for his sister, it was a work of perfection and elegance.

Despite having given up philosophy, Wittgenstein did not sever all ties with philosophy during his years as a schoolmaster, architect and gardener. In 1923 Frank Ramsey, a young man from Cambridge who had assisted in the translation of the *Tractatus*, visited Wittgenstein in Puchberg. Ramsey tried to persuade him to return to Cambridge, and repeated his visit the following year. Wittgenstein did then visit his English friends in Cambridge during the summer of 1925. At the same time, Moritz Schlick was writing to him, trying to arrange a meeting between Wittgenstein and the members of the 'Vienna Circle', a group of philosophers, mathematicians and physical scientists at the

University of Vienna. These men held seminars to discuss the *Tractatus* and its wider implications for their work and their own fields of endeavour. Although reluctant to do so, Wittgenstein finally agreed to meet with some of the members of the Vienna Circle in order to explain and discuss some points that puzzled them. It quickly became apparent, however, that Wittgenstein did not generally share the intellectual positions of the members of the Vienna Circle.[26] While these men viewed the *Tractatus* as supporting the logical positivism which they were developing, Wittgenstein came to dissociate himself from their ideas.

Early in 1929 Wittgenstein returned to Cambridge. He said that he had returned to philosophy because he felt that he could do creative work again. At first he was registered as a research student, a rather unusual position for someone who was widely regarded as the foremost living expert on his subject. Because of his renown and past accomplishments, it was soon decided that he could count his pre-war residence at Cambridge as credit towards his PhD, and could present the *Tractatus* as his dissertation. G. E. Moore, along with Russell the foremost Cambridge philosopher at that time, is reputed to have included in his examiner's report the following statement: 'It is my personal opinion that Mr. Wittgenstein's thesis is a work of genius; but, be that as it may, it is certainly well up to the standards required for the Cambridge degree of Doctor of Philosophy.'[27] Wittgenstein received his degree in 1929, and the following year was made a Fellow of Trinity College, Cambridge.

From the time he returned to Cambridge, Wittgenstein began to record his thoughts on philosophy in a series of notebooks in which he always wrote. While he wrote an enormous amount in the years that followed, the only philosophical writing that Wittgenstein himself published after the *Tractatus* was a paper, 'Some Remarks on Logical Form', published in 1929. As we will see, however, much of his later writing was published after his death. I will draw heavily on those writings in subsequent chapters.

Wittgenstein became a British citizen and, with several interruptions, lived the rest of his life in England. He left Cambridge in 1935 to spend a year in his hut in Norway, where he began to write what was to be his famous posthumous work, the *Philosophical Investigations*. Wittgenstein returned to Cambridge in 1937 from his trip to Norway and, two years later, succeeded G. E. Moore in the Chair of Philosophy. Before he could assume his chair, the Second World War broke out. Again he left Cambridge, this time to serve as a porter at Guy's Hospital in London. Later he worked in a medical laboratory in Newcastle, where he devised some useful technical innovations.

After the war, Wittgenstein assumed his chair at Cambridge, but remained only until the spring of 1947. He was away on leave in the autumn of that year, and from the end of the year ceased to be a professor. As I will indicate shortly, Wittgenstein had no real desire to be an academic philosopher. So he gave it up entirely to devote the rest of his life to his research and writing. As he had done before, he went to live in seclusion; first, on a farm in the Irish countryside during the winter of 1948; and after this, to live in a hut beside the ocean on the Irish west coast. Life there became too strenuous for him, however, and he moved into a hotel in Dublin. During the following year, he completed the second part of the *Philosophical Investigations*.

In the summer of 1949 Wittgenstein went to the United States where he stayed with his friend and former student Norman Malcolm and his wife, returning to England in October. Shortly after that, he learned that he had cancer. After spending a few months in Vienna, he returned to England. He spent part of 1950 in the house of his friend, G. E. M. Anscombe, then went to Norway for five weeks in the autumn of 1950. He returned to Cambridge and stayed in the home of his physician, Dr Bevan, dying there on 29 April 1951, three days after his sixty-second birthday. Wittgenstein's final words were 'Tell them [his friends] I've had a wonderful life!'

The above is obviously only a 'bare bones' outline of Wittgenstein's life and it tells us little of Wittgenstein the man. Let me now try to add some flesh to the skeletal outline provided above. While I have hinted at his extraordinary character, it is necessary to look more closely to fully appreciate this gifted man—for his life and character are indispensable for assessing his intellectual contributions. Consider first his physical appearance as described by Norman Malcolm:

> His face was lean and brown, his profile was aquiline and strikingly beautiful, his head was covered with a curly mass of brown hair . . . His face was remarkably mobile and expressive when he talked. His eyes were deep and often fierce in their expression. His whole personality was commanding, even imperial. In contrast, his dress was as simple as possible. He always wore light grey flannel trousers, a flannel shirt open at the throat, a woollen lumber jacket or a leather jacket. Out of doors, in wet weather, he wore a tweed cap and a tan raincoat. He nearly always walked with a light cane. One could not imagine Wittgenstein in a suit, necktie, or hat. His clothes, except

the raincoat, were always extremely clean and his shoes polished. He was about five feet six inches in height and slender.[28]

Consistent with this extreme plainness of dress was the austerity of his living. After his father's death in 1912, Wittgenstein inherited a great fortune. When he returned from the First World War, he gave away all of his money. From that time onwards, he lived a life of great simplicity. His rooms contained no easy chair, no reading lamp, no pictures, few books. His only furniture was a camp bed, a card table, two or three chairs, and a metal safe in which he kept his manuscripts. Flowers were the only decorative note in his rooms. Influenced by Karl Kraus, whose Vienna newspaper *Die Fackel* (*The Torch*) was dedicated to making its readers 'morally aware of the essential distinction between the chamber pot and an urn'; by Adolf Loos, an architect, whose ideas about ornament and decorations he found congenial; and by Tolstoy, whose work he greatly admired, Wittgenstein demanded personal integrity along with a commitment to egalitarianism and a concern for his fellow human beings. In addition, he acquired from these men a distaste for meaningless decoration and superfluity.[29]

Not surprisingly, he rebelled against many of the artificialities of intellectual life as well. It was his belief that academic activities did not represent 'real' or 'useful' work. Clearly his involvement in teaching young children, in designing his sister's house, working as a gardener, as a porter and in a medical laboratory, all revealed his strong doubts about the usefulness of his own academic and intellectual work. According to Malcom, Wittgenstein believed that a normal human being could not be a university teacher and remain an honest and serious person. He strongly discouraged his students from taking up academic philosophy as a career. Wittgenstein repeatedly tried to persuade Malcolm to give up philosophy as a profession. Being unsuccessful in his attempts, he gave Malcolm enough money to live on for several months until Malcolm returned to the United States. Wittgenstein's feelings about academic philosophy and his kindness towards his students are both revealed in a leter he wrote when he learned that Malcolm had been awarded the PhD in philosophy:

Congratulations to your Ph.D.! And now: may you make good use of it! By that I mean: may you not cheat either yourself or your students. Because, unless I'm very much mistaken, *that's* what will be expected of you. And it will be *very* difficult not to do it, & perhaps impossible; & in this case: may you have the strength to *quit*. This ends today's sermon.[30]

Despite his doubts about the human usefulness of academic philosophy, Wittgenstein was considered a remarkable teacher. Off and on, from the beginning of 1930, he lectured at Cambridge. Not unexpectedly, his lectures were highly 'unacademic'. First of all, he held his lectures in his own room or in the room of a friend. Students in the class brought in chairs or sat on the floor. The class met twice weekly, from 5 to 7 p.m. Wittgenstein demanded promptness and became angry if someone came in late. Those attending his classes were not only students in the usual sense, but also people who were highly expert in philosophy and other fields. And many of those students who attended his lectures were later to become leading philosophers in the United States and Europe.

Characteristically, Wittgenstein was never satisfied with his teaching. Sitting on a plain wooden chair in the middle of the room, he carried on a visible struggle with his thoughts. He frequently told his students that he felt confused and said such things as: 'I'm a fool!' or 'You have a dreadful teacher.' Not only was he impatient with himself, but also with his students and friends. He was fiercely insistent that anyone who disagreed with what he was saying should state his objections. But, as with many gifted persons, Wittgenstein's 'insistence' that people state their objections did not always mean that he made it easy for them to do so. Speaking of Wittgenstein's single-mindedness, Leavis comments:

> When one thought, as one often did, of 'singlemindedness' as a necessary descriptive word, there was apt to be some criticism of one's intention: 'He doesn't give one a chance.' . . . Argument once started, he exercised a completeness of command that left other voices little opportunity—unless (which was unlikely) they were prepared to be peremptory, insistent, and forceful.[31]

Despite the implied criticism in these remarks, Leavis speaks of Wittgenstein as a 'genius' and goes on to say that 'he was a complete human being, subtle, self-critical and un-self-exalting. When, in characterising him, one touches on traits that seem to entail adverse or limiting judgments, one is not intending to impute defects in his potential full humanity.'[32]

Wittgenstein's impatience and severity were undoubtedly connected with his absolute and relentless honesty, and his passionate love for truth. The architect Paul Engelmann, a friend of Wittgenstein's for many years, describes Wittgenstein as holding

an attitude to life that comes nearest perhaps to that sought by Tolstoy: an ethical totalitarianism in all questions, a single-minded and painful preservation of the purity of the uncompromising demands of ethics, in agonizing awareness of one's own permanent failure to measure up to them.[33]

Given Wittgenstein's high demands for himself, we can perhaps understand why he was always dissatisfied with what he had said at his lectures. Malcom describes Wittgenstein as being disgusted with what he had said, and with himself. Frequently he would rush off to the movies immediately after the class ended, imploring one or another friend to go with him. He always sat in the front row, so that the screen would fill his whole field of vision. This helped assure that he would become totally absorbed in the film, thus helping to free his mind temporarily from the philosophical thoughts with which he had been completely involved during his lectures. Wittgenstein loved movies, especially American westerns. And he also had a fondness for detective magazines. When Malcolm returned to the United States, he sent Wittgenstein detective magazines that could not be obtained in England during wartime. Wittgenstein's favourite was a detective magazine published by Street & Smith. He once wrote to Malcolm about the magazines: 'Your mags are wonderful. How people can read Mind [a philosophy journal] if they could read Street & Smith beats me. If philosophy has anything to do with wisdom there's certainly not a grain of that in Mind, & quite often a grain in the detective stories.'[34]

I hope that enough has been said here to provide at least a brief glimpse of the life and character of Ludwig Wittgenstein. In the remainder of this chapter, I will consider Wittgenstein's background somewhat further so that we can better understand his ideas as we encounter them in the following chapters. I share fully the viewpoint of Janik and Toulmin that 'those who are ignorant of the context of ideas are . . . destined to misunderstand them', and I draw heavily on their excellent book, *Wittgenstein's Vienna*, in the next few pages.[35]

Whereas most studies of the last days of the Austro-Hungarian Empire divide the subject matter according to separate 'fields of study', Janik and Toulmin make the assumption that

the distinctive features of the social and cultural situation in the Vienna of the early 1900's require us for once to question the initial abstractions involved in the orthodox separation of powers of, for example, constitutional history, musical composition, physical theory, political journalism and philosophical logic.[36]

They argue that to understand what philosophical problems were of central interest to Wittgenstein, it is necessary to look at the context (historical and social) in which he grew up. While we will not encounter Wittgenstein's ideas directly until the following chapter, it is important to locate them with regard to the social–historical context where many of them originated.

Janik and Toulmin suggest that the failure of political liberalism was perhaps the single most important factor accounting for the special character of Vienna's bourgeois society. In Heller's colourful language, 'Hungarian pig-breeders and Viennese stock-brokers were struggling for an intellectual articulation of their demands for greater profits.'[37] Not only Viennese culture, with its lack of articulate moral convictions and its receptivity to doctrines of racial purity, but the European empire itself was undergoing a process of upheaval and re-evaluation. In Vienna there was great concern among intellectuals for discovering who they were and where they were going. Janik and Toulmin assert: 'The problems of identity and communication plagued Viennese society at every level—political and social, individual and even international.'[38] A key to the solution of these problems was found in a critique of the accepted means of *expression*; this was true for Kraus, Schönberg, Loos and Wittgenstein alike.

Karl Kraus, as mentioned earlier, was the publisher of *Die Fackel*— a satirical fortnightly. In his view, the tastes of the Viennese in the arts reflected the moral duplicity existing throughout the society. Kraus employed polemics and satire as weapons to direct men away from what was superficial and dehumanising back to the 'origin' of all values. He used language and expression—polemics, aphorisms, satires, wit—in an attempt to educate his readers and to remind them of the hypocrisy of their times and of the contemporary crisis whose roots lay in a kind of spiritual malaise. Kraus was especially critical of those artists who, rather than being alienated *from*, were alienated *with* their whole social class. They lacked integrity, which was for Kraus the most important characteristic of what is moral and artistic. For those artists whose only interest was fame or financial success, he reserved a special scorn. Kraus believed that there should be a 'creative separation' between factual discourse and literary artistry, between the sphere of values and the sphere of facts. He expressed this in the statement:

> Adolf Loos and I—he literally and I grammatically—have done nothing more than show that there is a distinction between an urn and a chamber pot and that it is this distinction above all that provides culture with elbow room. The others, those who fail to make this distinction, are divided into those who use the urn as a chamber pot and those who use the chamber pot as an urn.[39]

As a polemical writer, Kraus always expressed his arguments with reference to particular individuals, for he believed that a man's art was intimately connected with his moral character. Again and again, he used the technique of taking whomever he criticised 'at his word', thus exposing the shallowness of his victim by citing the accused's own words and phrases. In Heller's words:

> He dealt with the practice of the law courts as though it were based upon justice; with the theatre as though it were concerned with the art of drama; with journals as though they intended to supply correct information; with politicians as though they desired to promote communal prosperity; and with philosophers as if they were seekers after truth.[40]

By criticising the way people used (or misused) language in Viennese society, then, he was implying a criticism of that society.

To fully appreciate the influence of Karl Kraus on the artists and writers of his day, we must realise that in the Vienna of that time these people were frequently close friends and spent a good deal of time together. The narrow specialisation and departmentalisation that characterise the intellectual life of great cities today were not to be found in Hapsburg Vienna. Among those who knew one another and acknowledged the inspiration of Karl Kraus were Loos in architecture and design; Schönberg in music; and the principal subject of our attention here, Wittgenstein in philosophy.

Adolf Loos battled against the notion of applied art, against excessive ornamentation and decoration in architecture and design. He held the view that, like any craftsman, the architect should take the plumber as his model, not the sculptor. Since the principles for designing objects for use would be purely factual and functional: 'I assert that use [is] the form of culture, the form which makes objects. . . . We do not sit in such-and-such a way, because a table maker has built a chair in such-and-such a way; rather, the table maker makes the chair

as he does, because someone wants to sit that way.'[41] That is, archi-
tects and builders must design and build to suit the contemporary way
of life, rather than men's ways of living being determined by the
buildings. All architecture, all utensils, Loos believed, must serve to
perfect the environment in which men live. This is not to say that Loos
preferred the plain and functional to the superfluous purely for aesthetic reasons—for simplicity, too, can become a fetish—or that he
was against changes in design, but that he believed that changes in
design must be rooted in the demands of social life. The main point
here with Kraus and Loos (and with Schönberg, the writer Robert
Musil, and several other important figures in Viennese thought and
art discussed by Janik and Toulmin) is that all these men were concerned with 'the problem of the nature and limits of *language, expression, and communication*'.[42]

A concern for a philosophical critique of language, then, was already widely recognised in Vienna prior to Wittgenstein's *Tractatus*.[43]
Thus Wittgenstein, while undoubtedly influenced by Frege and Russell,
had acquired a concern with the problems of a critique of language
from within the cultural context of life in Hapsburg Vienna.[44] The
means by which Wittgenstein could later formulate a generalised
critique of language, however, were provided by the logical symbolism
of Frege and Russell.

Later, as we shall see in the following chapter, Wittgenstein moved
away from a concern with logical symbolism to a focus on language
as behaviour. He wanted his readers to recognise for themselves what
was implicit in their own linguistic practices. He regarded philosophy
as a means to an end—namely, the liberation of men's minds.

As I noted earlier, the impact of Wittgenstein's later work can be
seen as a kind of *therapy*. He himself once noted that 'The philosopher's
treatment of a question is like the treatment of an illness.'[45] That is to
say, rather than answering a question, the philosopher 'treats' it. The
aim of philosophy is not completeness or comprehensiveness, nor is it
exactness; it is to help us untie the knots of our own thought. Wittgenstein was concerned that humans be released from those 'pictures'
which held them captive, that they get 'back to the rough ground'.
Rather than searching for essences, we must look at concrete cases,
uncovering similarities and differences which are important, perhaps
recognising and rearranging those things we already know.

It is not that something new has to be erected, or that something new
has to be discovered. We have to examine and compare things which
no one has ever bothered to examine or compare before, so as to see

hings *as they are now*. By seeing more than we did before, our philoso-
ohical dissatisfactions will disappear. 'The sickness of a time,' Wittgen-
tein wrote, 'is cured by an alteration in the mode of life of human
oeings, and it was possible for the sickness of philosophical problems
o get cured only through a changed mode of thought and of life, not
hrough a medicine invented by an individual.'[46] We can, he argued,
get cured only by abandoning our present habits of thinking. We must
recognise what it is to be human, even though it is certainly human to
want to avoid this recognition. We must recognise, as I will try to make
clear in chapter 9, that knowledge has no foundation, that grounds
come to an end in our actions. The essences for which men search are
made rather than found; they are not a discovery of reason but a
oroduct of will. One of Wittgenstein's goals, then, was to help us find
our way about, to recognise where (and what) we are. 'The philoso-
oher,' Wittgenstein said, 'is a man who has to cure himself of many
sicknesses of the understanding before he can arrive at the notions of
the sound human understanding. In the midst of life we are in death,
so in sanity we are surrounded by madness.'[47]

Wittgenstein, I have tried to show, was driven by an insistence on
truth and understanding. His life and work, his spiritual attitude,
showed that the world itself is an object worthy of man's thought.
Bertrand Russell characterises Wittgenstein as a Tolstoy and a Pascal
rolled into one:

> You know how fierce Tolstoy was; he hated competitors. If another
> novelist was held to be better than he, Tolstoy would immediately
> challenge him to a duel. . . . And you know how Pascal became dis-
> contented with mathematics and science and became a mystic; it
> was the same with Wittgenstein.[48]

Throughout his life, Wittgenstein struggled to free his mind in order
to understand the world fully, although he was always inclined to an
enormous pessimism as regarded the value of his own work. Malcolm
describes Wittgenstein's outlook on life in these words: 'A human
being should do the thing for which he has a talent with all of his energy
his life long, and should never relax this devotion to his job merely in
order to prolong his existence.'[49] Wittgenstein himself always observed
this sense of duty towards his work. While we shall consider Wittgenstein's philosophy in the following chapter, and the usefulness of his
ideas for helping us understand scientific knowledge in the remainder
of the book, it is important to remember that 'Wittgenstein the man'
was also a *moral* philosopher in the truest sense.

2 The 'Early' and 'Later' Wittgenstein

Our civilization is characterized by the word progress. Progress is it
form: it is not one of its properties that it possesses. It is typical of i
that it is building, construction. Its activity is one of constructing mor
and more complex structures. And even clarity serves this end, an
is not sought on its own account. For me on the other hand clarit
lucidity, is the goal sought.

LUDWIG WITTGENSTEIN

Although, as indicated in the preface, our interest is in the 'later' rathe
than the 'early' Wittgenstein, it is important to consider briefly th
ideas advanced in the *Tractatus* before going on to examine, in greate
depth, his subsequent views. Despite the enormous differences in hi
standpoints during the two phases of his work, his principal aim re
mained the achievement of clear understanding. And he always em
phasised that philosophy was not a science, but rather an activity o
elucidation and clarification. His concern in both phases was with th
same topic: the relation of language to the world.

The early Wittgenstein: the *Tractatus*

Wittgenstein's goal in the *Tractatus* was to present a comprehensiv
philosophical picture of the world. He wanted to show how proposi
tions succeed in presenting real states of affairs in the world, and ir
this sense he was part of an ancient tradition which conceived o
language as reference, as our way of referring to things in the world
He accepted that the world has a fixed structure,[2] and stated tha
'The great question round which everything that I write turns is: I

there an order in the world *a priori*, and if so what does it consist in?'[3] The world is represented to us, he argued in the *Tractatus*, by language, which is a picture of reality. If language is a picture of reality then, he reasoned, there must be a similarity of structure between that which pictures and that which is pictured. That is, the form of language must be the same as that of reality.

Wittgenstein sets out seven propositions in the *Tractatus*. A number is assigned to each, so that the first is 1, the second 2, and so on. Each proposition, with the exception of the last, is followed by a series of comments. The comments on proposition 1 are numbered 1.1, 1.2, and so forth. The same notation system is followed with the other propositions. Then there are comments on the comments, each numbered on the same principle; thus, comments on 1.1 are numbered 1.11, 1.12, etc. He apparently wished to proceed in his analysis from the nature of logic to the nature of language, and then to the nature of the world. Actually, however, the *Tractatus* shows almost the reverse of this order.

Wittgenstein begins with the proposition: 'The world is all that is the case.'[4] What is intended here is the following. If we ask someone 'What is the world composed of, from what is it built up?' we might get this type of answer: 'The world is composed of objects such as trees, people, animals, automobiles, books, tables, etc. All objects, considered together, make up the world.' This answer, according to the *Tractatus*, is wrong. While the world can be reconstituted from such objects, the mere collection of these objects is not sufficient. What is necessary is knowledge of the *combinations* in which objects are related to one another. In reality, a book or a table, for example, is not a fact, for a fact can occur only in combination, as in the proposition 'The book is lying on the table'. The book is a thing and the table is a thing, whereas it is a fact that the book is lying on the table. It is neither the book nor the table, but the book's lying on the table, which is one of the elements constituting the world. Such an element is a fact. Thus, Wittgenstein's second proposition: 'What is the case—a fact—is the existence of states of affairs.'[5] A 'state of affairs' is a fact that in itself does not consist of facts; it is a constellation of objects. It is a combination of things; and a thing is a simple, an irreducible entity. And a state of affairs that actually obtains is a fact. The book's lying on the table—rather than, say, in the street—is a state of affairs. If the book really lies on the table, instead of somewhere else, the state of affairs becomes a fact. Facts, then, may be positive or negative: a positive fact is the existence of a state of affairs; a negative fact is the non-existence of a state of affairs.[6]

Thus far we have seen that, following the *Tractatus*, the world consists of states of affairs—and not of objects. Objects are the constituents, so that changes in the combinations of objects yield changes in the states of affairs. So much for the world. Next we come to language, which is a *picture* or model of the facts: 'We picture facts to ourselves' and 'A picture is a model of reality'.[7] Just as states of affairs are the elements of the world, so propositions are the elements of language. Language is the totality of propositions. Propositions are pictures of that to which they refer. Complex propositions can be analysed into the basic units of language, elementary propositions. Consider this example. The proposition 'The book is lying on the table' refers to the state of affairs *that* the book is lying on the table, and by changing the relative positions of the elements in the proposition other propositions can be generated which picture different states of affairs: for instance, 'The table is lying on the book'. A proposition is a composite of names, not just any words (for example, 'big small out' is not a proposition) for they must be put together in the appropriate way, 'concatenated' like the links of a chain.[8] Further, there is a correlation between the elements of a picture and the elements of what is to be pictured. The correlation constitutes the pictorial relationship of the picture. Every sentence is a *picture* of a state of affairs. The objects in the state of affairs stand in a one-to-one correspondence with the terms in the sentence that refer to these objects.

Names are among the simple unanalysable elements of a proposition.[9] A name refers to an object; it is the proxy in the proposition for the object.[10] Not only are names correlated with objects, but also the relationships between the names in a proposition must be correlated with relationships between objects in facts.

> One name is representative of one thing, another of another thing, and they themselves are connected; in this way the whole images the situation—like a *tableau vivant*. The logical connection must, of course, be one that is possible as between the things that the names are representative of, and this will always be the case if the names really are representative of the things.[11]

What makes the linguistic picture (proposition) a picture of what it depicts is the similarity of *structure*. The proposition and the state of affairs it depicts have a common form. Propositions conveying false beliefs do so because they arrange names in ways in which the objects themselves are *not* arranged. The combination of names in a proposition which makes it a picture of the fact is referred to as the *logical form* of the sentence. 'What any picture, of whatever form, must have in common with reality, in order to be able to depict it—correctly or incorrectly—in any way at all, is logical form, i.e. the form of reality.' The logical form of the proposition and the logical form of the fact are identical: 'There must be something identical in a picture and what it depicts, to enable the one to be a picture of the other at all' and 'The fact that the elements of a picture are related to one another in a determinate way represents that things are related to one another in the same way'.[12] But for a proposition to be a proposition about a certain state of affairs, it must have '. . . . exactly as many distinguishable parts as in the situation that it represents'. If not, it would not be a proposition about *that* specific situation. Only elementary propositions can meet the requirement that there be a one-to-one correspondence between the elements of a proposition and those of the specific situation that it describes, for they alone consist entirely of names referring directly to objects. What makes something a proposition is that names are arranged in a *determinate* way, and 'What constitutes a picture is that its elements are related to one another in a determinate way'.[13]

Perhaps we can better understand what it is that enables propositions to be understood as pictures by considering von Wright's account of how the idea of language as a picture of reality occurred to Wittgenstein:

It was in the autumn of 1914, on the East front. Wittgenstein was reading in a magazine about a law-suit in Paris concerning an automobile accident. At the trial a miniature model of the accident was presented before the court. The model here served as a proposition; that is, as a description of a possible state of affairs. It has this function owing to a correspondence between the parts of the model (the miniature-houses, -cars, -people) and things (houses, cars, people) in reality. It now occurred to Wittgenstein that one might reverse the analogy and say that a *proposition* serves as a model or *picture*, by virtue of a similar correspondence between *its* parts and the world. The way in which the parts of the proposition are combined—the *structure* of the propositions—depicts a possible combination of elements in reality, a possible state of affairs.[14]

Wittgenstein's pictures in the *Tractatus* are not, however, spatial pictures like maps or photographs; rather, they are what he called 'logical pictures'. Thus the similarity between a picture and what it pictures is not visual but formal. The following give some idea as to how his picture theory is applied to language:

> At first sight a proposition—one set out on the printed page, for example—does not seem to be a picture of the reality with which it is concerned. But no more does musical notation at first sight seem to be a picture of music, nor our phonetic notations (the alphabet) to be a picture of our speech.
>
> And yet these sign-languages prove to be pictures, even in the ordinary sense, of what they represent.[15] A gramophone record, the musical idea, the written notes, and the sound waves, all stand to one another in the same internal relation of depicting that holds between language and the world.
>
> They are all constructed according to a common logical plan.[16]
>
> A proposition is a picture of reality: for if I understand a proposition, I know the situation that it represents. And I understand the proposition without having had its sense explained to me.[17]

It is important to point out that a picture is still a picture whether it depicts a truly existing fact or only a possible fact: 'In order to tell whether a picture is true or false we must compare it with reality', 'It is impossible to tell from the picture alone whether it is true or false', and 'There are no pictures that are true *a priori*'.[18] All non-elementary propositions are truth-functional compounds of elementary propositions. For example, take the proposition: 'The book is lying on the table and the table is in the room.' This proposition is a truth-function of the two propositions 'The book is lying on the table' and 'The table is in the room'. Since elementary propositions have sense only in so far as they can be compared to reality, all propositions must be capable of being true or false.

One of Wittgenstein's contributions from the *Tractatus*[19] has passed into textbooks of logic. One can devise the propositional connectives by setting out in a table the truth-conditions of propositions containing them. For example:[20]

p	q	p and q
T	T	T
F	T	F
T	F	F
F	F	F

Thus 'p and q' (for instance, 'The book is lying on the table and the table is in the room') is true in the case in which p ('The book is lying on the table') and q ('The table is in the room') are both true, and false if (a) p is false and q is true, (b) p is true and q is false, (c) p and q are both false. Wittgenstein offered, then, a decision procedure for propositional logic. In a sense, the picture theory required the truth-function theory. For if the end result of analysis is to be elementary propositions, there must be a way of determining their truth or falsity. And, since all propositions are truth-functions of elementary propositions, there must be a mechanical method to test whether the proposition has sense or not. Wittgenstein provided such a method.

To review, language consists of propositions. These propositions can be analysed into elementary propositions, and they are truth-functions of elementary propositions. The elementary propositions themselves are combinations of names, which refer directly to objects. Further, elementary propositions are logical pictures of states of affairs, which are combinations of objects. States of affairs combine to form facts of whatever complexity which constitute the world. Therefore language is truth-functionally structured and its essential function is to describe the world. 'The totality of true thoughts,' he believed, 'is a picture of the world'.

As mentioned earlier, Wittgenstein believed that he had found the definitive solution to the central problem of philosophy, namely, 'what can be expressed by propositions, i.e. by language (and, what comes to the same, what can be *thought*) and what cannot be expressed by propositions, but only shown . . . .'[21] In making the distinction between what can be *said* in language and what can only be *shown*, Wittgenstein tried to provide an exhaustive classification of the possible content of language. This viewpoint can be witnessed in the following:

A proposition *shows* its sense.
A proposition shows how things stand *if* it is true. And it *says that* they do so stand.[22]

Propositions can represent the whole of reality, but they cannot represent what they must have in common with reality in order to be able to represent it—logical form.
In order to be able to represent logical form, we should have to be able to station ourselves with propositions somewhere outside logic, that is to say outside the world.[23]

Propositions cannot represent logical form: it is mirrored in them.
What finds its reflections in language, language cannot represent.

What expresses *itself* in language, *we* cannot express by means o
language.
Propositions *show* the logical form of reality.
They display it.[24]

What *can* be shown, cannot be said.[25]

The *limits of my language* mean the limit of my world.[26]

Logical form, then, is something that a proposition can *show* but no
say. Propositions *say that* it is in reality as it is *shown* by their form
Wittgenstein believed that logical form is also the form of reality
Language can picture reality only because of sharing a common
logical structure with the world. Thus, the concept of logical form is
assumed to belong to ontology as well as to logic.

In the *Tractatus* Wittgenstein argued that the totality of true propositions constitutes the whole of natural science. By specifying the limits
of language, philosophy sets limits to the sphere of possible knowledge
Whether a proposition is true or false can be determined only by comparing it with reality. This implies a correspondence theory of knowledge, that is, that elementary propositions be compared with what
Wittgenstein called atomic states of affairs. This, as we shall see, leads
to considerable difficulties, for it requires that we be able to step outside
language in order to compare it with what it depicts. Wittgenstein's
general lack of concern with this problem and with epistemological
issues more generally in the *Tractatus* is one of the major differences
between this and his later work. Whereas the *Tractatus* directs us to
determine the truth-values of elementary propositions by comparing
them with reality, the later Wittgenstein came to preoccupy himsel:
with the epistemological issue of how we come to know what we know,
how it is that our cognitive claims are justified.

While the above exposition of the *Tractatus* is extremely cursory and
limited in scope, I hope that it provides some understanding of
Wittgenstein's concerns and general viewpoints as expressed in his
picture theory.

The later Wittgenstein: the *Philosophical Investigations*

Eventually Wittgenstein came to question these earlier views. Instru-
mental in helping him to recognise what he later regarded as 'grave
mistakes'[27] in the *Tractatus* were Frank Ramsey, with whom he discussed his 'new' ideas during the last two years of Ramsey's life; and

Piero Sraffa, an Italian economist who had come to Cambridge shortly before Wittgenstein returned there. Malcolm describes an incident between Wittgenstein and Sraffa that helped precipitate the destruction of the picture theory:

> One day (they were riding, I think, on a train) when Wittgenstein was insisting that a proposition and that which it describes must have the same 'logical form', the same 'logical multiplicity', Sraffa made a gesture, familiar to Neapolitans as meaning something like disgust or contempt, of brushing the underneath of his chin with an outward sweep of his fingertips of one hand. And he asked: 'What is the logical form of *that*?' Sraffa's example produced in Wittgenstein the feeling that there was an absurdity in the insistence that a proposition must literally be a 'picture' of the reality it describes.[28]

Hence Wittgenstein came to question the fundamental assumption of the *Tractatus* that language is a picture of reality, that its function is to represent the world to us. He came to believe that he had, by concerning himself with *formal analysis* of language as representation, given insufficient attention to the ways in which language is put *to use* in human life. Wittgenstein rejected his earlier view that language was a logically rigid essence concealed behind everyday discourse, and instead came to accept language as it actually is to be found in social life—serving a variety of human purposes. Rather than asking what the structure of reality was, he argued that one could only analyse the language in which people talked about it.

In the preface to the posthumously published *Philosophical Investigations*, Wittgenstein states that:

> The thoughts which I publish in what follows are the precipitate of philosophical investigations which have occupied me for the last sixteen years. They concern many subjects: the concepts of meaning, of understanding, of a proposition, of logic, the foundations of mathematics, states of consciousness, and other things. I have written down all these thoughts as *remarks*, short paragraphs, of which there is sometimes a fairly long chain about the same subject, while I sometimes make a sudden change, jumping from one topic to another . . . .[29]

The *Philosophical Investigations* is divided into two parts: the first, a series of remarks numbered from 1 to 693; the second, of fourteen remarks, some of them of considerable length.

Wittgenstein begins by noting that according to one view of human language, 'the individual words in language name objects—sentences are combinations of such names.—In this picture of language we find the roots of the following idea: Every word has a meaning. This meaning is correlated with the word. It is the object for which the word stands.'[30] This is, of course, the position advanced by Wittgenstein himself in the *Tractatus*. He believed that Augustine's *Confessions* (which he, for the most part, greatly admired) contained such a view of language. According to Augustine:

> When they (my elders) named some object, and accordingly moved toward something, I saw this and I grasped that the thing was called by the sound they uttered when they meant to point it out. ... Thus, as I heard words repeatedly used in their proper places in various sentences, I gradually learnt to understand what objects they signified; and after I had trained my mouth to form these signs, I used them to express my own desires.[31]

Wittgenstein comments on this view by saying: 'If you describe the learning of language in this way you are, I believe, thinking primarily of nouns like 'table', 'chair', 'bread', and of people's names . . . .'[32] He expresses his objection to Augustine's picture of the nature of language (and of his own earlier view) in the following remark:

> Augustine, we might say, does describe a system of communication; only not everything that we call language is this system. And one has to say this in many cases where the question arises 'Is this an appropriate description or not?' The answer is: 'Yes, it is appropriate, but only for this narrowly circumscribed region, not for the whole of what you were claiming to describe.'[33]

Wittgenstein's point is that language is not primarily a matter of naming, and, even when it is, naming is rather more complicated than simply attaching a name to an object:

> As if there were only one thing called 'talking about a thing'. Whereas in fact we do the most various things with our sentences. Think of exclamations alone, with their completely different function.
> Water!
> Away!
> Ow!
> Help!

Fine!

No!

Are you inclined still to call these words 'names of objects'?[34]

A word, then, is not simply a name for an object, although it can sometimes be used that way. But words can be used in many other ways as well.

Thus, Wittgenstein is highly critical of the picture view of language that he had advanced in the *Tractatus*. What, then, it might be asked, is a word's meaning? Wittgenstein answers: 'For a *large* class of cases—though not for all—in which we employ the word "meaning" can be defined thus: the meaning of a word is its use in the language.'[35] But words occur in sentences. And, Wittgenstein stressed in the *Tractatus*, they say something that is either true or false. He now rejects that earlier notion:

> But how many kinds of sentences are there? Say assertion, question and command? There are *countless* kinds: countless different kinds of use of what we call 'symbols', 'words', 'sentences'. And this multiplicity is not something fixed, given once for all, but new types of language, new language-games, as we may say, come into existence, and others become obsolete and get forgotten . . .
>
> Here the term 'language-*game*' is meant to bring into prominence the fact that the *speaking* of language is part of an activity, or a form of life . . .[36]

The point here is that we must consider speech as an activity, along with eating, sleeping, and other activities. There is not, Wittgenstein stresses, some correct usage for words that holds for all language-games. Thus the 'same' word may be used differently and have different meanings in the language-games of poetry, philosophy, and religion. To see what words mean, we must look at how they are actually used in specific situations.

But we should not conclude from Wittgenstein's assertion concerning meaning and use that he is *defining* the meaning of a word or expression in terms of its use. Rather, he is *recommending* that we pay close attention to the use of words and expressions in language. This can be seen in the following passage where the concept of meaning is related to the concept of use:

> But can't the meaning of a word that I understand fit the sense of a sentence that I understand? Or the meaning of one word fit the

meaning of another? Of course, if the meaning is the use we make of the word, it makes no sense to speak of such 'fitting'. But we understand the meaning of a word when we hear or say it; we grasp it in a flash, and what we grasp in this way is surely something different from the 'use' which is extended in time![37]

We must be sensitive to the unreflective use of concepts in abstraction from their proper framework. Thus, Wittgenstein cautions us to consider the circumstances or surroundings in which a concept appears:

> When philosophers use a word—'knowledge', 'being', 'object', 'I', 'proposition', 'name'—and try to grasp the *essence* of the thing, one must always ask oneself: is the word ever actually used in this way in the language-game which is its original home?
> What *we* do is to bring words back from their metaphysical to their everyday use.[38]

From the standpoint of Wittgenstein's thesis in the *Philosophical Investigations*, there are no independent or objective sources of support outside of human thought and human actions. Consider the following passages:

> And to imagine a language game is to imagine a form of life.[39]

> 'So you are saying that human agreement decides what is true and what is false?'—It is what human beings *say* that is true and false; and they agree in the *language* they use. That is not agreement in opinions but in form of life.[40]

There is no standard or objective reality (always fixed, never changing) against which to compare or measure a universe of discourse: 'What has to be accepted, the given is—so one could say—*forms of life*.'[41] Instead of assuming, as he did in the *Tractatus*, that the exploration of language provides us access to reality, Wittgenstein now argues that human language in a sense *creates* reality. Nothing exists outside of our language and actions which can be used to justify, for example, a statement's truth or falsity. The only possible justification lies in the linguistic practices which embody them: how people think and speak, and how they live. These notions about the status of 'external reality' are, I believe, difficult to grasp on first encounter, I only touch upon them here, but discuss them at length in later chapters.

There is not, then, any one specific feature common to all uses of language. Wittgenstein gives an example of the great variety of language-games:

Review the multiplicity of language-games in the following examples, and in others:

Giving orders, and obeying them—
Describing the appearance of an object, or giving its measurements—
Constructing an object from a description (a drawing)—
Reporting an event—
Speculating about an event—
Forming and testing a hypothesis— . . .
Play-acting— . . .
Guessing riddles—
Making a joke; telling it—[42]

Elsewhere in the *Investigations*, Wittgenstein gives other examples of language-games: ostensive definitions,[43] the expression of sensation,[44] the description of physical objects and the description of sense-impressions,[45] and the reporting of past wishes.[46] He says that 'lying is a language-game that needs to be learned like any other one'.[47] This multiplicity of language-games is not, of course, something fixed or established forever. 'We remain unconscious of the prodigious diversity of all the everyday language-games,' Wittgenstein notes, 'because the clothing of our language makes everything alike'.[48]

Language, to reiterate, is not a tool having one specific use or purpose, it is the name for a collection.[49] Not only is there a multiplicity of language-games at any given time, but part of what it means to learn about the world is to acquire skills in an increasing number of language-games:

When the boy or grown-up learns what one might call specific technical languages, e.g., the use of charts and diagrams, descriptive geometry, chemical symbolism, etc., he learns more language games. (Remark: The picture we have of the language of the grown-up is that of a nebulous mass of language, his mother tongue, surrounded by discrete and more or less clear-cut language games, the technical languages.)[50]

Language-games and forms of life

Since the terms 'language-games' and 'forms of life' have been used several times in the above discussion, and since they are important both to Wittgenstein's position and to the following chapters, it is useful to consider them at some length here.

In 'Notes for lectures', Wittgenstein says that: 'We call something a language game if it plays a particular role in our human life.'[51] Later, he extends his discussion of language-games:

> I shall in the future again and again draw your attention to what I call language games. These are ways of using signs simpler than those in which we use the signs of our highly complicated everyday language. Language games are forms of language with which a child begins to make use of words. The study of language games is the study of primitive forms of language or primitive languages.[52]

Then, in the *Philosophical Investigations*, Wittgenstein introduces *actions* as providing the linkage between language-games and forms of life: 'I will call these games 'language-games' and will sometimes speak of a primitive language as a language-game . . . . I shall also call the whole, consisting of language and the actions into which it is woven, the "language-game".'[53]

The uses of language, then, are like games. Because we use one word ('games') to apply to the vast variety of different games, we usually assume that they all have some common property. But, says Wittgenstein, this is not so. Considering what the word 'game' means, he writes:

> I mean board-games, card-games, ball-games, Olympic games, and so on. What is common to them all?—Don't say: 'There *must* be something common, or they would not be called "games"'—but *look* and *see* whether there is anything common to all.—For if you look at them you will not see something that is common to *all*, but similarities, relationships, and a whole series of them at that. To repeat: don't think, but look![54]

> I can think of no better expression to characterize these similarities than 'family resemblances'; for the various resemblances between members of a family: build, features, colour of eyes, gait, temperament, etc. etc. overlap and criss-cross in the same way.—And I shall say: 'games' form a family.[55]

Thus games, Wittgenstein argued, have only a family resemblance. Where there is a large collection of similarities, only a few of them will obtain between any two of the practices that we call games. But there is no single feature—say, skill, competition, entertainment—which is common to all games. A language-game is a simplified model of some particular aspect of our language, considered more or less in isolation by being conceived of as the total language of some group of people. Thus we can speak broadly of the language-game of science as distinguished, for example, from the language-game of religion. And within the language-game of science we can, for some purposes, speak of the language-games of physics, biology, and so on. Because the uses of language overlap even more than most games do, these are artificial abstractions. The *pieces*—that is to say, the words—we use in any one language-game might be used in many other language-games as well.

In other words, to understand a word or concept, it must be set in its linguistic context, and it must always be remembered that every word may figure in many different contexts. Words only have meaning, then, within language-games, within modes of human activity, governed by systems of rules. The language-game is 'the whole, consisting of language and the actions into which it is woven'.[56] A word or a concept, in short, is not a picture of anything. It has no fixed meaning.

Let us consider this further in terms of how a child learns language, remembering that Wittgenstein's remarks in the *Investigations* are directed against the views of Augustine and others who believe that a child learns his native language when it has learned to repeat a sound after us as we point. The problem is not how a child learns, for instance, a word like 'red' but how it learns to know what 'colour' *is*, that is, how to master a language-game. The child learns, Wittgenstein argues, not by explanation, but by *training*. It might be noted parenthetically here that Wittgenstein's experience in teaching small children undoubtedly had an important influence on his views. Wittgenstein describes the teaching of language this way:

> How do I explain the meaning of 'regular', 'uniform', 'same' to anyone?—I shall explain these words to someone who, say, only speaks French by means of the corresponding French words. But if a person has not yet got the *concepts*, I shall teach him to use the words by means of *examples* and by *practice*.—And when I do this I do not communicate less to him than I know myself.[57]

Elsewhere he says: 'One thing we always do when discussing a word is to ask how we were taught it. . . . Cf. How did we learn "I dreamt so and so"? The interesting point is that we didn't learn it by being shown a dream.'[58] We learn 'dreaming', 'beautiful', 'regular', and other words, by training. This training is largely non-verbal—involving gestures and facial expressions—although it also involves grunts, sighs, various tones of voice and other more-or-less verbal expressions. But training also involves the production of certain actions on the part of the learner. In the course of teaching the meaning of 'same' to someone, Wittgenstein emphasises that:

> I shall shew him the same colours, the same lengths, the same shapes, I shall make him find them and produce them, and so on. I shall, for instance, get him to continue an ornamental pattern uniformly when told to do so.—And also to continue progressions . . . . I do it, he does it after me; and I influence him by expressions of agreement, rejection, expectation, encouragement. I let him go his way, or hold him back; and so on.[59]

Of course, what makes something a word of 'approval' or an expression of 'encouragement' is the language-game and the form of life in which it appears. 'We don't start from certain words,' Wittgenstein says, 'but from certain occasions or activities'.[60] This means that words and language cannot be understood and characterised independently of certain occasions, activities, circumstances or 'forms of life' in which they are used. Wittgenstein never explicitly defines the notion of 'forms of life'. In fact the expression appears only five times in the *Investigations* and only occasionally in his other writings. Prior to the *Investigations*, he had spoken of 'circumstances' and 'occasions' rather than forms of life. Consider the following:

> It seems, whatever the circumstances, I always know whether to apply the word or not. It seems at first it was a move in a special game, but then it became independent of the game. (This reminds one of the way the idea of length became emancipated from any particular method of measuring it.) We are tempted to say: 'damn it all, a rod has a particular length however I express it.' And one could go on to say that if I see a rod I always see (know) how long it is, although I can't say how many feet, meters, etc.—But suppose I just say: I always know whether it looks tiny or big![61]

The point here, of course, is that 'tiny' and 'big'—like the concept of length (rods, feet, meters)—are context-bound; it is a matter of circumstances or forms of life.

Wittgenstein gives the example of understanding and translating a tribe's language:

> Whether a word of the language of our tribe is rightly translated into a word of the English language depends upon the role the word plays in the whole life of the tribe, the occasions on which it is used,

the expressions of emotion by which it is generally accompanied, the idea which it generally awakens or which prompts its saying, etc., etc. As an exercise ask yourself: in which cases would you say that a certain word uttered by the people of the tribe was a greeting? In which cases should we say it corresponds to our 'Good-bye', in which to our 'Hello'? In which cases would you say that a word of a foreign language corresponds to our 'perhaps'?—to our expression of doubt, trust, certainty? You will find the justification for calling something an expression of doubt, conviction, etc., largely though not of course wholly, consists in descriptions of gestures, the play of facial expressions and even the tone of voice.[62]

It would seem, then, that one must understand the meanings of 'gestures', 'facial expressions', 'tones of voice', and the like, on which understanding, doubt, trust or whatever is dependent. In other words, one must understand gestures, smiles, and so on, *before* one can understand a language. As Wittgenstein observes: 'If you went to Mars and men were spheres with sticks coming out, you wouldn't know what to look for. Or if you went to a tribe where noises made with the mouth were just breathing or making music, and language was made with the ears.'[63]

We know that children do learn the meaning of at least some gestures and signs—smiling, anger—before they acquire language. Unless there are some similarities between the non-verbal behaviour of an individual and of those whose language he is trying to learn and understand, the understanding and translation of that language would prove impossible. It is, on this account, impossible that we could understand either the 'gestures' or 'language' of stones. Perhaps with trees we are better off; at least they have (what we regard as) movement. And with animals, or other living creatures, we can at least imagine that, in some limited ways, they share our form of life. Wittgenstein remarks on this by saying:

Look at a stone and imagine it having sensations.—One says to oneself: 'How could one so much as get the idea of ascribing a *sensation* to a *thing*? One might as well ascribe it to a number!' —And now look at a wriggling fly and at once these difficulties vanish. . . .[64]

Or consider man's 'best friend', the dog:

Why can't a dog simulate pain? Is he too honest? Could one teach a dog to simulate pain? Perhaps it is possible to teach him to howl on particular occasions as if he were in pain, even when he is not. But the surroundings which are necessary for this behaviour to be real simulation are missing.[65]

Thus, one can teach a child to tell a lie, for instance, but not a stone, a tree or a dog, for the surrounding circumstances, the actions, the form of life, connected to it do not exist. Perhaps, then, we can grasp what Wittgenstein intends when he states that: 'The *speaking* of language is part of an activity, or of a form of life.'[66] And how we talk is part of it. 'Commanding, questioning, recounting, chatting, are as much a part of our natural history as walking, eating, drinking, playing.'[67] These shared forms of life have never been 'taught' us in any explicit manner, although we are all familiar with them. They are part of our 'natural history' which 'have escaped remark only because they are always before our eyes'.[68] Following a rule, making a report, giving an order, and so on, are customs, uses, practices or institutions. They presuppose a human society, and our form of life.

In order to help us recognise for ourselves the form of life lying behind our linguistic practices, the human decisions and conventions that have become 'second nature' to us, Wittgenstein employed parables or fables in teaching his students at Cambridge. Toulmin gives a rather lengthy example from one of Wittgenstein's lectures, which I quote in its entirety because of its persuasive power:

> Suppose an anthropologist finds the members of a tribe, whose language he does not yet understand, cutting up bolts of longitudinally striped cloth and exchanging them for small cubes of wood, uttering as they hand over the cubes the sounds 'cena', 'meena', 'mina', 'mo', and so on, always in the same regular sequence. And suppose he discovers that this exchange proceeds always up to the same point, regardless of whether the cloth is (as we should say) single-width or folded double. What should the anthropologist then conclude? Is he to infer that the tribe values cloth only by its length as measured along the stripes; or that the merchants who sell the cloth single-width are rogues; or that the tribe's arithmetic has a different structure from ours; or that 'eena', 'meena', 'mina', 'mo' are not their words for '1', '2', '3', and '4' after all; or that this is not really a commercial exchange, but some kind of ritual. . . ? Or might we have no effective way of deciding among the alternatives?[69]

The point with this example is that the hypothetical anthropologist would have no way of choosing among the various alternatives unless he were familiar with the 'forms of life' of the tribe. Could we imagine a form of life where men measured cloth by the length of its stripes, regardless of whether it was single-width, double-width or even triple-width? To do so would require that we also imagine the whole activity of 'measuring' to be far different from ours throughout that society.

When a form of life can no longer be imagined, its language can no longer be understood. Imagine that we ask: 'Has this table a length?' We cannot even imagine what a table without length would look like. But Wittgenstein asks, 'why do we say, "I can't imagine the opposite"? Why not: "I can't imagine the thing itself."'[70] To imagine every table having a length, I must simply imagine a table. Wittgenstein says: 'Only this picture, in connexion with the proposition "This table has the same length as the one over there". For here I understand what it means to have a picture of the opposite. . . .'[71] To imagine a different form of life, then, may often be to imagine the facts of nature being otherwise than as we have always experienced them. In Wittgenstein's words:

> I am not saying: if such-and-such facts of nature were different people would have different concepts (in the sense of a hypothesis). But: if anyone believes that certain concepts are absolutely the correct ones, and that having different ones would mean not realizing something that we realize—then let him imagine certain *very general facts* of nature to be different from what we are used to, and the formation of concepts different from the usual ones will become intelligible to him.[72]

All of this is intended to underscore the central point that the meaning of a concept (for example, length, measuring, regularity) grows out of its use in one or another form of life. 'Every sign *by itself* seems *dead*. *What* gives it life?—In use it is *alive*. Is life breathed into it there?—Or is the *use* its life?'[73]

Rules and grammar

One general similarity between language and games is that both involve the use of *rules*. This is not to say, however, that all aspects of either games or languages are bounded by rules. For example, there are rules in tennis; but no rules as to how high one throws the ball in serving. Rules, like games, have a 'family resemblance'; the terms cover many different but related things. With language, Wittgenstein notes, 'what we call a rule of a language-game may have very different rules in the game.[74] Usually, of course, we do not think about rules being involved when we are speaking. In fact, Wittgenstein points out, most of us would find it difficult to give such rules if asked. Imagine, for instance, the following. I tell someone that I lost my way when coming to visit him, and that we should go out and look for it. Imagine, further, that I tell him that I also lost my wallet, and that we should go and look for it as well. In the first case, the usage of the words 'look for' is nonsensical—one cannot 'look for' a lost way. What, then, are the rules that one follows in using these words? What rules have I violated in saying that I must look for my lost way?

Or imagine that I have 'lost my head' and must go and 'look for' it. Of course, I cannot do so; although had I—literally—lost my head, someone else might look for it. So I can look for lost wallets, books, combs, cigarettes and children; but not for lost ways, heads, bearing ('I lost my bearings'), tempers or composures. All of this points to our being unable to circumscribe clearly the concepts that we use. It is not that we do not know the real definitions of 'lose' or 'look for', but that they have no real definitions. The meaning of the expressions 'lose' or 'look for', then, may be different from context to context, depending on the speaker's point of view in saying them.

Central to the notion of following a rule is the idea that it is logically inseparable from the notion of *making a mistake*. Unless one can conceive of someone's making a mistake or doing something incorrectly, one cannot speak of someone's following a rule. For example, someone can make a mistake—that is, not follow the rules—with respect to scoring a tennis match or in serving the balls to the wrong court, but he cannot make a mistake by hitting the ball too hard or too soft. Similarly, there are no mistakes, and hence no rules, as to the correct way to daydream —although there may be rules as to when and where such behaviour is deemed inappropriate. To follow a rule is not the same as to interpret it, rather it is to *practise* it.

A language, according to Wittgenstein, is a set of activities defined by certain rules, the rules which govern its different uses in different circumstances. Rules are always 'public' in the sense that it must be possible for more than one person to learn to follow a rule. This means that the practice of following a rule must be teachable; unless it is possible to train a person to *use* a word, concept or language, we cannot say that it is language or a part of language. Wittgenstein argues that 'following a rule' involves what he terms 'agreement to go on in the same way'. Of course, there is a difficulty here. We can say that someone is following a rule if he always acts in the 'same' way in similar circumstances, but it is only in terms of a given rule that the word 'same' can acquire a definite sense. But one does not first learn 'rules', and then 'same', or *vice versa*. Rather, 'The use of the word "rule" and the use of the word "same" are interwoven'.[75] And, similarly, with rules and agreement: '. . . one learns the meaning of "agreement" by learning to follow a rule. If you want to understand what it means to "follow a rule", you have already to be able to follow a rule.'[76] Further, we learn what rule-governed activities *are* by participating in them. More specifically, we are trained to accept that there are right and wrong ways of doing things. This means that certain conventions must be accepted. More will be said about these conventions shortly.

Let me return now to the matter of 'going on in the same way' as evidence that one is following a rule. Wittgenstein discusses this by means of an example of language-games that involve expanding a mathematical series. Imagine that one person writes the following numbers on the blackboard: 2, 4, 6, 8, 10. He then asks the other person to 'go on in the same way'. Evidence that the second person has grasped the rule would be provided by his going on to write: 12, 14, 16, 18, and so on. But let us assume that we are not certain that he really understands the rule:

> Now we get the pupil to continue (the series) beyond 1000—and he writes 1000, 1004, 1008, 1012.
>
> We say to him: 'Look at what you've done!'—He doesn't understand. We say: 'You were meant to add *two*: look how you began the series!'—He answers: 'Yes, isn't it right? I thought that was how I was *meant* to do it.'—Or suppose he pointed to the series and said: 'But I went on in the same way.'—It would now be no use to say: 'But can't you see . . . ?'—and repeat the old examples and explanations.—In such a case we might say, perhaps: It comes natural to this person to understand our order with our explanations as *we* should understand the order: 'Add 2 up to 1000, 4 up to 2000, 6 up to 3000 and so on.'
>
> Such a case would present similarities with one in which a person naturally reacted to the gesture of pointing with the hand by looking in the direction of the line from finger-tip to wrist, not from wrist to finger-tip.[77]

This kind of learning is a matter of training, not of explanation. That is to say, the teacher can only *say* so much—beyond that, he must use examples: they constitute his knowledge. In every step in the learning process, 'the effect of any further *explanation* depends on his (the learner's) reaction'.[78] Stanley Cavell, writing about the same problem, says: 'We learn and teach words in *certain* contexts, and then we are expected, and expect others, to be able to project them into further contexts.'[79] Of course, nothing *guarantees* that these projections will occur. But that on the whole they do—that people do learn, that children are trained—is 'a matter of our sharing routes of interest and feeling, modes of response, senses of humour and of fulfilment . . . —all the whirl of organism Wittgenstein calls "forms of life". Human speech and activity, sanity and community, rest upon nothing more, but nothing less than this.'[80] That human beings can be trained to look in the direction of a pointing finger is a fact of human nature, just as it is a fact of nature that dogs, but not cats, can be taught to retrieve. Wittgenstein says:

> Imagine the gestures, sounds, etc., of encouragement you use when you teach a dog to retrieve. Imagine on the other hand, that you tried to teach a cat to retrieve. As the cat will not respond to your encouragement, most of the acts of encouragement which you performed when you trained the dog are here out of the question.[81]

Similarly with training children, the training which produces reaction is not explanation; instead, the reaction is presupposed by any interpretation. So we cannot teach cats to retrieve, tigers to talk or people to fly—although dogs are capable of learning to retrieve, people of talking and birds of flying.

We come now to *grammar*, which properly speaking cannot be separated from rules, language-games and conventions. Grammar, as Wittgenstein uses the term, refers to the unwritten, taken-for-granted rules that govern our language use—what we all know but cannot say. In Cavell's words: '. . . instead of accumulating new facts, or capturing the essence of the world in definitions, or perfecting and completing our language, we need to arrange the facts we already know or can come to realize merely by *calling to mind* something we know.'[82] This is not to say that Wittgenstein was not interested in essence. He was, but only '*essence* is expressed by grammar'.[83] Not that Wittgenstein wanted to talk only about words, for 'Grammar tells us what kind of object anything is'.[84]

Wittgenstein used the word 'grammar' in at least two senses. The surface grammar of a word is the superficial impression given in the way it is used in a particular utterance. We are often led to misunderstand the use of words because of our focus on their surface grammar.

Depth grammar is concerned with the language-game and circumstances in which a particular word plays a part. Wittgenstein emphasised the importance of considering a word's depth grammar if we are to understand fully how it is being used and what it means.

When we are confused about the grammar of an expression, Wittgenstein says, we experience conceptual puzzlement. If we are puzzled about this or that word, he recommends that we investigate expressions in which the word is *used* and, especially, that we ask: what is the process of 'getting to know' in this case? Questions about 'getting to know' are questions concerning the grammar of the words 'to know'. 'What do we *call* "getting to know?"' It is part of the grammar of the word "chair" that *this* is what we call "to sit on a chair", and it is part of the grammar of the word "meaning" that *this* is what we call "explanation of a meaning. . . ."[85] What is pointed to here, then, is the conclusion that the 'grammar' of one or another word includes the great variety of verbal expressions in which a word is generally used.

Consider the word 'house'. The grammar of this word includes 'to keep house', 'to clean house', 'to house-hunt', 'to housebreak', 'to have open house', but also 'to house a fugitive' and 'to house a complaint'. The grammar of 'house', however, tells us more than merely that a house is something, for example, that one can 'live in', but also what counts as 'living in a house'. After all, one can also be *living in* 'fear' or 'sin'. So, what makes something a house is not only that we can 'live in' it, but *how* we live in it (as compared to, say, living in fear). That is, you *can* live in fear, or in sin, but not in *this* way—not in the grammatical way that one lives in a house. This is what Wittgenstein means in the above quotation when he says that '*this* is what we call . . .'. Similarly, concerning our earlier example, one can 'lose' his wallet, his way, his memory or his temper. But one does not (grammatically) 'lose' these things in the same way.

Learning a word's meaning, then, involves learning the whole grammar that regulates its uses. Grammar is learned from cases, from experiencing words and phrases in certain verbal and social contexts. Pitkin makes an important observation in this regard:

[Grammar] is dependent on experienced reality; in that sense, our experience of reality is prior to language, prior to grammar. (It is, one might say, roughly one and a half to two years prior. The child has a backlog of preverbal experiences by the time it begins to talk.) But because in learning grammar we learn what will count as various circumstances, grammar is also prior to experience. Though not chronologically prior in learning, it is logically prior, once learned. It is prior not so much to what we can experience, but to what we can *say* (and therefore what we can think discursively) about our experience.[86]

Pitkin's point here deserves somewhat further attention, because the issue is complex. While Pitkin says on the one hand that grammar is prior 'to what we can experience', and on the other hand that it is prior 'not so much to what we can experience' as to 'what we can say', the general meaning of the statement can be seen, I believe, in the following example. Consider the matter of 'colour'. In some languages there are a larger or smaller number of words for colours than we are accustomed to in European languages. For instance, Nida states that in many African languages there are only three colour words.[87] This limits not only what the speakers of these languages can *say*, but also what they can experience and *see*. It is not that they see (what we call) 'rose', 'violet', 'pink' and 'red', and *call* all of these 'different' colours by one term, but rather that they *see* only one colour. There is a difference between a physical state and a visual experience. It is not a matter of different interpretations—different ways of thinking about something—but of seeing as an experiential state. Concerning such things as the duck-rabbit pictured below (which can be seen as a rabbit's head or a duck's), Wittgenstein remarks: 'Do I really see something different each time, or do I only interpret what I see in a different way? I am inclined to say the former. But why? To interpret is to think, to do something; seeing is a state.'[88] Thus certain African people (those described by Nida) and Europeans may, in a sense,

'look at' the same retinal/cordical/sense-data, but they may not 'see' the same thing. There is clearly more to seeing than meets the eyeball.

For Wittgenstein, grammar governs the possibilities of intelligible experience, and hence limits what the world could contain. Grammar, he says, governs 'the "*possibilities*" of phenomena' by regulating 'the *kind of statement* that we make about phenomena'.[89] Our concepts and their grammar determine what would *count* as an instance of this or that phenomenon. Wittgenstein asks, for instance, 'Can a machine have toothache?'[90] Our answer, of course, is that it cannot. What Wittgenstein draws our attention to is the use made of the word 'can' here. It is not only that all of our past experiences (and that of others known to us) have shown that machines do not have toothaches. Our saying 'no' is not an empirical generalisation; the impossibility is a logical one. Nothing that we could observe or experience would *count* as a machine's 'having a toothache'. At the same time that the grammar of machines and toothaches limits what is possible here, so might the grammar of 'cannot'. That is, someone who has lost all his teeth cannot have a toothache, but not in the same sense that a machine cannot. Consider another question: 'Is it possible for computers to think?' Again, this is not a matter of empirical research or experience. The question is nonsensical. A computer cannot—grammatically—think, or feel, or wish. Our language does not allow us to ascribe the words 'think', 'feel' or 'wish' to computers. This is not to say that there are not other forms of life and language-games where, for example, computers or trees or rocks 'think' and 'feel'—consider certain primitive peoples or the forms of life depicted in science fiction stories.

Conventions

This brings us to the matter of 'conventions' which I mentioned earlier. Language-games rest on human conventions. It is human beings who are responsible for the conventions by which language is used. Of course, language can, and in fact does, change. Wittgenstein makes this clear in the following statement: 'this multiplicity is not something fixed, given once for all; but new types of language, new language-games, as we may say, come into existence, and others become obsolete and get forgotten.'[91] But language, it must be emphasised, is always embedded in a situation, in human customs and institutions. And while language is conventional, this is not to say that it is arbitrary. Wittgenstein remarks: 'Orders are sometimes not obeyed. But what would it be like if no orders were *ever* obeyed? The concept "order" would have lost its purpose.'[92] And he goes on to offer the following examples:

[With regard to the application of 'above' and 'below' to the earth.] Here we have a quite clear idea of what 'above' and 'below' mean. I see well enough that I am on top; the earth is surely beneath men! (And don't smile at this example. We are indeed all taught at school that it is stupid to talk like that. But it is much easier to bury a problem than to solve it.) And it is only reflection that shews us that in this case 'above' and 'below' cannot be used in the ordinary way. (That we might, for instance, say that the people at the antipodes are 'below' our part of the earth, but it must also be recognized as right for them to use the same expression about us.)[93]

We say, for example: 'Experience teaches that there is rain when the barometer falls, but it also teaches that there is rain when we have certain sensations of wet and cold or such-and-such visual impressions.' In defence of this one says that these sense-impressions can deceive us. But here one fails to reflect that the fact that the false appearance is precisely one of rain is founded on a *definition*.[94]

The point here is not that our sense-impressions can lie, but that we understand their language. (And this language like any other is founded on convention.)[95]

If something is the criterion of this or that, then it is because men agree in certain *conventions*. 'Here we strike rock bottom,' Wittgenstein says, 'that is all we have come down to conventions'.[96]

But Wittgenstein also teaches something different: that, in a sense, concepts are dependent on the world. That is to say, language-games are dependent on what men and their world are like. For instance, Wittgenstein asks: 'How does it come about that this arrow ►——→ points?'[97] His remark is intended to show that, on the one hand, the 'pointing' of an arrow is a matter of human convention; but, on the other, it also has a deeper significance. Pitkin makes the point nicely:

For where does our convention come from, that arrows in diagrams and on signposts 'point' in the direction of the arrow tip? Arrows are something that human beings once used as instruments for hunting. They were made with a sharp tip at one end for this purpose, and to function they must be shot tip-first. So the convention about how an arrow points is not an arbitrary one. To be sure, if this planet's physics were very different, if what we call hunting had a totally different purpose than it now has, one might need very different 'arrows' or might shoot arrows in some radically different way. So arrows that point are conventional; but that convention is not just based on an arbitrary agreement that might just as well have been arranged in some other way.[98]

An excellent example of the dependence of concepts on the world is found in *Cosmicomics*, the work of the wonderfully inventive novelist Italo Calvino. In a chapter entitled 'Without colours', Calvino paints the following picture of the earth as it was before its atmosphere, which now filters the sun's murderous light, had been formed. The narrator speaks:

> Among the countless indispensable things we had to do without, the absence of colors—as you can imagine—was the least of our problems; even if we had known they existed, we would have considered them an unsuitable luxury. The only drawback was the strain on your eyes when you had to hunt for something or someone, because with everything equally colorless no form could be clearly distinguished from what was behind it or around it.[99]

Not only did the lack of atmosphere mean an absence of colours, but this lack asserted itself in other ways. Calvino continues, 'you take meteors for example: they fell like hail from all the points of space, because then we didn't have the stratosphere, where nowadays they strike, as if on a roof, and disintegrate. Then there was the silence: no use shouting! Without any air to vibrate, we were all deaf and dumb.'[100]

An absence of colours and total silence! This is indeed a different world from the world we know today. Later, as Calvino moves further in his imaginative portrayal of the earth's birth, we get a description of 'betting' between the narrator and Dean(k)yK:

> We bet on what events would or would not take place; the choice was virtually unlimited, because up till then absolutely nothing had happened. But since there wasn't even a way to imagine how an event might be, we designated in a kind of code: Event A, Event B, Event C, and so on just to distinguish one from the other. What I mean is: since there were no alphabets in existence then or any other series of accepted signs, first we bet on how a series of signs might be and then we matched these possible signs with various possible events, in order to identify with sufficient precision matters that we still don't know a thing about.

We also didn't know what we were staking because there was
nothing that could serve as a stake, and so we gambled on our word,
keeping an account of the bets each had won, to be added up later.
All these calculations were very difficult, since numbers didn't exist
then, and we didn't even have the concept of numbers, to begin to
count, because it wasn't possible to separate anything from anything
else.[101]

Calvino's *Cosmicomics* serves as an apt example of the ways in which
our language and concepts are dependent on what men and the world
are like. In Calvino's 'world', there are no colours, no sounds, no
happenings, no alphabets or other signs, no numbers. In fact, he tells
us, nothing could be separated from anything else. Elsewhere in his
novel, Calvino's narrator discusses people who refer to others as
'immigrants', and asserts: 'This was mere unfounded prejudice—that
seems obvious to me—because neither before or after existed, nor any
place to immigrate from, but there were those who insisted that the
concept of "immigrant" could be understood in the abstract, outside
of space and time.'[102] Without the notion of 'place', then, immigration
is (grammatically) impossible. Of course, as Calvino notes, some persons
see the concept of 'immigrant' and other concepts as existing outside
time and space—as, in a sense, did Wittgenstein in the *Tractatus*, and
as do many positivists at the present time.

Now, some may argue that Calvino's account is totally unrealistic
and far-fetched. But consider another example. Imagine that a living
arrangement is created in which all 'property' (books, automobiles,
clothing, toothbrushes, and so on) is communal property; it belongs
to everyone and there is no notion of private property. Imagine further
that this continues for several generations, so that eventually the notion
of this or that 'belonging' to some individual plays no part in their form
of life. One day a sociologist arrives on the scene to do a study of this
community focusing on the issue of how much 'stealing' there is among
these people. But among these people the question is idle. There is no
'stealing'—the concept does not exist for them. Stealing does not exist,
cannot be created, among those who have no concept of personal
belongings. The typical (positivistic, picture-following) sociologist would
perhaps argue: 'But when A takes B's comb or book or toothbrush,
that is "really" stealing.' Perhaps that is so within the language-game
familiar to the sociologist. For those belonging to our imaginary community, however, there is no stealing—just as there is no casting of
spells by sociologists on one another (that is to say, there is nothing

that *counts* as 'casting a spell' in the language-game of academic sociology).

Thus, language and life rest on conventions. While they have no necessity beyond what human beings do (which should, I think, be sufficient), they are not arbitrary. It is not that all the members of a society could (even if it were physically possible) get together and take a vote as to what the forms of life should be—and therefore their language—and what they should consider painful or humorous, or insulting or interesting, for example. In referring to social arrangements as conventional, then, we must also recognise that they are natural. (This will be considered further in subsequent chapters.) The *Investigations* represents Wittgenstein's rejection of the views expressed in the *Tractatus* that the conceptual frameworks which human beings employ can be objectively justified. Rather, he argues that the request for such justification is without foundation; we use the frameworks we do because we are the creatures we are.

Private language and understanding

Mind-matter dualists like Descartes and Locke held that subjective experiential data are the primary source of knowledge. Subjective experiences, they thought, constitute the basis for public things and qualities. This view rests on an argument by analogy: when I see that there are other bodies (constructed out of my sense-impressions) which resemble mine, and further that these bodies behave as I do in similar circumstances, I *infer* that these bodies are possessed by minds which think and feel in ways similar to mine. *My* point of view, therefore, is given as the inescapable basis of knowledge.

What is immediately given is *my* experience, especially *my* sense-impressions and perceptions. With regard to language, we have the following formulation. Since the knowledge of the objective world or the public world is somehow derived from subjective experiences, ordinary intersubjective languages which refer to public things and qualities must have been *preceded* by subjective or private languages referring to subjective experiences only. Hence, 'private language' is taken to mean a language logically *prior* to any public, intersubjective language.[103]

Wittgenstein rejects this epistemological tradition, noting that purely subjective, incommunicable experiences have no place in the public, intersubjectively understandable language in which we speak, for example, about our thoughts and feelings. He directs the following argument against the private language idea:

> Let us imagine the following case. I want to keep a diary about the recurrence of a certain sensation. To this end I associate it with the sign 'S' and write this sign in a calendar for every day on which I have the sensation.—I will remark first of all that a definition of the sign cannot be formulated.—But still I can give myself a kind of ostensive definition.—How? Can I point to the sensation? Not in the ordinary sense. But I speak, or write the sign down, and at the same time I concentrate my attention on the sensation—and so, as it were, point to it inwardly.—But what is this ceremony for? for that is all it seems to be! A definition surely serves to establish the meaning of a sign.—Well, that is done precisely by the concentration of my attention; for in this way I impress on myself the connexion between the sign and the sensation.—But 'I impress it on myself' can only mean: this process brings it about that I remember the connexion *right* in the future. But in the present case I have no criterion of correctness. One would like to say: whatever is going to seem right to me is right. And that only means that here we can't talk about 'right'.[104]

> What reason have we for calling 'S' the sign for a *sensation*? For 'sensation' is a word of our common language, not of one intelligible to me alone. So the use of this word stands in need of a justification which everybody understands.—And it would not help either to say that it need not be a *sensation*; that when he writes 'S', he has *something*—and that is all that can be said. 'Has' and 'something' also belong to our common language.—So in the end when one is doing philosophy one gets to the point where one would like just to emit an inarticulate sound.—But such a sound is an expression only as it occurs in a particular language-game, which should now be described.[105]

Therefore, the question about the existence of something about which nothing can be said in any language turns out to be a spurious one. If someone invents a rule and tries to follow it, then he has no independent checks on whether or not he is following the rule *correctly* (and without the notions of correct and incorrect, there are no rules). Since the so-called 'private rule' follower cannot know whether or not his memory is deceiving him, everything that would seem correct to him would be correct. However, to think that one is following the rule correctly is, of course, entirely different from following the rule correctly. Wittgenstein says:

> And hence also 'obeying a rule' is a practice. And to *think* one is obeying a rule is not to obey a rule. Hence it is not possible to obey a rule 'privately': otherwise thinking one was obeying a rule would be the same thing as obeying it.[106]

Consequently, there can be no private rules. All rules must be (at least potentially) social and public. Further, this makes it clear that such concepts as 'understanding' and 'knowledge' are inseparable from outward criteria, in that rules for showing that one understands or knows must be intersubjective or public. Let us consider the question of understanding.

What is it, Wittgenstein asks, to 'understand' something: a word, a sentence, a proposition? Does 'understanding' involve some special psychological process which accompanies the words, sentences or propositions, or is it something else? And if it is something else, what is it? Wittgenstein considers these questions, writing:

> It is a prevalent notion that we can only imperfectly *exhibit* our understanding; that we can only point to it from afar or come closer to it, but never lay our hands on it, and that the ultimate thing can never be said. We say 'Understanding is something *different* from the expression of understanding. *Understanding* cannot be exhibited; it is something inward and spiritual.'—Or 'Whatever I do to exhibit understanding, whether I repeat an explanation of a word, or carry out an order to show that I have understood it, these bits of behaviour do not *have* to be taken as proofs of understanding.' . . . But the impossibility spoken of here is supposed to be a logical one. 'Isn't it the case that the expression of understanding is always an incomplete expression?' That means, I suppose, an expression with something missing—but the something missing is essentially *inexpressible*, because otherwise I might find a better expression for it. And 'essentially inexpressible' means that it makes no sense to talk of a more complete expression.[107]

The view which Wittgenstein is trying to combat is that which argues that the 'real', 'final', 'essential' (or whatever) understanding is an inner process that takes place when understanding occurs. The grammar of the word 'understand', he cautions us, is not the grammar of an 'inner process' or a 'state of consciousness', but something different. There is only one way to learn it: to look and see how the word is used in practice. It is not as if, when we understand something, a bell rings somewhere in our minds or a certain feeling passes over us, and we carry around a picture of this ringing or feeling, so as to be able to judge when it occurs. Instead, understanding is a phenomenon of learning and using our human language.

Consider the question of whether someone understands a particular game:

> What's the sign of someone's understanding a game? Must he be able to recite the rules? Isn't it also a criterion that he can play the game, i.e., that he does in fact play it, even if he's baffled when asked for the rules? Is it only by being told the rules that the game is learnt and not also simply by watching it being played? Of course a man will often say to himself while watching 'oh, so that's the rule'; and he might perhaps write down the rules as he observes them; but there's certainly such a thing as learning the game without explicit rules.[108]

Understanding a game, then, may mean knowing the rules, but it may also mean knowing how to play it. Similarly, understanding words or sentences may mean: *knowing* how they are used; *being able* to apply them. But it still might be asked: 'Isn't there something special that happens when one does understand?' Wittgenstein indicates that a multiplicity of things may happen:

> 'I cannot carry out the orders because I don't understand what you mean.—Yes, I understand you now.'—What went on when I suddenly understood him? Here there are *many* possibilities. For example: the order may have been given in a familiar language but with a wrong emphasis, and the right emphasis suddenly occurred to me. In that case perhaps I should say to a third party: 'Now I understand him: he means . . .' and should repeat the order with the right emphasis. And when I grasped the familiar sentence I'd have understood the order,—I mean, I should not first have had to grasp an abstract sense.—Alternatively: I understood the order in *that* sense, so it was a correct English sentence, but it seemed preposterous. In such a case I would say: 'I do not understand you: because you can't mean *that*.' But then a more comprehensible interpretation occurred to me. Before I understand several interpretations, several explanations, may pass through my mind, and then I decide on one of them.[109]

Thus when we understand something (a word, a sentence, an order, a proposition) there is no instantaneous grasp of grammar or anything else that occurs. In fact, there is no one single characteristic which is common to all acts of understanding. In the case of understanding words ('beauty', 'regular', 'high'), this generally involves being able to use them on certain occasions in a special tone of voice. Wittgenstein asks: 'What does it mean to understand the word "perhaps"?'

> Do I understand the word 'perhaps'?—And how do I judge whether I do? Well, something like this: I know how it's used, I can explain its use to somebody, say by describing it in made-up cases. I can describe the occasions of its use, its position in sentences, the intonation it has in speech.—Of course this only means that 'I understand the word "perhaps"' comes to the same as: 'I know how it is used etc.'; not that I try to call to mind its entire application in order to answer the question whether I understand the word.[110]

What Wittgenstein emphasises again and again is that a word's meaning is its role in the language, or more specifically in a particular language-game. He rejects the idea that concepts like 'understanding' and 'meaning' refer to mental activities. That is, he rejects the view that these verbs refer to or assume some invisible, inner, private activity, accessible only to the individual himself. Consider again the example where one person writes down a series of numbers (1, 3, 5, 7, 9) and another person is supposed to continue the series correctly. Perhaps at first the man is watching in a somewhat puzzled manner, then suddenly says: 'Now I've got it' or 'Now I understand it'. What, then, has changed? Uttering those words does not appear fully to constitute his understanding; so we try to 'get hold of the mental process which seems to be hidden behind the coarser and therefore more visible accomplishments'.[111] But Wittgenstein asks, what will we find when we look 'inward'? We may find any number of thoughts and feelings, or none at all. It need not be assumed that a man who says 'Now I understand' is giving us a report on some internal state or activity that he has just himself observed. In fact, 'It would be quite misleading . . . to call the words a "description of a mental state":— One might rather call them a "signal"; and we judge whether it was rightly employed by what he goes on to do.'[112]

The central point here is that understanding or meaning, for example, are not activities with duration that take place while we speak. 'If we say to someone "I should be delighted to see you" and mean it, does a conscious process run along these words . . .? This will hardly ever be the case.'[113] Understanding, meaning, knowing, and the like, are not usually processes that have duration, like running a foot-race or sleeping. 'Suppose it were asked: *When* do you know how to play chess? All the time? or just while you are making a move? And the *whole* of chess during each move? How queer that knowing how to play chess should take such a short time, and a game so much longer!'[114] All of this is to say that the grammar of words like 'mean' and 'understand' is more complex than usually assumed. These words are not simply labels for some inner processes recognisable only by the individual actor, but they are dependent on the language-games in which they are found. They rest on the human condition and the language-games in which they form a part.

In this connection, it is perhaps appropriate here to make some preliminary remarks about the work of Peter Winch, whom I consider in a later chapter. Winch's *The Idea of a Social Science* was the first book which argued for the importance of Wittgenstein's work as it pertained to the social sciences. By reminding us that 'meaning' and 'understanding' can only be grasped by considering the social relationships and situations in which actions take place, Winch has followed Wittgenstein's lead. Unfortunately, however, Winch fails to recognise that in the practice of science it is the scientists themselves who are the ultimate arbiters of 'scientific' truths and knowledge. As I will try to show later, Winch stops short of carrying the implications of Wittgensteins's views to their logical conclusion. I will return to this issue later.

Wittgenstein's method

The later Wittgenstein conducts a dialogue with the Wittgenstein of the *Tractatus*; there is a kind of dialectic, where his earlier and later views are compared and contrasted. In fact, Wittgenstein himself says that he had wanted to publish the *Tractatus* and the *Investigations* together because, in his words, '. . . the latter could be seen in the right light only by contrast with and against the background of my old way of thinking. For since beginning to occupy myself with philosophy again . . . , I have been forced to recognise grave mistakes in what I wrote in the first book.'[115]

Wittgenstein tells us that 'There is not *a* philosophical method, though there are indeed methods, like different therapies'.[116] What he means by methods are apparently things like imagining a language or a form of life different from our own,[117] 'finding and inventing intermediate cases',[118] imagining 'certain very general facts of nature to be different from what we are used to, and the formation of our concepts different from the usual ones',[119] or calling attention to some well-known facts which are forgotten. These different methods are methods for acquiring self-knowledge. Cavell remarks that 'the nature of self-knowledge—and therewith the nature of the self—is one of the great subjects of the *Investigations* as a whole'.[120] For Wittgenstein, as for Socrates, self-understanding is both the method and the goal of philosophising. Wittgenstein's method is not, of course, a recipe or a formula. It is an *art*. He created a new style of thinking, a new way of looking at things. Like Socrates, Freud and Marx, he is engaged in persuasion and conversion. Speaking of psycho-analysis, Wittgenstein says, 'If you are led by psycho-analysis to say that really you thought so and so or that really your motive was so and so, this is not a matter of discovery, but of persuasion'.[121] And, speaking of himself, he stated in one of his lectures: 'I am in a sense making propaganda for one style of thinking as opposed to another. I am honestly disgusted with the other . . . (Much of what we are doing is a question of changing the style of thinking.)'[122]

An emphasis on the richness of language and its many possible uses is one of the qualities that so clearly distinguishes Wittgenstein from other philosophers. Cavell expresses it nicely:

> The first thing to be said in accounting for his style is that he *writes*: he does not report, he does not write up results. Nobody would forge a style so personal who had not wanted and needed to find the right expression for his thought. The German dissertation and the British essay—our most common modern options for writing philosophy— would not work; his is not a system and he is not a spectator . . . [The *Investigations*] contains what serious confessions must: the full acknowledgement of temptation ('I want to say . . .'; 'I feel like saying. . . .'; 'Here the urge is strong. . .'). . . (The voice of temptation and the voices of correctness are the antagonists in Wittgenstein's dialogues.) In confessing you do not explain or justify, but describe how it is with you. And confession, unlike dogma, is not to be believed but tested, and accepted or rejected. Nor is it the occasion for accusation, except of yourself, and by implication those who find themselves in you. There is exhortation ('Do not say: "There *must* be something common" . . . but *look* and *see*'), not to belief, but to self-scrutiny. And that is why there is virtually nothing in the *Investigations* which we should ordinarily call reasoning.[123]

What we find in Wittgenstein, then, is confession, doubt, exhortation, as well as irony, metaphor, paradox, humour, parable and dialogue. In short, we find human speech—not the language of the expert or the professional. We find an insistence on the language and life of ordinary people.

In the following chapters, we will encounter again many of the themes introduced in the present chapter: form of life, language-games, rules and conventions. It is hoped that the overview of Wittgenstein's philosophy presented in these pages will serve as a basis for dealing with the issues to be raised in the remainder of this book.

3 Two Images of Science

Until relatively recently, descriptions of science have been characterised by an ahistorical approach, with a heavy emphasis on logic, on the
unified nature of science, on the principle of empiricism and on formal
analysis. Science, from this perspective, is an enterprise controlled by
logic and empirical facts, whose purpose is to formulate truths about
the laws of nature. This dominant view has long been firmly entrenched
and taken for granted. It has enjoyed the support not only of philosophers of science but of practising scientists as well. Slowly, however, this image of science is being replaced by a new image, where
science is viewed as a social activity. This new image is represented by
Thomas Kuhn, Michael Polanyi, Paul Feyerabend, Stephen Toulmin
and others. As I will indicate in the following pages, it shares many
characteristics with that part of sociology which is referred to as the
sociology of knowledge.

In this chapter I will consider both the old (or dominant) and the
new images of science. My reason for doing so is quite simple: both
images lead to conclusions that are at odds with a more Wittgensteinian
conception, even though there are similarities to some of Wittgenstein's ideas in both positions. Further, and more importantly, careful
examination of some of Wittgenstein's ideas in the following chapter
will indicate the extent to which his views may help us resolve certain
problems raised by these two competing images of science.

The dominant image

The general image of science in Western society has been strongly
influenced by certain notions about the nature of scientific development, practice and progress. While it is difficult to characterise the
dominant image with any one all-inclusive term, I will use the word
'positivism' as the term best describing it.[1] It is interesting in this
regard that the terms 'positivist' and 'positivism' are seldom used by
scientists in describing their own work or their own position. However,

the terms are frequently used nowadays to express disapprobation in criticising the work of those with whom one disagrees. That is, they are used by many critics of contemporary science as shorthand terms for designating work with which they are not in sympathy.

For the most part, there are few attempts to set out and discuss the elements of positivism which serve to differentiate it from other views or standpoints. The fact that neither the advocates nor the critics of positivism take the trouble to make explicit their usage of the term make it difficult to be clear as to what is intended when the terms 'positivist' and 'positivism' are employed. Since I want to contrast the dominant (positivistic) image of science with what I term the 'new image', it is important to try to lay out, albeit roughly, the major elements of positivism.

It is not my intention here to discuss or trace the history of positivism, but instead to consider some of its major characteristics. Still, it is useful to say something about its origin, because of the profound consequences for the field of sociology which followed from the influence of Auguste Comte, who is credited with being the inventor of the term 'positivism'. He viewed history as progressing through three stages: the religious, the metaphysical and the scientific. For Comte, the scientific was the last and superior stage. That is, science provided the standards by which the earlier two stages could be examined and evaluated. In the theological or religious stage, men explain phenomena by referring them to the acts of spiritual beings; in the metaphysical stage, spiritual beings are replaced by 'powers' or 'essences'; while in the scientific (positive) stage, men come to see that explanation involves a description of the coexistence and succession of phenomena. The general methods used in physics and chemistry, Comte argued, could be used in the study of society. These 'positive' sciences rejected undisciplined speculation and, instead, emphasised the importance of tested and systematic experience. Just as men in the Middle Ages turned to the Church and theology, men of the nineteenth century turned to Science. Comte wanted to transfer to the study of social phenomena the methods and concepts of the natural (positive) sciences.

Three major principles of positivism are stressed in Comte's formulation:

[T]he first characteristic of the Positivist Philosophy is that it regards all phenomena as subject to invariable natural *Laws* . . . . Our real business is to analyze accurately the circumstances of phenomena, and to connect them by the natural relations of succession and resemblance . . . . Its secondary and general aim is this: to review what had been effective in the sciences, in order to show that they are not radically separated, but all branches from the same trunk . . . . The only necessary unity is that of Method, which is already in great part established.[2]

With the third principle of positivism, the 'human mind' is to be studied, not by introspection, but by practising the positive method itself.

Underlying Comte's positivism was his desire to change, reform and improve the quality of life by criticising the dominant institutions and practices of his day. He sought new bases for social norms and authority. Part of Comte's task was to oppose what he regarded as the 'negative' philosophy of the seventeenth and eighteenth centuries, to contravene 'all those individualistic ideas that had flowered during the Enlightenment and which were the driving force of the Revolution'.[3] His six-volume *Positive Philosophy* was directed at the negative, revolutionary philosophy represented by the Hegelian dialecticians. However, Comte's influence on sociology has come less from his philosophy of history ('the law of three stages') than from his emphasis on society as the primordial reality, with the 'individual' being regarded as a mental construct. 'Social facts' are to be recognised as realities *sui generis*, referring not to individuals but to the collectivity. This methodological principle is also seen in Durkheim's powerful influence on the development and practice of sociology. Durkheim admonished sociologists 'to treat phenomena as things is to treat them as data, and these constitute the point of departure of science'.[4]

Positivism in the twentieth century has come to be known as *logical positivism* or *logical empiricism*, thus placing a heavy emphasis on rationality with which logic is seen to be synonymous. The term 'logic' was added because it was thought that the work of Frege, Russell and others in modern logic would prove central to the development and practice of positivist science. It was hoped that the new logic would help to reveal the disorder of language, thus making it possible to display logically the structure of reality (a task very much akin to the focus of Wittgenstein's *Tractatus*). As represented by the members of the Vienna Circle (Schlick, Carnap, Neurath, Frank), logical positivism or logical empiricism was characterised by the methodological requirement of 'strong reductionism'. This meant that all theoretical statements should, in principle, be totally reducible to observation statements. More recent positivists, like Hempel and Nagel, reject the reductionist requirement, as does Karl Popper. Rather than conceiving of science as some sort of inventory of inductive generalisations based on observation, they stress the importance of constructing theories. These theories, however, have deductive consequences which are indirectly testable by observation. All of these philosophers of science share the viewpoint that the various sciences are characterised by common methods of explanation and prediction.

Like the early Wittgenstein, modern positivists seem to hold that 'science is the totality of true propositions'. For the logical positivists, statements are cognitively meaningful only if they are verifiable. 'The principle of verifiability', the principle that the meaning of a proposition lies in its method of verification, came to be regarded as the central tenet of logical positivism. The logical positivists thought they had derived the verification principle from Wittgenstein's *Tractatus*. He had written that 'to understand a proposition means to know what is the case, if it is true'. But this is not at all the same as to identify a proposition's meaning with its method of verification. After all, Wittgenstein claimed that he was not advancing a *theory* about meaning.

Whatever the origin of the verification principle, for the logical positivists *scientific* meaning is viewed as a property only of propositions that can be tested, directly or indirectly, by means of observation. Positivists presuppose a common and easily intelligible 'observation language' which is both the basis of scientific theories and the ultimate criterion for settling the claims of various theories. The truth of different propositions rests on their correspondence to what exists in the outside world. The actual practice of science involves the division of propositions into two disjunctive classes, accepted and nonaccepted propositions. The emphasis on logic and observation is, of course, part of the positivists' rejection of metaphysics. They viewed 'metaphysics' as a concern with those entities which lie beyond the reach of any possible experience, and they wanted to eliminate as meaningless all references to entities which are not accessible to observation.

For logical positivists, the world we know is a collection of individual facts. Science has the goal of ordering these facts, and it is only because of this ordering activity that a practice becomes a 'true' science. The facts themselves are what they are no matter what scientists call them. In this view, words are labels and language our means of referring to what exists 'out there' in the world. Hence, language and the world are separate, although correlatable. Truth, then, is correspondence with the facts as disclosed by experience or observation; knowledge of extralogical truths must be *empirical*. Further, it is believed that, in principle, everything can be said in the language of physics, that is, by reference to processes in time and space. According to the 'Unity of Science' principle, what cannot be expressed in the language of physics is either tautologous or nonsensical. Methodological monism, the idea of the unity of scientific method amid the diversity of subject matter, is a cardinal tenet of positivism. Science has but one method, one language.

So far as most positivists are concerned, explanation and prediction are quite similar, in that both require *deducing* a proposition that refers to a *particular* event from other propositions referring to general regularities, together with particular propositions referring to specific events ('antecedent conditions'). Thus there is an epistemological symmetry between explanation and prediction; they are two sides of the same coin. To explain is to cover an instance with a generalisation; to predict is to deduce an instance from a generalisation. The proposition which refers to regularities is *tested* by determining whether or not a logically independent item of evidence corresponds to the *predictions* that have been deduced from these posited regularities, supplemented by certain propositions (sentences) referring to antecedent conditions. Logical positivism emphasises the importance of 'confirming' regularities (universal hypotheses) then, through observation.

In saying above that an item of evidence is 'logically independent', it is intended that the evidence must not be contained in the antecedent conditions. That is to say, the relation between evidence and antecedent conditions must be 'empirical', that is, based on *observation*. A regularity employed in prediction is *confirmed* if it is found to be *empirically* true, if, in other words, a logically independent piece of evidence corresponds to it. Explanation (as distinct from prediction) is involved when it is possible to *identify* those regularities and antecedent conditions which are referred to by the propositions which provide for the *deduction* of the particular propositions pertaining to the event to be explained. As with the prediction of an event, the explained event must stand in an empirical relation to its own antecedent conditions. Regularities are also said to be 'explained' when the universal hypotheses which refer to them are deduced from some other, more abstract, universal hypotheses.

As noted earlier, positivists hold that the natural and social sciences share a basic methodology, that they share the same logic of inquiry and similar research procedures. They believe that the application of 'the scientific method' should be the same at all times, in all places, under all conditions. However, the term 'scientific method' should not be taken to suggest that there is any one correct source of empirical evidence but, rather, that all scientific propositions, in Hempel's words,

> must be checked against the facts of our experience, and they are acceptable only if they are properly supported by empirical evidence. Such evidence is obtained in many different ways: by experimentation, by systematic observation, by interviews or surveys, by psychological or clinical testing, by careful examination of documents, inscriptions, coins, archeological relics, and so forth.[5]

The purpose of all this, of course, is to describe, explain and predict the occurrences in the world we live in. To repeat, our theories must be checked against 'the facts'.

This emphasis on the facts as existing 'out there' as part of reality can be seen clearly in Durkheim, who has been the major influence on the development of positivistic sociology. The world is viewed as a collection of individual observable facts which science aims at ordering. Discovery of these facts will reveal the laws governing them. Thus Durkheim holds that

> The scientist does not create different realities by thinking of the same phenomena in different ways. Rather, the realities come first and our ideas and concepts are simply more or less accurate reflections of the reality to which they correspond and which they ultimately represent.[6]

Durkheim, in his thesis concerning social facts, assumes the existence of a social reality existing independently of the consciousness of individuals, something external to human inquirers. He instructs us that 'to treat phenomena as things is to treat them as data, and these constitute the point of departure of science'.[7] We locate these data, Durkheim says, through 'the eradication of all preconceptions' and by finding and investigating 'a group of phenomena defined in advance by certain common external characteristics'.[8]

Positivists, then, hold that there exists an external reality, a world of nature, which is independent of the human observer. Nature is what it is and would be what it is, according to positivists, without the existence of human observers. Further, positivists believe that there is *a* correct or true version of the world and that truth lies in nature. Scientists are involved in discovering or locating what exists independently in nature, and comparing that reality with their theories or hypotheses.

According to positivists, there exist not only independent data or brute facts in nature but also 'regularities'. Brute facts and regularities, alike, are considered to be independent of any human observer. Durkheim, for example, states that 'when we come into contact with social phenomena one is . . . surprised by the astonishing regularities with which they occur under the same circumstances'.[9]

The assumption of independent facts and regularities in nature is also seen in the emphasis among some logical positivists on causal laws. Individual cases can be subsumed under hypothetically assumed general laws of nature. Hempel states that 'all that a causal law asserts is that any event of a specified kind, i.e., any event having certain specified characteristics, is accompanied by another event which in turn has certain specified characteristics'.[10] Reichenbach says: 'Since repetition is all that distinguishes the causal law from a mere coincidence, the meaning of a causal relation consists in the statement of an exceptionless repetition, it is unnecessary to assume that it means more.'[11] This emphasis on causal laws can also be seen among many sociologists. For instance, Labovitz and Hagedorn state that 'cause, in one way or another, is central to the goal of establishing scientific laws. In general terms, causation refers to the factors that make designated phenomena happen or change.'[12] And Leik notes that 'if X is a causal variable in a general relationship with Y, then changes in X should be sufficient to produce changes in Y'.[13]

Just as logical positivists believe that there exist observer-independent data, they believe that scientists obtain knowledge of these brute facts through the use of theory-independent observational statements. The idea here is that 'theorising' does not enter into observations at all, and that observational terms have their own meaning, independent of the meaning of other terms. Similarly it is assumed that observational statements, made up of observational terms, may be replaced by an alternative framework without altering their meaning. Thus, Nagal states that an experimental law 'retains a meaning that can be formulated independently of the theory; and it is based on observational evidence that may enable the law to survive the eventual demise of the theory'.[14] Carnap holds the same view. Observational statements, of course, refer to perceived things and processes, while theoretical statements typically postulate unobservable elements. The function of the theoretical statements is to explain the laws which generate the phenomena to be observed. Any two theories of the same domain of phenomena may be compared to see which is more successful in accounting for the facts (obtained by observations). Thus the distinction between observational and theoretical language is another central feature of logical positivism. Positivists, then, view reality in mechanistic terms, and assume the existence of a sharp dividing line between scientists and the data they observe.

Logical positivists hold that the theory of science itself *is* a logic, and that the philosopher of science has the goal of disclosing its structures. Since science is a justified form of knowledge, that which justifies it must, in principle, be capable of expression in formal rules of inference (that is, a logic). Associated with this thesis is the distinction, formulated by Reichenbach,[15] between the 'context of discovery' and the 'context of justification'. These two contexts must be kept separate, and only the latter is of concern to the philosopher of science. The thought-processes which lead to discovery are of no interest to the philosopher, because the gist of the scientific method is proof and validation, not discovery. The process of justification is considered to be a rational process which needs to be carefully distinguished from the more erratic processes involved in scientific discovery.

The dominant image of science also rests on the assumption that science must begin from a foundation where certain things are beyond doubt, whether this foundation be first principles, sense-datum statements or something else. Because, it is argued, there are neutral and unquestionable basic propositions in science, different theories can be put in *direct* confrontation with one another, that is, 'commensurability' is possible. Scientific progress is guaranteed by working from this foundation and by introducing hypotheses or theories which then must be closely examined both for their logical consistency and for their corroboration in reality.

Positivist sociologists, like other positivists, hold that the ultimate criterion for a sociological theory is its ability to predict patterns in reality. That is to say, one's hypotheses or theories are tested as to their representativeness in the empirical domain. In Riley's words: 'Guided by the conceptual model and the objective, the researcher then applies the empirical methods he has selected in order to obtain the research findings. These findings consist of facts drawn from the multitude of phenomena in the real world.'[16] In the 'real world' exist the facts which are to be discovered by application of the proper rules of scientific procedure. Thus, Labovitz and Hagedorn state that 'to achieve the major goal of science, which is to establish causal laws, facts and relations between variables must be established. The criteria to establish facts and relations are the procedures of the scientific method.'[17] And Smelser, in discussing the 'common language' of the social sciences, notes that 'The language that I have employed is the language of the ingredients of science: dependent variables, independent variables, theoretical frameworks, and research methods.'[18] Speaking specifically of social facts, Durkheim says that their study 'merely adds to physical, chemical, biological and psychological forces, social forces which like these act upon men from without'.[19] As do other scientists, the sociologist can 'discover' these facts and the relations among them by the use of objective variables which lend themselves to the sort of scientific analyses used in the positive (natural) sciences.[20] Positivism abdicates all reflection, with the result that the 'facts' are absolutised and the existing order reified.

To review briefly, the dominant (positivist) image of science includes several central features: direct observation of perceived things and processes provides the ultimate link between scientific knowledge of the world and the world itself, the reality of the world of which we have knowledge is independent of the observer, and there are observational terms which are themselves theory-independent units of meaning. In addition, the dominant image holds that the actual practice of science —involving the process of justification, the testing and validation of scientific theories and hypotheses—is a *rational process*, far different from what goes on in more common, everyday activities. Finally, the dominant image sees science (and various specific scientific disciplines) as cumulative; new facts are added to old ones, and new theories broaden and extend previous theories. Science, on this view, is cumulative and progressive; it represents a solid growth of knowledge.

Let me now turn briefly to the matter of scientific knowledge and scientific practice as conceived of by sociologists of science, the sociological sub-speciality concerned specifically with science. We have seen that positivism teaches that words are labels, referring to things in the world. The scientist's task is to discover the meaning of what exists in the world. The object of discovery, true knowledge, is viewed as eternal, as out there, to be discovered by anyone who uses the proper procedures in the correct manner. Science, from this perspective, is a systematic body of acquired knowledge. Hence, Ben-David states that science is 'knowledge that can be written down, forgotten, and learned again, with its form or content remaining unchanged. Moreover, scientists are engaged in discovering "laws of nature" that cannot be changed by human action.'[21] Further, the way by which scientists discover these laws of nature is by following the rules of the scientific method. These rules assure the discovery of nature's laws—although, as Ziman points out, nature may be very tenacious of her secrets—through the testing and refutation of various hypotheses so as to establish which ones are valid.[22] Science, from this perspective, is *governed by reason and logic*, by the timeless principles of logico-empirical methodology.

Sociologists of science and knowledge have generally accepted the positivist ideal of science, while ignoring the substance of scientific thought. Even though sociologists have emphasised the social influence of norms, values, behaviour and ideas in other segments of society, they have generally exempted scientific knowledge from social influences. As Klima has recently observed: 'The scientific "norms and values" themselves as well as the contents of the scientific ideas produced under their rule were taken as non-problematic for sociology, ceding the investigation of the conditions of their development to the historians and philosophers of science.'[23] For sociologists of science like Ben-David and Barber, the truths of science are seen as permanent and immutable, and the methods of science as beyond question.[24] Thus Ben-David's statement that: 'In science one obtains interpersonally valid knowledge through the subjection of personal ideas and explanations of reality to public test by logic, experiment or empirical observation. Thus personal biases and mistakes are corrected, and gradually eliminated.'[25] Merton expresses a similar viewpoint: 'The institutional goal of science is the extension of certified knowledge. The technical methods employed toward this end provide the relevant definition of knowledge: *empirically confirmed and logically consistent statements of regularities* (which are, in effect, predictions).'[26]

The new image of science

A new image of science has emerged in recent years, an image owing much to the work of Thomas Kuhn, but also associated with people like Hanson, Feyerabend, Polanyi and Toulmin. Until about 1960, there was a sharp separation between the philosophy of science and the history of science, with the consequence that most philosophers of science had long illustrated the correctness of their position by drawing on a very limited number of examples from studies of the history of science. In the work of Kuhn, Hanson and the others mentioned above, there has been a convergence in the philosophy and history of science.

Norwood Russell Hanson was one of the first to pursue analyses from this standpoint. For example, he argued that the search for answers to the question 'What is *the* cognitive status of a law of nature' was fundamentally misguided. To ask such a question, he said, is rather like asking 'What is *the* use of rope?'[27] Hanson considered the

Newtonian laws of motion from this viewpoint, and concluded that
these laws had been put to a *variety* of uses—depending on the purpose
at hand. He pointed out that expressions are not accompanied by labels
which read 'empirically significant' or '*a priori* true'. Rather, the cognitive status of an expression must be evaluated with regard to the
system of statements in which it is located. Furthermore, Hanson
attacked the discovery/justification dichotomy, arguing that discovery
has its own characteristic cognitive processes, and that justification
cannot (as the positivists claim) be reduced to any explicit set of
formal rules. Hanson's work has been built upon and extended in
recent years, most especially by the historian of science Thomas Kuhn.
Since Kuhn is the best known and most influential of those advocating
the new image of science (especially as far as the social sciences are
concerned), I will focus mainly on his views in considering the new
image of science.

Kuhn argues that instead of considering science as 'the totality of
true propositions' or as governed by unchanging principles of logico-
empirical methodology, there is another way of looking at science: *as a
human activity*. The practice of science, he holds, is not guided by timeless and ahistorical canons of scientific method. Instead, science is
heavily influenced by what he terms 'paradigms'. By paradigms, Kuhn
means 'universally recognized scientific achievements that for a time
provide model problems and solutions to a community of practitioners'.[28] These are not fully articulated explications of principles,
rules or theories, he says, but are generally unanalysed, taken-for-
granted aspects of scientific practice, including 'laws, theory, application, and instrumentation together'.[29] For Kuhn, then, an individual
learns science not from following abstract, universal, solidly-estab-
lished rules or principles of scientific method, but by being *socialised*
into the shared paradigm of his scientific community with its shared
rules of scientific practice. These rules, Kuhn points out, gain their significance only from the cases and circumstances in which they are
learned and utilised. Science can be seen as a fully human activity,
governed by rules, conventions and grammar—like any other human
activity. Science is a game in which the rules are changed as we go
along.

At any given time in a scientific discipline there are 'particular
coherent traditions of scientific research', which Kuhn terms 'normal
science', that take their shape from paradigms. These paradigms 'are
the source of the methods, problem-field, and standards of solution
accepted by any mature scientific community at any given time. As a

result, the reception of a new paradigm often necessitates a redefinition of the corresponding science.'[30] Such paradigms 'provide scientists not only with a map but also with some of the directions for map-making. In learning a paradigm the scientist acquires theory, methods, and standards together, usually in an inextricable mixture.'[31] A paradigm indicates the existence of a coherent, unified viewpoint, which seems to determine the way a science's practitioners view the world and practise their craft.

Since scientists acquire theory, methods and standards in 'an inextricable mixture', the whole positivist notion of theory-independent observations gets called into question. Kuhn conceives of a theory as 'a conceptual network through which scientists view the world'.[32] He asserts that 'People do not see stimuli: our knowledge of them is highly theoretical and abstract'.[33] Similarly, Feyerabend notes that:

> Introducing a new theory involves changes of outlook both with respect to the observable and with respect to the unobservable features of the world . . . Scientific theories are ways of looking at the world; and their adoption affects our general beliefs and expectations, and thereby also our experiences and conceptions of reality.[34]

Both Kuhn and Feyerabend emphasise that what *counts* as an observation of this or that is theory-dependent. There are, then, no raw data, no brute facts, but only data 'analyzed, modelled, and manufactured according to some theory'.[35] Hence, they question the minimal positivist assumption that there is some description of the facts which is neutral between competing explanatory theories. Facts are essentially facts-as-interpreted. Kuhn and Feyerabend, it is clear, are suggesting that the hypothetico-deductive method of explanation rests on an untenable assumption: that meaning remains invariant throughout the process of explanation. Instead, they argue, in adopting a new theory we inevitably alter the concepts and the 'facts' from which we started.

Learning a paradigm means learning a specific way of looking at the world: one sees the world differently (or one sees a different world) from within one paradigm than from within another. Considering paradigm-changes, Kuhn remarks: 'Paradigm changes . . . cause scientists to see the world of the research-engagement differently. In so far as their only recourse to that world is through what they see and do, we may want to say that after a [scientific] revolution scientists are responding to a different world.'[36] Galileo serves as an example for Kuhn's thesis:

Since remote antiquity most people have seen one or another heavy body swinging back and forth on a string or chain until it finally comes to rest. To the Aristotelians, who believed that a heavy body is moved by its own nature from a higher position to a state of natural rest at a lower one, the swinging body was simply falling with difficulty. Constrained by the chain, it could achieve rest at its low point only after a tortuous motion and a considerable time. Galileo, on the other hand, looking at the swinging body, saw a pendulum, a body that almost succeeded in repeating the same motion over and over again *ad infinitum*.[37]

Making use of the relatively new theory of motion—the 'impetus theory'—allowed Galileo to 'see' what the Aristotelians could not. Until the impetus theory 'was invented, there were not pendulums, but only swinging stones, for the scientist to see'.[38] What Kuhn does here is to show that scientists' conceptual language and perceptions are affected by particular paradigms existing under different social-historical conditions.

Kuhn's work makes clear the extent to which the natural and biological sciences share with the social sciences the feature of being fully social activities and, consequently, always subject to the influence of social circumstances and conventions. In fact, Kuhn's investigations are very much in keeping with the aims of sociological inquiry. Consider his statement that 'the type of question I ask has . . . been: how will a particular constellation of beliefs, values, and imperatives affect group behaviour?'[39] Lakatos, Popper, Shapere and Scheffler have strongly criticised Kuhn's 'sociological' analyses, partly on the grounds that they *are* sociological.

The 'new image' of science, as represented by Kuhn, conceives of science as a social enterprise, with an organised consensus of scientists determining what is and is not to be considered scientific, what is and is not to be warranted as knowledge. Since scientists belong to communities, traditions and paradigms, what they can think, see and say are all dependent on the game as played at a particular time and place. Whereas those holding the dominant view of science, like the early Wittgenstein, are concerned with establishing rules of correspondence between language and the world which will then result in true statements, Kuhn, Feyerabend and others in the new image of science hold that it is the consensus of one's fellow scientists (in Kuhn's terminology, those sharing a particular paradigm) who determine whether a statement or proposition is true or not. The problem with the dominant image of science, with its correspondence theory of truth, where propositions are held to be objectively and eternally true pictures of the world, is that it requires a *transcendental* criterion of truth; there must exist extralinguistic criteria which allow for the separation of true propositions (statements, theories) from false ones. But the new image of science appears to have a serious problem of its own: that of relativism.

Kuhn's views, especially, seem to lead to a kind of relativism in science. By stressing the determinative influence of paradigms, as they affect the ways in which scientists view the world, Kuhn apparently denies the possibility of comparing and making judgements about the choice of paradigms. That is, since there are no such things as 'independent' facts, or any other independent features or standards, there can be no 'good reasons' for choosing one paradigm over another. For, according to Kuhn, what constitutes a good reason is itself established by the paradigm in which a scientist practises his craft. For instance, Kuhn states that 'the competition between paradigms is not the sort of battle that can be resolved by proofs'[40] and adds that 'in these matters neither proof nor error is at issue'.[41] Furthermore, he asserts, 'we may . . . have to relinquish the notion, explicit or implicit, that changes of paradigms carry scientists closer to the truth'.[42]

Since Kuhn regards paradigms as sovereign, as providing alternative world-views, this means that those scientists working within one paradigm do not fully share theoretical concepts with scientists working under its rival or predecessors. Lacking a common vocabulary, they may be unable to even formulate topics for discussion or disagreement. From Kuhn's standpoint, there is simply no vocabulary for comparing and contrasting the respective theoretical positions of people operating under different scientific paradigms; there is no way of establishing the superiority of one scientific theory over another. Thus the assumption of the logical positivists that 'commensurability' between different theories is a major characteristic of science is called into question. It is for this reason that the charge of relativism has been directed at Kuhn.

Kuhn has responded to accusations of relativism by asserting that 'one scientific theory is not as good as another for doing *what scientists normally do*'.[43] But this statement is highly ambiguous. Does it mean what scientists *usually* (ordinarily) do, or what they *ideally* (properly, normatively) do? If he means what they 'usually' do, then there is no basis for criticising the actual practices of a scientific community. If he means what they 'ideally' do, then apparently he is an absolutist, holding that there are abstract, timeless criteria of rationality. Should the latter be Kuhn's meaning, then he is abandoning his original thesis.

Leaving the problem of relativism aside for consideration in a later chapter, it is important to dwell on the full consequences of the work of Kuhn, as well as that of Feyerabend, Toulmin and other recent critics of the dominant image of science. They raise strong objections to the assumption that there exists a class of entities which are distinguished by their capacity of being observed *directly* by human observers through their direct sensory equipment. The new image of science argues that all scientific observations are no less problematic than scientific theories. Since scientists work *within* a specific paradigm or tradition, none of the observations, experiments or discoveries can lead directly to the overthrow of that particular paradigm. After all, these observations, experiments, and so on, are themselves framed and expressed in terms of that dominant paradigm, and presuppose various tacit and unarticulated assumptions.

By calling into question the logical positivists' distinction between discovery and justification, the emphasis on commensurability, the assumption of a common and easily intelligible observation language, and the doctrine that the objectivity of science lies in a neutral methodology, capable of being made explicit in a set of logical rules, the new critics have challenged the dominant image of science. Kuhn especially, coming at science from what he terms a 'sociological' perspective, has raised serious questions about earlier conceptions of science and scientific practice.

Kuhn's work makes explicit the community structure of science. Scientists group themselves into specialists' communities, 'bound together by common elements in their education and apprenticeship, aware of each other's work, and characterised by the relative fullness of their professional communication and the relative unanimity of their professional judgement'.[44] These groups produce scientific knowledge. The members of various scientific communities (or subspecialities) must be prepared to appeal to the agreed-upon criteria within their particular communities for warranting scientific truth and knowledge. But, as Kuhn emphasises, scientists differ from other people in the language-games they play, in the way they carve up the world, and in the manner in which they go about deciding what is and is not to be accepted as constituting knowledge. As Kuhn notes: 'Science is not the only activity the practitioners of which can be grouped into communities, but it is the only one in which each community is its own exclusive audience and judge'.[45] Kuhn's writings help emphasise the point that scientific truth and knowledge exist *only* by virtue of being warranted by one or another scientific community. Consistent with the teachings of Wittgenstein, Kuhn rejects the idea of science as a private activity and of knowledge as a private product. Instead, science is recognised as a communal enterprise and scientific knowledge as a product of specialists' communities.

Kuhn's work bears many similarities to the views of two sociologists of knowledge, Karl Mannheim and C. Wright Mills. Both anticipate many of Kuhn's central themes. For example, Mannheim holds that the individual not only *speaks* the language of his group, but he also *thinks* in the manner in which his group thinks—having at his disposal only certain concepts and their standardised meanings within that group. Further, Mannheim observes that people's *perceptions* are dependent upon their historical and social locations: 'Every epoch has its fundamentally new approach and its characteristic point of view, and consequently sees the "same" object from a new perspective.'[46] (We find echoes of this observation in Kuhn's statement that 'When Aristotle and Galileo looked at swinging stones, the first saw constrained fall, the second a pendulum.'[47]) Mannheim notes that every perception is ordered and organised into categories, and that the extent 'to which we can organize and express our experiences in such conceptual forms is in turn dependent upon the frames of reference which happen to be available at a given historical moment'.[48] And he adds: 'the approach to a problem, the level on which the problem happens to be formulated, the stage of abstraction and the stage of concreteness that one hopes to attain, are all in the same way bound up with social existence.'[49] Unlike Kuhn, however, Mannheim exempts the natural sciences from the determinative influence of particular social–historical perspectives.

Mills's sociology of knowledge shares with Mannheim's a concern with the social determinants of ideas and mentality. For example, rather than regarding the rules of logic as an innate expression of the human mind, or as having a timeless and unchanging character, he views them as human and conventional. 'No individual can be logical,' Mills notes, 'unless there be agreement among the members of his universe of discourse as to the validity of some general conceptions of good reasoning'.[50] What we term 'illogicality' is very much like immorality; both are to be seen as deviations from social norms. Correspondingly, the criteria of logicality may be different at other times and in other groups. Mills lays heavy emphasis on the crucial place of language in social life: 'Our behavior and perception, our logic and thought, comes within the control of a system of language.'[51] Mills recognises that language precedes any given actor; a socially sustained system of meanings has a priority over any given individual. In Mills's words, 'Meaning is antecedently *given*; it is a collective "creation"'.[52] This is what Kuhn is talking about when he views a paradigm as establishing what constitutes 'similarity', 'new facts', and the like.

Mills emphasises that 'truth' and 'objectivity' have meaning only with reference to some accepted system of verification. 'Criteria, or observational and verificatory models,' he asserts, 'are not transcendental'.[53] Mills observes that, for the most part, individual thinkers and scientists do not consciously select a verificatory model, anticipating Kuhn, who stresses that the very criteria for verification at different times and in different scientific communities are dependent on the paradigm in which the criteria are located. Like Mannheim, Mills emphasises the influence of social–historical factors on perception:

> In acquiring a technical vocabulary with its terms and classifications, the thinker is acquiring, as it were, a set of colored spectacles. He sees a world of objects that are technically tinted and patternized. A specialized language constitutes a veritable a priori form of perception and cognition, which are certainly relevant to the results of inquiry. ... Different technical elites possess different perceptual capacities.[54]

The sociology of knowledge espoused by Mannheim and Mills, like Kuhn's new image of science, seems to lead inevitably to relativism. Both positions have the paradoxical flavour of most all-or-nothing views. For they both have the form: we can never be sure of *x* because we are sure of *y*, in that *y* turns out to be an instance of *x*. Whereas those holding the dominant (positivist) view of science seem to deny history, by emphasising a formal, axiomatic, deductive account of scientific theories, and by ignoring the consequences of conceptual and historical variety, those with a more 'sociological' and historical approach appear to bow completely to history. Recognising the determinative influence of social–historical conditions on what men and women can think, say, perceive, and so on, they come to see various criteria, standards, and so forth, as completely local, temporary and, therefore, 'relative'. Mannheim and Mills in a sense later 'escaped' the relativism problem by turning away from the consequences of the sociology of knowledge to a preoccupation with entirely different sorts of sociological problems. Nevertheless, the charges of relativism have continued to be made against sociologists of knowledge and most especially against Mannheim. Kuhn, too, has been widely accused of embracing relativism—particularly by Karl Popper. Popper states:

> Kuhn suggests that the rationality of science presupposes the acceptance of a common framework. He suggests that rationality *depends* upon something like a common language and a common set of assumptions. He suggests that rational discussion, and rational criticism, is only possible if we have agreed on fundamentals. This is a widely accepted and indeed a fashionable thesis: the thesis of *relativism*. And it is a *logical* thesis. I regard the thesis as mistaken.[55]

Kuhn, as noted earlier, denies being a relativist, or at least he acknowledges that it is possible to make judgements as to one historical theory being superior to another. But, he says, there is another step which he refuses to take. Many philosophers of science, Kuhn observes, wish to compare theories as representations of nature, of statements about 'what is really out there'. In other words, Kuhn refuses to see various competing theories as better or worse approximations to the 'truth'.[56]

Despite his denials about being a relativist, Kuhn's work, like that of sociologists of knowledge, does raise serious questions about the status of scientific standards and intellectual viewpoints. Kuhn, Mannheim and Mills all argue that people think in terms of the intellectual and social 'universes of discourse', 'technical languages' or 'paradigms' available to them in their own culture or group. These determine what people can see, what they regard as evidence, as compelling, as consistent, and so on. But if people's standards and preferences vary between different cultures and historical milieux, what intellectual or social authority can be claimed for one set of standards or preferences rather than another? The thoroughgoing relativist concedes final authority to the standards current in a particular milieu, at the same time denying that those standards have any special relevance or authority outside that milieu. This is almost precisely the position taken by Mannheim and Mills with what they call 'relationalism', when they argue that intellectual criteria can only be formulated in terms of the perspective of a given situation. It is also the position to which Kuhn's remarks on paradigms seem inevitably to lead. Not only do the sociology of knowledge and the new image of science lead to relativism, but also to a totally deterministic view of social and scientific life, where the individual is epistemologically locked into the milieu in which he lives and the paradigm under which he practises science. These issues will be considered in greater depth in the following chapters. Also reserved for consideration in later chapters is a concern with 'possibilities'. Suffice it for now to remark that what is presented here is not a concrete description of the way things 'really' are in the world. Instead it is a possible version, a possible way of looking at science and scientific practice (or at different images of science). As Wittgenstein once pointed out: '[T]he fact that it can be described by Newtonian Mechanics tells us nothing about the world; but this tells us something, namely, that the world can be described in that particular way in which as a matter of fact it is described.'[57]

4 Relativism and Wittgenstein

I noted in the previous chapter that the new image of science, especially as represented by Kuhn, shares certain characteristics with the sociology of knowledge. Most importantly, they both appear to lead to relativism. In this chapter, I will consider the relativism issue at greater length, and then will introduce some of Wittgenstein's ideas which, I believe, are helpful in this regard.

Relativism and the sociology of knowledge

To begin, it is not at all clear that the sociology of knowledge constitutes a unique and distinctive approach to the study of social phenomena. The basic tenet of this subdiscipline of sociology is that people's ideas, viewpoints, and so on, are influenced by their social and historical locations. This also appears, however, to be a primary assumption of sociology more generally. Of course, the sociology of knowledge is more explicitly and self-consciously concerned with the relationship between people's location in the social structure and their ideas and viewpoints, but whatever weaknesses exist with regard to the sociology of knowledge will apply as well to many other areas of sociological inquiry. In fact, some of the criticisms launched against the new image of science are criticisms resulting from taking seriously the implications of a fully sociological approach to scientific practice.

Karl Mannheim is certainly one of the best known of the sociologists of knowledge, and in the English-speaking world his name is synonymous with that approach. Influenced by Marx, Weber and Lukács, he began with a concern with the social determinants of ideology. Whereas Marx believed that his own ideas were scientific and those of his opponents only 'rationalisations' based on class interest, Mannheim extended Marx's conception to include the possibility that our own ideas, as well as those of our opponents, could be ideological. He used the term 'ideological' to refer to systems of ideas which positively evaluate either the existing social order and various interests of specific groups, or some past social order. But Mannheim also differed from Marx in his rejection of the idea that intellectual attitudes and beliefs could be accounted for *solely* by material interests. 'We cannot relate an intellectual standpoint directly to a social class,' he says, 'although what we can do is to find out the correlation between the "style of thought" underlying a given standpoint and the "intellectual motivation" of a certain social group.'[1] Mannheim associates 'style of thought' with *social* strata which he distinguishes from *intellectual* strata. By intellectual stratum, he means 'a group of people belonging to a certain social unit and sharing a certain "world postulate" . . . who at a given time are committed to a certain style of economic activity and of theoretical thought'.[2]

Ideology, for Mannheim, is *distorted* knowledge. This can be seen when it 'fails to take account of the new realities applying to a situation, and when it attempts to conceal them by thinking of them in categories which are inappropriate'.[3] Given that different social groups have different world pictures, the sociology of knowledge is defined by Mannheim as 'a discipline which explores the fundamental dependence of each intellectual standpoint on the differentiated social group reality standing behind it, and which sets itself the task of retracing the evolution of the various standpoints',[4] Mannheim extended his analyses beyond ideology, in the usual sense, to include the whole conceptual apparatus with which people operate. He notes that every perception is ordered and organised into categories, and that the extent 'to which we can organize and express our experiences in such conceptual forms is, in turn, dependent upon the frames of reference which happen to be available at a given historical moment'.[5] And he adds that 'the approach to a problem, the level on which the problem happens to be formulated, the stage of abstraction and the stage of concreteness that one happens to attain, are all and in the same way bound up with social existence'.[6]

What one finds in Mannheim is an acute sensitivity to the paramount influence of social factors on the various modes of social thought and knowledge. One sees further an emphasis on the impossibility of considering any element of social life—whether language and meaning, perception, knowledge, truth—outside of a communal or social context. It is not surprising, then, that Mannheim stressed that 'every point of view is particular to a certain definite situation. . . '.[7] But how then does one distinguish truth from falsehood? As does Kuhn more than thirty years later, Mannheim appears to reject the idea that there exist firm, unchanging, ultimate 'truths'. The very notion of truth has a social character. 'We see, therefore,' says Mannheim, 'not merely that the notion of knowledge in general is dependent upon the concretely prevailing form of knowledge and modes of knowing expressed therein and accepted as ideal, but also that the concept of truth itself is dependent upon the already existing types of knowledge'. Thus, 'we must reject the notion that there is a "sphere of truth in itself" as a disruptive and unjustifiable hypothesis'.[8]

Mannheim was very conscious of the problems raised by this 'relativistic' definition of truth, and wished to avoid the consequence that objective truth was impossible. While he emphasised that various points of view are always particular to specific social groups, he believed that there was one social group which was able to free itself from the influences of such particularisms: 'the free-floating intelligentsia'. Because they belong to a stratum which does not constitute a special class, they can, on the basis of their own social consciousness, construct a *total* view of the whole social process. Because the free intelligentsia have been educated in such a way as to allow them to go beyond the world-views of the groups from which they have come, they can function as an independent entity. Thus, Mannheim argued, they can emancipate themselves from the effects of extra-cognitive influences so as to have a clear and undisturbed view of social reality; that is, they function as a group *above* other social groups. The free intelligentsia, therefore, are some sort of supermen, who are not affected by the factors which influence ordinary mortals. When Mannheim tells us that we have to 'recognize that every point of view is particular to a certain definition and to find out through analysis of what this particularity consists', he is presupposing the possibility of confronting a distorted image of reality (that held by others) with an image that is clear and undistorted. In other words, the epistemologically privileged position of the free intelligentsia, by which they acquire a kind of 'purified' vision, allows them access to undistorted social reality, which they can then compare with the distorted images held by others.

Despite Mannheim's efforts to save his assertions from the charge of relativism, his *Ideology and Utopia* was severely attacked. In reviews appearing shortly after the book's publication in English, von Schelting and Becker raised questions about the epistemological status of the sociology of knowledge.[9] The tenor of these criticisms is echoed in Merton's observation, originally published in 1941, that Mannheim's view 'leads at once, it would seem, to radical relativism with its familiar vicious circle in which the very propositions asserting such relativism are ipso factor invalid'.[10] Noting Mannheim's remarks about men speaking in categories which are inappropriate, Merton points out: Moreover, determination of the "appropriateness" or "inappropriateness" of categories presupposes the very criteria of validity which Mannheim wishes to discard.'[11] Hinshaw puts the matter succinctly:

> If one claims that relativism is true, then either this very claim is relative and hence, relativism—if true at all—is not absolutely true; or perhaps, relativism itself is the only position which can be upheld. But, in that case, we can never know it to be so, since all our 'knowledge' would be relative.[12]

Most sociologists seem to reject the relativist implications of the sociology of knowledge, assuming instead that objective truth is possible and, thereby, adopting the 'absolutist' standpoint. That is, they see scientific truth as objective and independent of all social influences, rather than as relative to time, place and situation. This absolutist idea of truth is the polar opposite of the relativist view, holding that scientific truth is independent of social–historical circumstances. For the most part, however, sociologists have not been concerned with the epistemological consequences of the sociology of knowledge (which means that, in a sense, they ignore the epistemological consequences of sociology itself). A notable exception was Wright Mills, who asserted that: 'There have been and are diverse canons and criteria of validity and truth, and these criteria, upon which determinations of the truthfulness of propositions at any time depend, are themselves, in their persistence and change, legitimately open to social–historical relativization.'[13] More typically, epistemological questions are either totally ignored or seen as off-limits for sociology and the sociology of knowledge. For example, Berger and Luckmann, while boldly stating that '*The sociology of knowledge must concern itself with everything that passes for "knowledge" in society*',[14] at the same time explicitly exclude epistemological questions from their purview. Epistemological questions, they claim, 'properly belong to the methodology of the social sciences, an enterprise that belongs to philosophy and is by definition other than sociology, which is indeed an object of its enquiries'.[15]

Not only most sociologists, but most philosophers of science as well, hold to the view that objective truth is possible. Even though the sociology of knowledge has generally exempted the truths of the natural sciences from the influence of social factors, Karl Popper has long been extremely critical of the directions it has taken. For example, he asserts that the sociology of knowledge 'shows an astonishing failure to understand its main subject, the *social aspects of knowledge*, or rather of scientific method. It looks upon science as a process in the mind or "consciousness" of the individual scientist or perhaps as the product of such a process.'[16] What Popper is calling attention to is the public character of science, with its necessary reliance on procedural rules or what he refers to as 'scientific method'. Popper shows his position most clearly in contrasting his view with what he regards as the sociological view:

> If scientific objectivity were founded, as the sociologistic theory of knowledge naively assumes, upon the individual scientist's impartiality, or objectivity, then we should have to say good-bye to it. . . . No, what we usually mean by the term rests on different grounds. It is a matter of scientific method. . . . Scientific objectivity can be described as the inter-subjectivity of scientific method. But this social aspect of science is almost entirely neglected by those who call themselves sociologists of knowledge.[17]

Relativism and Kuhn

While sociologists of knowledge, with the exception of Mills and the early work of Merton,[18] have indeed neglected the social aspects of science, this accusation is most assuredly not correct for those philosophers and historians of science advocating what I have referred to as the new image of science. In fact the 'social aspects of science', which Popper advocates studying, have been the express focus of concern to Thomas Kuhn, whose standpoint, like that of sociologists of knowledge, seems to lead directly to relativism. Recall that Kuhn raises serious objections to the dominant view of science by arguing that scientists within a given paradigm share certain assumptions that are not empirically testable, and that furthermore these assumptions vary within different paradigms and under differing social–historical conditions. Kuhn says:

> To the extent . . . that two scientific schools disagree about what is a problem and what a solution, they will inevitably talk through each other when debating the relative merits of their respective paradigms. In the particularly circular arguments that regularly result, each paradigm will be shown to satisfy more or less the criteria it dictates for itself and to fall short of a few of those dictated by its opponent.[19]

since each paradigm dictates specific criteria for itself, rational detachment (and comparisons of paradigms) is deemed impossible. The relativist implications of Kuhn's views can be seen clearly in the following tatement concerning scientific knowledge:

> Can we not account for both science's existence and its success in terms of evolution from the community's state of knowledge at any given time? Does it really help to imagine that there is some one full, objective, true account of nature and that the proper measure of scientific achievement is the extent to which it brings us closer to that ultimate goal? If we can learn to substitute evolution-from-what-we-do-know for evolution-toward-what-we-wish-to-know, a number of vexing problems may vanish in the process.[20]

.t appears here that Kuhn is simultaneously denying the possibility of objective knowledge while, at the same time, continuing to speak of knowledge.

Whatever the ambiguities in Kuhn's position, there is the implication hat scientific truth is relative. His critics have been quick to note this. Scheffler observes that the upshot of Kuhn's position 'is that there can be no real community of science in any sense approximating that of the standard view, no comparison of theories with respect to their observational content, no reduction of one theory to another, and no cumulative growth of knowledge, at least in the standard sense'.[21] He goes on to add: 'Independent and public controls are no more, communication has failed, the common universe of things is a delusion, reality itself is made by the scientist rather than discovered by him.'[22] Trigg similarly argues that Kuhn's work challenges the idea that scientific theories can be objective in the usual sense.[23]

While not sharing the general standpoint of Kuhn's critics, I do agree with their charge that Kuhn's work implies the relativity of scientific truth. But his work goes beyond merely raising questions about scientific truth. For his views call into question the very *concepts* involved in communication among people from different groups, from different societies and from different scientific communities. Contrary to what Kuhn seems to believe, this *is* a problem. If as Kuhn and, in an inconsistent manner, Mannheim and Mills argue, the concepts and standards accepted as authoritative in different milieux lead scientists to define the world in different ways, how can one find an impartial standpoint of rationality and thus escape the throes of relativism? How can one, for instance, compare scientific theories and decide which is the best? From what standpoint can this be done? If the

members of different societies or within different paradigms indeed liv
in 'different worlds', there will not necessarily be any point of contac
between the concepts of one group and those of another.

Consideration of both Kuhn's writings and the work of Mannheir
and Mills seems to me to lead inevitably to the necessity for philosopher
of science and sociologists of knowledge to choose between the *relativi*
approach, where the particular conceptual and theoretical system
current in one's own scientific milieu are treated as locally sovereign
and the *absolutist* approach, where certain abstract, ideal, universa
standards are imposed on all milieux alike. If one accepts the basi
canons of the sociology of knowledge and the conclusions of Kuhn'
research and other work in the new image of science, then one mus
choose the relativist position. Choosing the absolutist position, on th
other hand, involves rejection of the basic tenets of the sociology c
knowledge and of recent studies, like Kuhn's, in the history of science

As between these two extremes, I prefer the relativist position. But
believe that there is a middle ground between the absolutist and rela
tivist extremes, a position represented in the work of Wittgenstein. Le
us, then, return to a further consideration of some of Wittgenstein'
ideas.

Wittgenstein against relativism

Wittgenstein's later work is directed against the idea that the words i
an utterance are in some way correlated with the objects for which th
words stand. This idea assumes that all language has a particular us
or employment, and Wittgenstein insists that there is a 'multiplicity o
language-games'.[24] Further, he emphasises repeatedly that language i
a concrete social activity, expressive of human needs. That is, languag
is used not only as a device for constructing and talking about th
world, but also as a means of communication within the world. Languag
cannot be divorced from the wider human context in which it is located
Another way of saying this is to state that 'form of life' in some wa
underlies and precedes 'language-games'. Form of life, although neve
clearly defined by Wittgenstein, can be seen as referring to variou
differences in biological and mental properties among differen
organisms. Wittgenstein frequently refers to these in terms of th
'natural histories' of the human species. What, then, are some of thes
properties which belong to *our* natural history?

First of all, *thinking* belongs to this natural history. Wittgenstei
writes: 'What does a man think for? What use is it? . . . But we are no

interested in causes,—we shall say: human beings do in fact think.'[25] He continues: 'Does man think, then, because he has found that thinking pays?—Because he thinks it advantageous to think? (Does he bring his children up because he has found it pays'?)[26] Man simply thinks; that is a fact of our human history.

Secondly, *language* belongs only to our natural history—not to the natural history of animals:

> It is sometimes said that animals do not talk because they lack the mental capacity. And this means: 'they do not think, and that is why they do not talk.' But—they simply do not talk. Or to put it better: they do not use language—if we except the most primitive forms of language.—Commanding, questioning, recounting, chattering, are as much a part of our natural history as walking, eating, drinking, playing.'[27]

Thirdly, the existence of language is presupposed for some forms of thinking. Consider, for example, the following:

> One can imagine an animal angry, frightened, unhappy, startled. But hopeful? And why not?
> A dog believes his master is at the door. But can he also believe his master will come the day after tomorrow?—And *what* can he not do here? . . .
> Can only those hope who can talk? Only those who have mastered the use of a language. That is to say, the phenomena of hope are modes of this complicated form of life.[28]

The point here is that hope is an instance of a kind of consciousness which requires language, as do calculating, betting, making predictions, guessing and a number of other things which are only possible for human beings who have language. The use of language, then, is a species-specific characteristic which represents another element in our natural history.

A fourth aspect of our natural histories concerns what Wittgenstein calls 'agreement in judgements'. That is, it is simply a fact of our natural history that human beings do generally make the same judgement in certain specific situations. For instance, unless human beings agreed in judging pain to be unpleasant and unless there were similarly characteristic responses to pain, the concept of 'pain' would be unintelligible among human beings. Wittgenstein writes:

> The concept of pain is characterized by its particular function in our life. Pain has *this* position in our life; has *these* connexions; (That is to say: we only call 'pain' what has *this* position, *these* connexions). Only surrounded by certain normal manifestations of life, is there such as an expression of pain. Only surrounded by an even more far-reaching particular manifestation of life, such a thing as the expression of sorrow or affection. And so on.[29]

But it is *natural* for us, Wittgenstein says, that people cry and moan when they are in pain. And it is also natural for human beings like ourselves that others treat the pain that hurts:

> It is a help here to remember that it is a primitive reaction to tend, to treat, the part that hurts when someone else is in pain; and not merely when oneself is—and so to pay attention to other people's pain-behaviour, as one does *not* pay attention to one's own pain-behaviour.
>
> But what is the word 'primitive' meant to say here? Presumably that this sort of behaviour is *pre-linguistic*: that a language-game is based *on it*, that it is the prototype of a way of thinking and not the result of thought.[30]

As with pain, similarly with grief:

> 'Grief' describes a pattern which recurs, with different variations in the weave of our life. If a man's bodily expression of sorrow and joy alternated, say with the ticking of a clock, here we should not have the characteristic formation of the pattern of sorrow or the pattern of joy.[31]

We could, of course, imagine a form of life where there were human beings different from ourselves who had no concept of pain or grief who did not find unpleasant that which we call pain and did not express joy or sorrow. We can imagine the facts of nature to be such that some of our concepts simply would not exist. But it is a contingent fact for us that the concepts of pain and grief connect up with a certain uniformity of judgement among human beings. Recall Wittgenstein's remarks about natural facts:

> I am not saying: if such-and-such facts of nature were different people would have different concepts (in the sense of a hypothesis). But: if anyone believes that certain concepts are absolutely the correct ones, and that having different ones would mean not realizing

something that we realize—then let him imagine certain very general facts of nature to be different from what we are used to, and the formation of concepts different from the usual ones will become intelligible to him.[32]

Another aspect of our natural history concerns our *common interests*. Wittgenstein considers the example of our concept of 'shamming':

> Imagine that the people of a tribe were brought up from early youth to give no expression of feeling *of any kind*. They find it childish, something to be gotten rid of. Let the training be severe. 'Pain' is not spoken of; especially not in the form of a conjecture 'Perhaps he has got. . . .' If anyone complains, he is ridiculed or punished. There is no such thing as the suspicion of shamming. Complaining is so to speak already shamming.[33]

> 'Shamming,' these people might say, 'What a ridiculous concept!' (As if one were to distinguish between a murder with one shot and one with three.)[34]

> For here life would run on differently.—What interests us would not interest *them*. Here different concepts would no longer be unimaginable. In fact, this is the only way in which *essentially* different concepts are imaginable.[35]

Again, we see that it is a fact of *our* natural history that this and not that is possible. Our notion of shamming is dependent on the fact that we do, sometimes at least, give expression of feeling. Were we different from the way we are, so that we never gave expressions of feeling, suspicions of shamming could not exist (just as stealing cannot exist without the concept of property).

For Wittgenstein, various language-games are partly dependent on certain contingent facts of nature: that human beings think, use language, agree in judgements and reactions, and share certain common interests. In this sense, language is a *product* of human activity in the world; it is a product of the facts of human and physical nature. But, at the same time, language is also a *producer* of meaning and new forms of human activity. Wittgenstein, then, does not want to endorse a position which holds that facts of nature *completely* determine language; nor, on the other hand, does he want to say that the facts of nature are *totally* creations of our language. Whereas the relativist refuses to separate the 'facts of nature' from language, so that language determines what is real, and the absolutist sees particular concepts as determined by nature, Wittgenstein's position is different. While he gives many examples of imaginary peoples with forms of life differen from our own and, therefore, with such basically different conception of the way things are that they can be said to live in a 'different world' this is not the case in the world in which *we* live. Of course, there are different language-games among us, but there are certain facts o nature which have a priority to all language-games.

In other words, nature has something to say, although it does no determine what we can say. I think that Kuhn partially recognises thi in his response to his critics, where he writes: 'Most of the puzzles o normal science are directly presented by nature, and all involv nature indirectly. Though different solutions have been received a valid at different times, nature cannot be forced into an arbitrary set o conceptual boxes.'[36] Whereas Kuhn, for the most part, considers i impossible to speak of 'nature' independently of a particular theory o paradigm, here he does at least point to the constraints and limit which nature establishes. While Kuhn uses nature as a touchstone he does not feel we have to listen to it and heed its voice.

What is of crucial importance to our interests here, however, i Wittgenstein's conception of facts of nature as providing an importan *prior grounding* for language. In fact, 'form of life' can be seen as a con cept referring to the fact that, by and large, the human race is on biological species. The existence of people who show certain commor characteristics, interests and responses provides a kind of grounding which restricts the possible forms which language can (logically) take

'It is as if our conception involved a scaffolding of facts.' That would presumably mean: If you imagine certain facts otherwise, describe them otherwise, than the way they are, then you can no longe imagine the application of certain concepts, because the rules fo their application have no analogue in the new circumstances.[37]

There are, then, non-arbitrary aspects of language-games; they are rooted in the pre-linguistic world. Wittgenstein remarks that 'it is ou *acting*, which lies at the bottom of the language-game'.[38] But this acting is not something conditioned by prior-held beliefs; it is primitive, pre linguistic behaviour of the human species.

Wittgenstein, I have tried to indicate, did not hold that the world i completely the creation of our language. While I emphasised in chapter 2 the ways in which Wittgenstein sees our language-games a the products of human agreements about the state of things, here have been pointing to his concern with the non-arbitrary aspects o language and language-games. Just as Wittgenstein opposed the idea of individual solipsism and privileged first-person immediacies, he also opposed the idea of collective or aggregative solipsism. Whereas individual solipsism relativises all assertions about the world to those of the speaking subject (an impossible position to defend, as I show in chapter 9), collective solipsism relativises them to the social level. With the first, each of us is non-trivially conditioned by his *own* world-view; with the second, each of us is fully conditioned by *our* (collective) world-view—whether it be social class, paradigm, or whatever. Collective solipsism has the consequence that even another world-view (paradigm, language-game) is only accessible to us from within our particular world-view; we are epistemologically locked into seeing things the way we do in fact see them.

At the same time that Wittgenstein denies the notion that the facts of nature are completely the creation of our language, he also denies that language is uniquely determined by external facts of nature. Wittgenstein tries to strike a balance between these two positions. He writes:

> Do I want to say, then, that certain facts are favourable to the formation of concepts; or again unfavourable? And does experience teach us this? It is a fact of experience that human beings alter their concepts, exchange them for others when they learn new facts; when in this way what was formerly important to them becomes unimportant, and *vice versa*.[39]

When people learn new facts, they may alter their concepts, they may come to see the world differently (that is, partially through these new concepts). Wittgenstein's middle position is reflected in the following remarks:

> We have a colour system as we have a number system. Do the systems reside in *our* nature or in the nature of things? How are we to put it?—*Not* in the nature of numbers or colours.[40]

> Then is there something arbitrary about this system? Yes and no. It is akin both to what is arbitrary and to what is non-arbitrary.[41]

Later, in speaking of people's unwillingness to acknowledge a colour intermediate between red and green, he writes:

> Yes, but has nature nothing to say here? Indeed she has—but she makes herself audible in another way.

'You'll surely run up against existence and non-existence somewhere!' But that means against *facts*, not concepts.[42]

Existence, then, is not entirely the creation of concepts or language.
Nor is our language uniquely determined by the facts of nature.
Language does have an enormous freedom to create its own reality,
but language is nevertheless built upon the facts of human and physical
nature.

Wittgenstein's recognition of the dialectical relationship between
nature and language also serves to undermine those *deterministic* explanations where either nature or language *causes* us to act (and see,
and talk) as we do. Unless people can give reasons for doing things as
they do, then we must search for causes. If, indeed, everything we say
and do were *entirely* a consequence of certain facts of nature which
impress themselves upon us or of the conceptual apparatus available to
us within the group or society in which we happen to live, then we would
be locked into a deterministic system. There is much in the work of
sociologists of knowledge and in Kuhn's writings which appears to
entail determinism. By emphasising the continuing tension between
nature and language, Wittgenstein helps us avoid a commitment to
determinism. This tension between language and the facts of nature
will be considered further in our discussion of mathematics in chapter 6.

For now, let us continue to consider the issue of relativism. In so
doing, it is necessary to return to the notion of language-games. As
noted earlier, Wittgenstein's use of the concept 'language-game' is
enormously equivocal. In the *Blue and Brown Books* he restricts the
term to elementary 'components' of language, such as the games which
are played by children in learning their natural (everyday) language.
At other places, he speaks of specific 'technical' languages which people
come to learn above and beyond their basic natural languages. And
elsewhere, Wittgenstein refers to the 'everyday language-game'. In
addition, he remarks on language-games with physical objects, colour
words, cardinal numbers, inductive reasoning; and further, giving
orders and obeying them, reporting an event, asking, thanking, cursing,
greeting, praying, solving a problem in practical arithmetic, forming
and testing a hypothesis, presenting the results of an experiment in
tables and diagrams. All of these language-games involve the employment of rules and, hence, the concepts of mistake, error or wrongness.

Nowhere does Wittgenstein provide us with a clear, unequivocal
definition of language-games, but perhaps he could not. After all, he
emphasises that while games have a family resemblance there is no

one common feature—say, competition, skill or entertainment—which is common to all games. Language shares with games, Wittgenstein says, the presence of a family resemblance and the absence of any one particular feature in common although, speaking more generally, all language-games involve human action, meaning and communication. There is frequently an overlap among language-games, so that there is no particular 'place' where one language-game ends and another begins. Rather, they must be seen as discrete and bounded for particular purposes.[43] That is to say, we can draw the boundaries and define the limits. With regard to 'prediction and confirmation', for example, Wittgenstein sometimes speaks of these as *part* of the language-game of mathematics and arithmetic and, at other times, as a *special* language-game.[44] Similarly we can, if it serves our purpose, speak of mathematics as a special language-game or as part of the language-game of science. Thus on one level we can consider science as a language-game containing a variety of language-games such as physics, biology, psychology, and so on. Each of these particular language-games can, in turn, be said to be compounded of a large number of intersecting, supporting (and perhaps conflicting) language-games, among them: asking questions, calculating, theorising, giving and following orders, and testing hypotheses. None of these latter language-games is really *peculiar* to science, let alone to a specific discipline. All of them are found in what might be loosely referred to as the language-game of everyday life.

The various scientific disciplines and specialities are special language-games which seek an ordered understanding of some particular bounded region of the world. Each discipline has the task, then, of constructing a language for describing and explaining that particular portion of the world 'as it really is'. Each concrete language-game (sociology, physics, philosophy) has a history and an internal dynamic. Each has its own grammar. At the same time, of course, there is some overlap among these extraordinary (technical) languages and also an overlap with the language-game of everyday life. That is, to repeat a point made earlier, the boundaries between ordinary and extraordinary languages and between various extraordinary languages must always be drawn for a specific purpose (thus we can speak of the natural and social sciences, for some purposes, and of psychology, sociology and political science, among the social sciences, for other purposes, or even, within sociology, of structural-functionalism, ethnomethodology and symbolic-inter-actionism, as particular language-games).

In this connection, it is important to recognise the *primacy* of ordinary

language and the general language-game of everyday life. This language
is not only primary in our everyday lives, it is also the foundation upon
which other (extraordinary) languages are based. That is, we can only
learn to play the language-game of physics or sociology, for example
through the use of ordinary language. This ordinary language, Witt
genstein stresses, is beyond justification (although what we say *within*
ordinary language is not). Wittgenstein warns:

> Here we are in enormous danger of wanting to make fine distinc
> tions.—It is the same when one tries to define the concept of a
> material object in terms of 'what is really seen'.—What we have
> rather to do is to *accept* the everyday language-game, and to note
> *false* accounts of the matter as *false*. The primitive language-game
> which children are taught needs no justification; attempts at justifica
> tion need to be rejected.[45]

Our everyday language-game, in short, is not based on grounds. It is
there—like our life.

The everyday language-game constitutes the very rock bottom of
our knowledge and experience. It would simply make no sense to ask
whether it is 'true' (or 'false'), for there is no transcendental criterion
—which would have to stand beyond or outside language—by
which such a judgement could be made. Wittgenstein writes: 'I want
to say: It is *primarily* the apparatus of our ordinary language, of our
word-language, that we call language; and then other things by
analogy or comparability with this.'[46] There is no self-justifying
foundation outside our ordinary language:

> When I talk about language (words, sentences, etc.) I must speak
> the language of every day. Is this language somehow too coarse
> and material for what we want to say? *Then how is another one to be
> constructed?*—And how strange that we should be able to say anything
> at all with the one we have!
>
> In giving explanations I already have to use language full-blown
> (not some sort of preparatory, provisional one); this by itself shows
> that I can adduce only exterior facts about language.
>
> Yes, but then how can these explanations satisfy us?—Well, your
> very questions were framed in this language; they had to be ex
> pressed in this language, if there was anything to ask!
>
> And your scruples are misunderstandings. Your questions refer
> to words; so I have to talk about words.
>
> You say: the point isn't the word, but its meaning, and you think

of the meaning as a thing of the same kind as the word, though also different from the word. Here the word, there the meaning. The money, and the cow that you can buy with it. (But contrast: money, and its use.)[47]

Hence, *the everyday language-game has an epistemological and ontological primacy.* The importance of this will be seen in the following chapter, where the 'incommensurability' of paradigms is considered. For now t is enough to repeat that the language-game of everyday life underlies and provides a foundation for such extraordinary language-games as science, art, law and religion.

This emphasis on the everyday language-game must, however, be distinguished from Schultz's interest in the common-sense thinking of everyday life and his idea that the reality of everyday life is the *one* paramount reality. For him, 'There is only one external world, the public world, and it is given equally to all of us'.[48] In his view, there are signs and expressions which are meaningful and intelligible in their own right, regardless of whether anyone is thinking of them or using them. The extent of my disagreement with this viewpoint will become apparent in my discussion of the social nature of mathematics in chapter 6.

With regard to Kuhn's notion of paradigms and Wittgenstein's concern with language-games, it is worth noting—parenthetically—that Kuhn himself has pointed to the similarity between paradigms and the notion of 'family resemblance' in Wittgenstein's work. In considering the problem of how a paradigm can guide research without there existing any full set of explicit rules, Kuhn notes that Wittgenstein asked the question: what need we know 'in order that we apply terms like "chair," or "leaf," or "game" unequivocally and without provoking argument'?[48] Wittgenstein's answer, says Kuhn, is that games, and chairs, and leaves are natural families, each constituted by a network of overlapping and crisscross resemblances'.[50] Kuhn goes on to write:

> Something of the same sort may very well hold for the various research problems and techniques that arise within a single normal-scientific tradition. What these have in common is not that they satisfy some explicit or even some fully discoverable set of rules and assumptions that gives the tradition its character and hold upon the scientific mind. Instead, they may be related by resemblance and by modeling to one or another part of the scientific corpus which the community in question already recognizes as among its established

achievements. . . . Paradigms may be prior to, more binding, and more complete than any set of rules for research that could be unequivocally abstracted from them.[50]

What is interesting here is the resemblance between Kuhn's notion of paradigm and Wittgenstein's concept of language-game. Neither paradigms nor language-games can be described completely in terms of a set of explicit *rules*. Answering the objection that he has nowhere said what the essence of a language-game, and hence of language is, Wittgenstein states:

> Instead of producing something common to all that we call language I am saying that these phenomena have no one thing in common which makes us use the same word for all,—but that they are *related* to one another in many different ways. And it is because of these relationships, that we call them all 'language'.[52]

It is surprising that no one has pointed to the similarity between paradigms and language-games, although, as noted above, Kuhn has seen the similarity between paradigms and family resemblances. It seems to me that there is a definite similarity between language-games and paradigms, and it therefore seems appropriate to conceive of scientific paradigms as particular language-games played within various scientific disciplines.

I have observed that both the sociology of knowledge and the new image of science are at odds with the dominant image of science. Whereas the positivist tradition in science presupposes a common and easily identifiable observation language, Kuhn and Feyerabend have seriously called into question the meaning invariance of observational terms as well as the whole distinction between observations and theories. These studies lead to a rejection of many of the presuppositions of the positivist philosophy of science. The sociology of knowledge has the same consequence.

It is also characteristic of the new image of science that discussions of the criteria of 'truth' are replaced by discussions of consensus among scientists and scientific elites (as we shall see in chapter 7). It seems to me inescapable that the new view of science leads to the conclusion that scientific truth and knowledge are fully the products of consensus within scientific communities. While scientists do speak of discovering laws which explain this or that, it is not 'laws' or 'theories' which explain; it is physicists who 'explain' physical phenomena, biologists who 'explain' biological phenomena and sociologists who 'explain' social phenomena. Or, more correctly, it is *scientists* (physicists, biologists, and so on) who provide 'scientific' explanations of these phenomena. After all, the man in the street may also set forth explanations. But he is playing a different language-game from the language-game of science. This is an important consideration, and will concern us later in this volume.

At this point, I want to emphasise that the explanatory activities of a scientific discipline—including their theories, procedures and techniques—are collective activities which make *communal* sense. Although this viewpoint is implicit in the work of Kuhn, Feyerabend and Polanyi, it is explicitly the position of the physicist John Ziman: 'The objective of Science is not just to acquire information nor to utter all non-contradictory notions; its goal is a *consensus* of rational opinion over the widest possible field. . . . It is not a subsidiary consequence of the "Scientific Method;" it *is* the scientific method itself.'[53] A scientific truth, on this view, is one that is warranted as such by the consensus of a scientific community. Since there are different scientific communities with different standards for warranting truth, it follows that truth is completely relativised. This is obviously a long way from the dominant view in science that truth refers to that which is objectively and eternally true. In the dominant view, there exist some extra-linguistic criteria which can separate true propositions or statements from false ones. Thus we are back to our central concern in this chapter: transcendental versus consensus criteria of scientific truth.

It is important to point out here that consensus always exists within a concrete language-game (say, sociology or physics, or a particular paradigm in one of these disciplines) with shared standards, meanings and activities. Scientific truth and falsehood have their life within this intersubjective system. These concrete language-games, which can be isolated for purposes of discussion, do not, however, exist in total isolation from other language-games. They overlap with the language-game of everyday life, and they must to some extent rely upon the facts and certainties of our ordinary language. The constructed, extra-ordinary language-games of science, in other words, cannot exist in total isolation from concrete everyday language employed by human beings. And this everyday language, I have tried to indicate, is itself partly dependent on certain facts of physical and human nature.

Whereas sociologists of knowledge and various advocates of the new image of science are relativistic in that they seem to see various language-games—paradigms, scientific disciplines, and so on—as creations entirely of language, Wittgenstein is at great pains to emphasise the dialectic of language-games with nature. The dialectical quality of Wittgenstein's position is captured nicely in his comments on the role of truth and justification:

> Well, if everything speaks for an hypothesis and nothing against it —is it then certainly true? One may designate it as such.—But does it certainly agree with reality, with the facts? With this question you are already going round in a circle.
>
> To be sure there is justification; but justification comes to an end.[54]

Various sciences, disciplines and paradigms must be seen for what they are: artificial, constructed languages which create 'possible' worlds. Each of these extraordinary languages expresses a possible way of constructing the world or some portion thereof (consider, for example, Marxism or Freudianism), each will speak of certain things and be silent about others. But there are limits to what is possible, as I have tried to point out. Wittgenstein's account of language, therefore, is most certainly not a relativist account. Nor is it a conventionalist account—if we mean by that an account where any statement at all can be assured of truth by meddling at sufficient length with the meanings of other statements in the system. Instead, there are constraints which exist prior to conventions; there is a non-arbitrary element, based on various facts of nature and on our certainties.

5 Paradigms and Incommensurability

One of the consequences of the new image of science has been an emphasis on the 'incommensurability' of paradigms. As we have seen, advocates of the new image challenge the view that statements, including scientific theories, have some atomic, fixed meanings; they argue that statements have meanings only by virtue of their relations to other statements in the system to which they belong. Further, Kuhn and Feyerabend stress the very *impossibility* of comparing, contrasting and discussing different observational languages, theories and standards when different scientific paradigms are involved. Scientists work within these paradigms, and the paradigms determine the scientists' views of the world. A scientist working within a given paradigm simply cannot, on Kuhn's account, transcend his own particular situation. In his words: 'Though most of the same signs are used before and after a [scientific] revolution—e.g. force, mass, element, compound, cell—the ways in which some of them attach to nature have changed. Successive theories are thus, we say, incommensurable.'[1] Feyerabend is in general agreement with Kuhn, acknowledging that 'succeeding paradigms can be evaluated only with difficulty and that they may be altogether incomparable'.[2] He goes on to speak of incommensurable theories whose 'content cannot be compared'.[3]

In this chapter, I will try to show that some of Wittgenstein's views can be used to lead us away from the enormous difficulties ensuing from the incommensurability thesis, and towards the formulation of a position different from and less deterministic than the Kuhn/Feyerabend standpoint. The incommensurability problem will be considered here in terms, first, of perception in science; second, of the closed nature of paradigms; and third, of Kuhn's own ability to transcend the limits which he imposes on others.

93

Kuhn and incommensurability

Central to Kuhn's analysis are the notions of normal science and paradigms, the practice of normal science depending on commitment to paradigms which provide scientists with the conceptual language by which they view the world. 'Normal science', writes Kuhn, 'means research firmly based upon one or more past scientific achievements, achievements that some particular scientific community acknowledges for a time as supplying the foundation for its further practice'.[4] Paradigms, as noted in chapter 3, refer to accepted examples of actual scientific practice, including laws, theories, standards, and so forth, which guide scientific inquiry and research.[5] Paradigms, with their shared consensus and commitment to the same rules and standards for scientific practice, are prerequisites for normal science. Without paradigms, there is simply no way of practising science; one cannot do research without some notion of what constitutes a theory or a fact, for example. The fuller implications of a scientific commitment to one or another paradigm are spelled out elsewhere.[6] Here I want to consider only the matter of the 'incommensurability' of different paradigms.

Kuhn states: 'The normal-scientific tradition that emerges from a scientific revolution is not only incompatible but often actually incommensurable with that which has gone before.'[7] Because scientists with different paradigms live in different worlds, they tell us different things about the universe and the behaviour of its inhabitants. Thus there are substantive differences among various paradigms. But, in addition to differences concerning nature and the world, paradigm differences are reflected in the methods, problems and standards of solution accepted by any mature scientific community at a given time. Neither the content nor the practice of science, then, can be compared with regard to different paradigms. In fact, according to Kuhn, one cannot even understand what goes on within a specific scientific community—with its particular paradigm—unless one belongs to it. (Needless to say, this should call Kuhn's whole account into question— at least, if we took him literally. I shall have more to say about this point later.)

So with regard to scientific theories, it is impossible for someone simultaneously to understand two theories formulated from within different paradigms. People holding different theories 'see different things, and they see them in different relations to one another'.[8] He continues:

That is why a law that cannot even be demonstrated to one group of scientists may occasionally seem intuitively obvious to another. Equally, it is why, before they can hope to communicate fully, one group or the other must experience the conversion that we have been calling a paradigm shift.[9]

But this 'paradigm shift' is not something that is 'made a step at a time, forced by logic and neutral experience. Like the gestalt switch, it must occur all at once (though not necessarily in an instant) or not at all.'[10] Different paradigms carry different conceptions of science and community life, and one cannot reject one paradigm, says Kuhn, without accepting another at the same time. Indeed, 'To reject one paradigm without simultaneously substituting another is to reject science itself'.[11] Kuhn emphasises that the conversion experience of paradigm change is similar to a change in visual gestalt; what was once seen, for example, as a bird is now seen as an antelope, or *vice versa*. But he adds: 'That parallel can be misleading. Scientists do not see something *as* something else; instead, they simply see it.'[12] In other words, from within one paradigm one sees a bird, and from within another paradigm, an antelope. Or, in the case of science, Kuhn says:

> After the assimilation of Franklin's paradigm, the electrician looking at a Leyden jar saw something different from what he had seen before. The device had become a condenser, for which neither the jar shape nor glass was required. . . . Lavoisier . . . saw oxygen where Priestley had seen dephlogistated air and where others had seen nothing at all.[13]

Since Galileo saw a pendulum whereas the Aristotelians saw only a heavy body swinging back and forth, these men, then, worked in different worlds. Thus, according to Kuhn, natural scientists are completely locked into the particular paradigms within which they practise science. Before arguing against this viewpoint, it is first necessary to briefly compare the realist and conventionalist accounts of conceptual truths.

Realism and conventionalism

For realists, any statement which has a definite sense must have something in virtue of which either it or its negation is true. With regard to mathematics, for example, mathematical objects are there and stand in certain relationships to one another, independent of knowing subjects. We human beings have the task of discovering these objects and their relations to one another. According to the realist account, then, conceptual truths are about the world and not about language. For conventionalists, on the other hand, necessity is not imposed by reality but by us. That is, necessary truths are imposed by us upon our language, so that a mathematical formulation is necessarily true by virtue of our having chosen to regard nothing as counting as falsifying it. A criticism of the conventionalist viewpoint is its inability to explain the non-arbitrary element in conceptual truths; conventions cannot simply be altered at will. This suggests that in some sense they are, indeed, non-arbitrary and necessary. Let us now examine the 'sense' in which this may be true.

Michael Dummett, who accuses Wittgenstein of conventionalism, describes the way in which a conventionalist would respond to a rigorous mathematical proof:

> At each step we are free to choose to accept or reject the proof; there is nothing in our formulation of the axioms and of the rules of inference, and nothing in our minds when we accepted them before the proof was given, which of itself shows whether we shall accept the proof or not; and hence there is nothing which *forces* us to accept the proof.[14]

A realist will hold that there exists either a proof or a disproof for a statement of some mathematical theory. Hence the fact that a statement is true, if it is true, consists in the existence of such a proof even if we have yet to discover it. But, says Dummett,[15] Wittgenstein would argue that whatever is yet to be discovered, 'it is still up to us to decide whether or not we wish to count it as a proof'.

Dummett is correct in stating that Wittgenstein would hold that it is up to us to decide what counts as a proof (or as a this or a that). This is not to say, however, that someone can regard a proof in any way he chooses. On the contrary, it is central to Wittgenstein's views that not just any old result is allowed as correct in counting, calculating, and the like. He says:

> 'Then according to you everybody could continue the series as he likes; and so infer anyhow!' In that case we shan't call it 'continuing the series' and also presumably not 'inference'. And thinking and inferring (like counting) is of course bounded for us, not by an arbitrary definition, but by natural limits corresponding to the body of what we call the role of thinking and inferring in our life.[16]

Wittgenstein's position is generally to show that our present ways of counting, calculating, inferring, and the like, are not the only possible ones. And while he gives numerous examples to show the *possibility* of ways of counting, calculating, and so forth, different from ours, this does not imply that our doing these things as we do is solely a result of our having chosen certain more or less arbitrary conventions to which there exist clear and intelligible alternatives. The point here is that things could have been otherwise, yet, at the same time, as we saw in our lengthy discussion in the previous chapter, there is often a kind of necessity (what Wittgenstein refers to above as 'natural limits') in what we do. Wittgenstein provides the following example of people whose ways of conducting business are very much different from ours:

> Imagine people who used money in transactions; that is to say coins, looking like our coins, which are made of gold and silver and stamped and are also handed over for goods—but each person gives just what he pleases for the goods, and the merchant does not give the customer more or less according to what he pays. In short this money, or what looks like money, has among them a quite different role from among us. We should feel much less akin to these people than to people who are not yet acquainted with money at all and practice a primitive kind of barter.—'But these people's coins will surely also have some purpose!'—Then has everything that one does a purpose? Say religious actions—.
>
> It is perfectly possible that we should be inclined to call people who behaved like this insane. And yet we don't call everyone insane who acts similarly within the forms of our culture, who uses words 'without purpose'. (Think of the coronation of a King.)[17]

Certainly one can imagine the possibility of people transacting business in the way Wittgenstein describes. But this does not mean that their way of conducting business represents an alternative *within our form of life*. To consider fully what it would be like to be one of those merchants who gives out the same amount of goods no matter how much money he receives, is to lead us to an abandonment of many of our own ways of thinking. In other words, those rules by which people calculate and transact business in Wittgenstein's example do not constitute a set of genuine alternatives which people like ourselves could have chosen. Thus, the kinds of examples set forth by Wittgenstein are intended to oppose the realist view—that conceptual truths are about the world and not about our language—while, at the same time, showing a language-game of counting or calculating which belongs to a specific form of life. In a sense, then, our ways of counting, calculating, and so forth, *are* contingent on our form of life.

That Wittgenstein recognised this can been seen in remarks like the following: 'What we are supplying are really remarks of the natural history of men: not curiosities, however, but rather, observations on facts which no one has doubted and which have only gone unremarked because they are always before our eyes.'[18] What he seems to have in mind here is that certain human behaviours might not have obtained if we were different from what we are. He makes this clear with regard to activities like counting, calculating, making inferences, and the like, when he states that 'mathematics is after all an anthropological phenomenon'.[19] That is, certain facts of human nature make it possible for calculating, inferring, and so forth, to occur at all. For instance, Wittgenstein says that 'I practically never get into difficulties in correlating what I have drawn as groups of five'; 'our memory is generally good enough for us not to take numbers twice in counting up to "12," and not to leave any out; and so on'.[20] These are among the examples of what Wittgenstein refers to in speaking of the 'psychological' and 'physiological' facts that make calculating possible.[21] Further, it is simply a fact of nature that almost everyone has sensory organs capable of distinguishing between 'add' and 'sad', or 'subtract' and 'detract'. That much must simply be taken as given. So the correctness of the rules in calculating cannot be ultimately traced, on the one hand, to certain 'truths' which are firmly established for everyone everywhere or, on the other hand, to truths which are accepted without foundation. Instead: 'The limits of empiricism are not assumptions unguaranteed, or intuitively known to be correct: they are ways in which we make comparisons and in which we act.'[22]

The only foundation for our ways of counting, calculating, and the like, then, is the 'ways in which we make comparisons and in which we act'. That is simply the kinds of creatures we are. And while Wittgenstein tells us that to imagine a language-game is to imagine a form of life, so that we can further, perhaps, imagine the form of life in which this could play a part, these different language-games may not represent possible alternatives for people like ourselves—with our natural histories. Thus, on this reading, Wittgenstein is certainly not a realist, in that we can never establish that our own ways of calculating, for example, are true; nor is he a conventionalist, in that our way of calculating is not—*for us*—merely one of an unlimited number of available alternatives.

What I am arguing here is that the language-games of which

Wittgenstein speaks—giving orders and obeying them, reporting an event, making a joke, doing mathematics—are part of a form of life which, in a sense, underlies them.[23] Again, consider an example:

'There are 60 seconds to a minute.' This proposition is very *like* a mathematical one. Does its truth depend on experience?—Well, could we talk about minutes and hours, if we had no sense of time; if there were no clocks, or could be none for physical reasons; if there did not exist all the connexions that give our measures of time meaning and importance?[24]

What I find significant here is that part of the quotation where Wittgenstein says, 'if we had no sense of time'. For while we can invent language-games where people have different notions of time, or even perhaps where they have no notion of time at all, we cannot, I submit, formulate a form of life for ourselves where time plays no part. A 'sense of time', then, is simply another example of our natural histories and forms of life. 'Compare a concept with a style of painting,' suggests Wittgenstein. 'For is even our style of painting arbitrary? Can we choose one at pleasure? (The Egyptian, for instance?) Is it a mere question of pleasing and ugly?'[25] Perhaps we could learn to paint like an Egyptian. But could we learn to see like an Egyptian, and what would be necessary to learn to do so?

Perception in science

The above discussion suggests that our form of life limits what is (conceptually) possible for us. This awareness of the relation between various language-games and the forms of life in which they play a part may cast some light on the general problems of paradigms and in-commensurability discussed earlier. Let us consider this in regard to *perception* and, most especially, perception in science.

Not only do the universes of discourse, language-games, and so on, available to people influence what they can think, what they will regard as evidence, as compelling, as consistent, and so on, but they also determine what people can *see*. Kuhn argues that paradigm changes cause scientists to see the world differently. He states: 'Insofar as their only recourse to that world is through what they see and do, we may want to say that after a revolution scientists are responding to a different world.'[26] The dominant view of science has long held that there are raw data or brute facts, existing independently of the observer, which can be observed and then compared with various theories. The true theory is that which best 'fits' these neutral data. Kuhn is highly critical of the notion of theory-independent observation. Wittgenstein, of course, rejects the very possibility of drawing a line between the empirical and the conceptual; there is simply no line to be drawn. And this indeterminacy can be seen in perception as well. Wittgenstein remarks:

Take as an example the aspects of a triangle. This triangle can be seen as a triangular hole; as standing on its base, as hanging from its apex; as a mountain, as a wedge, as an arrow or pointer, as an over-turned object which is meant to stand on the shorter side of the right angle, as a half parallelogram, and as various other things.

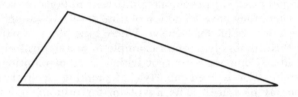

'You can think now of *this* now of *this* as you look at it, can regard it now as *this* now as *this*, and then you will see it now *this* way, now this.'—*What* way, There *is* no further qualification.—

But how is it possible to *see* an object according to an *interpretation*?— The question represents it as a queer fact; as if something were being forced into a form it did not really fit. But no squeezing, no forcing took place here.[27]

At issue, then, is not how we see something, but rather that there is a difference between a physical state and a visual experience. It is not a matter of different interpretations—different ways of thinking about something—but of seeing as an experiential state. Wittgenstein says: 'Do I really see something different each time, or do I only interpret what I see in a different way? I am inclined to say the former. But why? To interpret is to think, to do something; seeing is a state.'[28]

It seems clear that there are cognitive elements in perception, but there are also limits to the cognitive influence that can be imposed on perception. Consider, for instance, Köhler's famous goblet-and-faces drawing, which to some people represents a goblet and, to others, two men staring at one another. Different people viewing the drawing 'see' different things. And the same person, at different times, may see either the goblet or the two men. I look and see two men facing one another.

Later I look again and see the goblet but not the two faces. The drawing has not changed. What has changed is what I 'see'. Some might ask: But what is it 'really'? Such a question makes no sense here. In order to see this or that, we must already have certain types of knowledge. Unless one is familiar with faces or goblets, he will see neither. Imagine that someone is familiar with faces but has never seen a goblet (or a picture of one). We ask him repeatedly: 'Don't you see that goblet?' He says no, and then tells us that he does not know what a goblet is. We might tell him that a goblet is something like a glass or a bowl. That could help. But unless he is familiar with glasses or bowls, this similarity will not help him either. This is not to say that in Köhler's drawing an individual will always see faces if he is unfamiliar with goblets. For people can be blind to what others see.

The limits of one's perception, then, are in one sense empirically established. The language-games into which we are trained set a limit on the possible ways in which we can see this or that. All of us acquire a language as part of growing up; we are socialised into the use of language within a given form of life. This provides us with the conceptual apparatus (rules, meanings, conventions) which constitute our perceptual possibilities. What this means is that as we encounter other human practices (say, science) we acquire an ability to play these other 'language-games' only through an appeal to and reliance upon the rules and conventions governing the language-game in the form of life where we originally acquired language. This is, at least initially, the case. Within the language-game as played, as part of a form of life, we can always employ the established rules and conventions for dealing with or explaining new rules or conventions encountered *both* within that (original) language-game and within a *new* language-game into which we are being trained.

In other words, there is a sort of meta-language in use which underlies our learning of new ways of thinking and seeing. And while the training of infants into the most general behaviour of the human species does not initially involve this meta-language, all future training into other language-games builds upon this meta-language. So, for example, training individuals to see something as a 'this' or a 'that' is dependent upon the (meta-) language which allows us to understand the notion of giving a particular interpretation in the first place. If we think of one element in the initial training of a child into a language-game as teaching him to 'see', then future training into other language-games can be thought of as learning to see anew. Seeing, then, is dependent on training into a language-game. Therefore, learning to see 'this' where one previously saw 'that' is dependent upon training into a new language-game. I wish to suggest, however, that an intermediate step between seeing this and seeing that is the ability to 'see as'. I conceive of 'seeing as' here as the acquired ability to play two language-games.

Now let us briefly consider this in terms of science. Mills points out that 'Different technical elites possess different perceptual capacities'.[29] And Kuhn notes that—making use of the 'impetus theory'—Galileo could see what the Aristotelians could not.[30] Hanson gives the example of Kepler and Tycho Brahe standing on a hill watching the sun:

> Kepler regarded the sun as fixed: it was the earth that moved. But Tycho followed Ptolemy and Aristotle in this much at least: the earth was fixed and all other celestial bodies moved around it. *Do Kepler and Tycho see the same thing in the east at dawn?*[31]

This is not a question as to whether or not they 'interpreted' what they see differently.

Imagine that the same two men are shown a certain physical object—(what we regard as) a lead cylinder. In one sense, both men 'see' this object—that is to say, unless they are blind or conceptually blind in the sense of not even being able to see it as something. But while Tycho Brahe sees a mere lead pipe, Kepler sees a telescope—an instrument he has learned about from Galileo. It is not that Kepler sees it as a lead pipe and then interprets it as a telescope; no, he *sees* a telescope. They may share a common visual experience, but their perceptions are different. I am not suggesting, however, that Kepler could not see it 'as' a lead pipe. During a discussion of what it 'really' is, for example, Kepler might say: 'Look, I know that it looks like a lead pipe, I understand why you might see it *that* way. But it isn't a lead pipe, it's a telescope.' All that Tycho could say would be: 'A telescope? What's that? It's a lead pipe.' One can at least conceive of Kepler being able to see it 'as' a lead pipe, while holding that it *is* a telescope. But one can also conceive of someone being trained to see it 'as' a telescope, and then, after a while, being able to see only a telescope.

Someone may, that is, see X, later be trained to see X as Y, and still later see Y. Thus, we have seeing, seeing as, and then seeing again: X, X as Y, Y. In the second phase, where we see X as Y, the perceived object originally categorised as an X is placed into the language-game which is a necessary condition for its being seen as Y. At the very least, then, we can say that 'seeing as' marks the transition from one perceptual language-game to another. At the very most, we might argue that 'seeing as' is the ability to play more than one language-game at a time. This is not to say, however, that 'seeing as' is seeing plus an interpretation—for neither is an interpretation. If, as many scientific views of observation hold, seeing as is merely seeing with an interpretation added, then it should be possible to specify the seeing *simpliciter* which forms the basis for the 'added' interpretation. But this we cannot do. There is no neutral sense-datum language in which we can state what we saw before we added the interpretation.

We must be careful, though, in our distinction between seeing and seeing as, not to confuse the two in cases where something like Köhler's goblet–faces is involved. Let us say that the drawing is shown to someone who has never encountered it (or heard about it) before. We ask him, 'What do you see here?' He tells us: 'I see two faces looking at one another' or, perhaps, 'I see a goblet'. He would not answer: 'Now I see it as a goblet' or 'Now I see it as two faces'. Instead, he simply describes his perception. But imagine that someone who tells us he sees two faces looking at one another is later *trained* to see a goblet instead of two faces. Perhaps we show him goblets and pictures of goblets. After a while we may show him the drawing again, and ask him what he sees: 'I see a goblet,' he says. Then we inform him that what we have been showing him is Köhler's famous goblet-and-faces drawing, and that it can be *seen as* either a goblet *or* two faces (that is, we and others like us can see the drawing as one or the other). We train him further, pointing to the drawing, telling him: 'Look again. O.K., look away, and then take another look,' or maybe, 'Close your eyes. Now open them and tell us what you see.' After enough training into this language-game, he may begin to answer our inquiries by saying: 'Now I see it as a goblet', 'Now I see it as two faces', or even 'Now I see it as the Köhler drawing'. (This is what Wittgenstein terms 'the dawning of an aspect'.) Thus an ambiguous figure like the Köhler drawing is an excellent example, because it straddles two language-games. Again, however, the difference between seeing and seeing as is not a situation where we have seeing and seeing plus interpretation. Seeing Köhler's drawing is just as much an experiential state as seeing it 'as' a goblet, as two faces, or even as Köhler's drawing. The crucial difference here is between (1) *seeing*, which is the result of an actually played language-game into which one has been trained and which is largely independent of other language-games, and (2) *seeing as*, which is the ability to play more than one language-game with the same object (that is, the 'something' in question).

Before moving on to confront some of the issues with regard to Kuhn and paradigms, let us consider one further example, again from the work of Norwood Hanson:

> A trained physicist would see one thing: an X-ray tube viewed from the cathode. Would Sir Lawrence Bragg and an Eskimo baby see the same thing when looking at an X-ray tube? Yes, and no. Yes—they are visually aware of the same object. No—the *ways* in which they are visually aware are profoundly different. Seeing is not only the having of a visual experience; it is also the way in which the visual experience is had.

> At school the physicist had gazed at this glass-and-metal instrument. Returning now, after years in University and research, his eye lights upon the same object once again. Does he see the same thing as he did then? Now he sees the instrument in terms of electrical circuit theory, thermodynamic theory, the theories of metal and glass structure, thermionic emission, optical transmission, refraction, diffraction, atomic theory, quantum theory and special relativity.[32]

In this example we cannot say, of course, what the Eskimo baby would see. But the physicist student would first 'see' a glass-and-metal instrument, which he would then be trained to 'see as' an X-ray tube with all that it implies in terms of electrical circuit theory, and the like. Hanson notes that 'The infant and the laymen can see: they are not blind. But they cannot see what the physicist sees; they are blind to what he sees.' What Hanson does not point out, however, is that the physicist may *become* blind to what they see. Looking at the X-ray tube, the experienced physicist may no longer be able to see it as a 'glass-and-metal instrument'.[33] Here we have what I consider the crux of the matter with regard to the problem of perception and theory-independent observation. It is not a matter of whether observation is theory-independent or not, for I cannot even conceive of such a thing. No, the crucial question, once we are trained into a language-game, is whether (1) we are able to see only what we have been trained to see within that language-game, or (2) we are able to see it 'as' something else because we had earlier learned to 'see' it that way. In this case we must be able to straddle two different language-games at once. If (1) is correct, then our highly experienced physicist *sees* an X-ray tube and that is all. He is incapable of seeing the object *as* a glass-and-metal instrument. If (2) is correct, then he *sees* the X-ray tube but is also able to see it *as* a glass-and-metal instrument. The critical distinction here is between being trainable into one as compared with multiple language-games.

Let us now return to Kuhn's thesis regarding the matter of paradigms and seeing. Recall that, for Kuhn, a scientist working under one paradigm cannot seriously entertain a new paradigm. But, once he has undergone a 'conversion', a paradigm-switch, he then looks at the world from the vantage point of the new paradigm. This paradigm-switch, Kuhn states, is a 'relatively sudden and unstructured event like the gestalt switch',[34] and 'the transition between competing paradigms cannot be made a step at a time'.[35] This sudden switch from one paradigm to another means the acceptance of a new paradigm and the total rejection of the paradigm that has dominated the scientist's thinking up until the switch. On this account, someone who once viewed the world in one way now views it in another. This creates an incommensurability between supporters of the older and newer paradigms; since those with different paradigms share no common scientific language, no common viewpoint, no common gestalt, neither can understand the point of view of the other. Neither can understand the way the other sees the world. Since, according to Kuhn, no rational discussion is possible between paradigms, the scientist is logically forced to accept the impossibility of a critical comparison of two paradigms.

Popper has been highly critical of Kuhn's views, and argues against them as follows:

> I do admit that at any moment we are prisoners caught in the framework of our theories; our expectations; our past experiences; our language. But we are prisoners in a Pickwickian sense: if we try, we can break out of our frameworks at any time. Admittedly, we shall find ourselves again in a framework, but it will be a better and roomier one; and we can at any moment break out of it again. The point is that a critical discussion and a comparison of the various frameworks is always possible.[36]

According to Popper, then, while we may be caught in one or another paradigm ('framework'), we can 'break out at any time'. What is a logical impossibility for Kuhn is only a matter of slight difficulty for Popper. Given the incompatibility of these two viewpoints, let us examine the problem more closely.

Conversion and incommensurability

Kuhn refers several times to conversion, a process of rejecting one paradigm and accepting another, something that happens all at once. For example, he states:

> Scientists then, often speak of the 'scales falling from the eyes' or of the 'lightning flash' that 'inundates' a previously obscure puzzle, enabling its components to be seen in a new way that for the first time permits its solution. On other occasions the relevant illumination comes in sleep.[37]

Indeed, something like this may occur among those individuals who are responsible for *inventing* or formulating a new paradigm. But one wonders about the practitioners of normal science who, having practised within one particular paradigm, later reject that paradigm and accept another. Kuhn treats it as a (logical) impossibility that transference of allegiance from one paradigm to another can occur other than by means of a conversion experience.

This strikes me as highly dubious, in that just as one can be *trained* to straddle or play two language-games, so can one, I believe, be trained to grasp—albeit not wholly—two different paradigms. To see this, let us consider Kuhn's discussion of scientific training and education. Kuhn points out that scientific education involves exposure to general literatures in the field, to various traditions, to men working on the problems of normal science, and so on. All of this involves, in addition to the concepts, laws and theories which men are explicitly taught, a great number of taken-for-granted viewpoints and practices which students *learn*, although no formal teaching may be involved. Through contact with working scientists, the apprentice scientist is trained—although, again, not only explicitly, but by example—to view the world in a certain manner. Recall, however, that this training to play the language-game of physics or chemistry, or whatever, is dependent upon having mastered an earlier language-game (what I referred to earlier as a meta-language) upon which the extraordinary (scientific) language of a paradigm is imposed.

Preparation in a particular scientific sub-speciality, then, involves acquiring a scientific paradigm, a way of viewing the world, that may—initially, at least—be at odds with the language-game already played. But it is simply not the case that someone learning physics, for example, undergoes a conversion experience by which he is totally unable to view the world as he did previously. The physicist who has learned to *see* an X-ray tube can still see the object *as* a glass and metal instrument. In fact the dynamics of perception are obviously rather complex. For perceptual readiness, both to see and to see as, is dependent on the likelihood of events or objects learned by an individual in the past, as well as his needs at a particular time. An example of the first is provided in a study by Bruner and Minturn where subjects were presented with a stimulus which could be perceived as the letter B or the number 13: a broken capital B with a slight separation between the vertical and curved component of the letter. Whether the subjects saw a B or a 13 was highly influenced by whether they had previously been presented with letters or with numbers in the experiment.[38] As regards needs, or what has been termed 'functional salience', a study by Bruner and Goodman found that poor children overestimated the size of coins considerably more than did rich children.[39] It seems to me that similar influences must exist in science and with perception in science. Of course, it may be argued that in my earlier discussion I have compared the language-game as played (the meta-language) with learning a scientific paradigm, and that things are otherwise when two or more scientific paradigms are at issue. But are things really that different? Can one not be trained to accept one paradigm and to abandon another one, or is conversion, as Kuhn says, a necessary condition?

Imagine someone practising normal science from within a particular paradigm, who becomes aware of certain anomalies or violations of expectation that seem—*to him*—to threaten the practice of his sub-speciality as he knows it. He finds it more and more difficult to take his paradigm for granted. In short, he experiences a crisis. This is not necessarily to say, however, that there exists a large-scale crisis within the scientific community to which he belongs. But *his* feeling of crisis loosens his commitment to the paradigm. This loosening, following from his dissatisfaction with the existing paradigm, may result in his 'looking around' so that he becomes more focally aware of work going on at 'the fringe' or the 'cutting edge'—depending on its subsequent success—of his speciality area. Further, he may begin to look at work outside his own discipline, perhaps even at work that is considered non-scientific. In doing all of this, he is of course looking here and there through the spectacles provided by the paradigm in which he practises science. Yet his uneasiness, his dissatisfaction, his doubts about the paradigm—or at least about his own work within it—and the subsequent loosening of his commitment to it, make him more receptive to new ways of viewing the world than he had been previously, and more receptive than are his colleagues, for whom the paradigm is non-problematic.

Such an individual, who may not even be able fully to articulate the reasons for his vague feelings of dissatisfaction, is, I believe, a prime candidate for *training* into a different world-view. True, he may be ripe for conversion (a gestalt switch) but, more importantly, he is open and receptive to other world-views (paradigms). But this is not necessarily, as Popper states, a matter of choosing to break out of an existing framework whenever one wants. It is most definitely not a matter of being able, at least initially, to compare and contrast one's old views in terms of one's new views, for one has yet to have become fully aware of or accepted a new framework. It is, in fact, a period of 'dis-ease' where one leans away from the old framework (paradigm) without necessarily having any clear idea of what is wrong or what is desired. For Kuhn, of course, there is in a sense nowhere else and no other way to look. If there is only one paradigm, there exist no possible alternatives. And even if they existed, one could not see them from within the framework of one's present paradigm. So, for Kuhn, we are caught in the frameworks of our theories and can only get out by converting to another framework within which we are similarly captive; while, for Popper, we can break out of the framework any time we choose.

Of these two viewpoints, I find Kuhn's preferable but not fully satisfactory. Instead, I prefer an alternative viewpoint where scientists ready themselves, often not fully consciously or deliberately, for a sort of receptivity to other frameworks. In saying this, I am not suggesting that there must be another scientific paradigm already available. That is to say, it is not necessary to conceive of 'paradigms' as externally existing essences which can be discovered and then utilised. What I have in mind is the growing awareness among dissociated individuals that there may be other ways of looking at the world that are, for them, more preferable, more liberating, more beautiful, or whatever. These people do not, as yet, constitute a scientific community; for there can be no community without agreement about rules, methods, theories, standards, and so forth (paradigms, in short). But as long as these people are able to learn from one another (even in the sense of reading one another's work without face-to-face contact) so that they become aware of one another's unease with the paradigm within which they all work, there exists the possibility of their acquiring new ways of looking at and thinking about the world.

Now I have mentioned scientists being *trained* to view the world in a different way. But how would this work? One way might be by reading the work of earlier scientists, philosophers or even poets. However, I will focus on another possibility. Perhaps the dissatisfied scientist reads a paper by another scientist who does not practise within his (the first scientist's) paradigm. And he finds that he cannot understand, cannot make sense of, this paper; the man simply views the world and the subject-matter of his scientific inquiry in a way that is foreign to our hypothetical reader. Yet the reader—prepared by his feelings of dissatisfaction within the paradigm under which he works—concludes: 'It's interesting', or 'Maybe there's something there', or 'I wonder what he means', or 'I wonder what he's getting at'. Perhaps he makes contact with the author of the paper, and asks him for further elaboration, elucidation, clarification or examples. Or maybe he thinks he has some idea of what is intended and asks the author: 'Do you mean this? or 'Is this an example of what is intended?'

To make our hypothetical example easier, imagine that these two scientists actually get together, and that our first scientist makes a further commitment to learning to view the world in the same way as the author of the paper does—not necessarily because he wants to or is willing to accept fully that way of viewing the world, but because he thinks that it is perhaps an interesting viewpoint that he would like to understand better. In short, let us say that he agrees—though not necessarily in a formal, explicit manner—to be *trained* into this other way of looking at the world. I am not denying that the second scientist may have himself arrived at this 'new view' by means of a dream, a flight of fantasy, or what have you. Whatever the act of creation that generated his viewpoint, the question here is whether another scientist (or scientists) can come to accept it without the kind of conversion process that Kuhn emphasises. I have been arguing that he can, if he is open and receptive and, therefore, willing to be trained into a new vision.

Remember that the language-game of everyday life underlies the various language-games of science. And while each concrete scientific discipline and each sub-speciality has its own grammar, there is some overlap among these extraordinary (technical) languages and also an overlap with the language-game of everyday life. Once people have acquired language, they can use the rules and conventions of that language to explain and teach an extraordinary language like mathematics or a different world-view as in the above example. In the case of scientists practising within two different paradigms, they will not only share an ordinary language but there will be, I believe, almost always some overlap in the technical languages which they each employ. There is, however, no *a priori* guarantee that two persons brought up in the same language community—let alone two persons operating within different paradigms—will use words with the same meanings in all situations.

Thus our first scientist may find that there are many terms which he and the second scientist use unproblematically; these terms elicit no disagreements or requests for clarification. With other terms, however, there may be a kind of 'communication breakdown'. This may necessitate a mutual exploration of how the two scientists react verbally and visually to different terms, different objects, and so forth. Say, for example, that scientists from within two different paradigms are speaking of 'free fall'. Each will use the word 'fall' in a way that is consistent with the theory within his particular paradigm. Nevertheless, in terms of their shared everyday language and certain shared experiences, they will use the word 'fall' in a way that is mutually intelligible. Both will employ the word in such a way as to indicate that objects fall from above to below and not *vice versa*. And should they disagree about how they are using the term 'fall' here, it may be necessary for each to show what he means. Presumably each of them will illustrate the meaning of the term 'fall' by dropping stones from an outstretched arm in the direction of his feet, throwing a ball into the air and referring to its downward flight as 'fall', and the like. In other words, it is what men *do*, the ways they proceed, which ultimately underlies their communication and understanding. All of this is to say that language-games overlap, that there are intersections among them, and that individuals can learn to play more than one language-game. As I indicate later in this chapter, I consider it a mistake to regard paradigms as closed systems. This is not to say, however, that different paradigms are learned through some sort of neutral and independent observation language— even though, as I indicated in the previous chapter, the everyday language-game does have an epistemological and ontological primacy.

Let us, then, consider the matter more closely, utilising Kuhn's discussion of 'seeing'. I will first quote Kuhn at length here, and then discuss his remarks. Kuhn says that when paradigms change, the world itself changes:

Led by a new paradigm, scientists adopt new instruments and look in new places. Even more important, during revolutions scientists see new and different things when looking with familiar instruments in places they have looked before. . . . Insofar as their only recourse

to that world is through what they see and do, we may want to say
that after a revolution scientists are responding to a different world.
. . . What were ducks in the scientist's world before the revolution
are rabbits afterwards. The man who first saw the exterior of the
box from above later sees its interior from below. Transformations
like these, though usually more gradual and almost always irre-
versible, are common concomitants of *scientific training*. Looking at a
contour map, the student sees lines on paper, the cartographer a
picture of a terrain. . . . Only after a number of such transformations
of vision does the student become an inhabitant of the scientist's
world, seeing what the scientist sees and responding as the scientist
does.[40]

Notice that Kuhn speaks here of transformations brought about by
'scientific training'. He goes on to add:

Therefore, at times of revolution, when the normal-scientific tradition changes, the scientist's perception of his environment must be
re-educated—in some familiar situations he must learn to see a new
gestalt. After he has done so the world of his research will seem, here
and there, incommensurable with the one he had inhabited before.[41]

Learning to see a new gestalt, then, is something that requires what
Kuhn terms 're-education', or what I have referred to as 'training'
into another way of looking at the world.

In referring to gestalts and to different ways of viewing the world,
the assumption is that the units of perception are people, trees, goblets,
instruments, ducks, rabbits—not innumerable sensory elements. That
is, a mosaic of stimuli may be grouped in a variety of ways, so that the
unity of some physical object, for example, does not in itself account
for the unity of the perception. Thus a gestalt switch involves the reorganisation of stimuli so that 'this' rather than 'that' is seen. Whereas
Kuhn believes that this reorganisation must be all at once, I doubt that
this is often the case. Nevertheless, we both share the viewpoint that
all perceptual experiences at a given moment are, to a large extent,
dependent on what a person has experienced in the past. This means
that particular kinds of experience are a necessary, though not sufficient,
condition for seeing things in one or another way. In short, unorganised
experience cannot organise perception. Thus while on Kuhn's account
a gestalt switch may be sudden, it still requires having had certain
experiences that allow for a new way of seeing. Without the experience
of familiarity with goblets or X-rays tubes, or whatever, one cannot

suddenly 'see' them. Some sort of direct (or at least vicarious) experience is a condition of all perception and all inquiry, both in our everyday life and in our scientific activities.[42]

Kuhn treats the acquisition of new and wider experiences not only as providing a necessary condition for new ways of seeing, but also as providing for the impossibility of 'seeing' things 'as' we did in the past within previous paradigms. Speaking of paradigm changes, Kuhn remarks:

> Looking at the moon, the convert to Copernicanism does not say, 'I used to see a planet, but now I see a satellite'. That locution would imply a sense in which the Ptolemaic system had once been correct. Instead, a convert to the new astronomy says, 'I once took the moon to be (or saw the moon as) a planet, but I was mistaken'. That sort of statement does recur in the aftermath of scientific revolutions. If it ordinarily disguises a shift of scientific vision or some other mental transformation with the same effect, we may not expect direct testimony about that shift. Rather we must look for indirect and behavioural evidence that the scientist with a new paradigm sees differently from the way he had seen before.[43]

I fail to see why Kuhn regards it as a serious failing for the convert to Copernicanism to report that he used to 'see' a planet but now can 'see' a satellite. Kuhn says that such a locution would imply that the earlier (Ptolemaic) system 'had once been correct'. But, in a sense, it was correct. From within the paradigm in which the convert had previously viewed the world, it was correct. Of course, it is no longer so within his new paradigm. A scientist may, as Kuhn suggests, state that he once saw the moon as a planet but was mistaken. But he might also state that he once saw the moon as a planet but now sees a satellite. Whether the scientist reports his experience in the locution suggested by Kuhn or in some other manner, Kuhn makes too little of the possibility of someone's being able to see something in one way and, *at the same time*, maintaining the capacity to see it 'as' something else, the 'something else' being the way he used to see it within the old paradigm. This, in a sense, is what Wittgenstein does in the *Philosophical Investigations* where he conducts a dialogue with the author (himself) of the *Tractatus*. He shows his ability to play two different language-games.

What I have tried to suggest above, in short, is that different paradigms need not be incommensurable, at least not for that individual who has moved from one to another and has the experience of them both; so that with regard to scientific perception, he can straddle two paradigms just as someone can straddle two language-games. At the very least, the scientist who sees *this* in the new paradigm can draw upon his previous experience to see it also *as that*. In fact, I believe that Kuhn himself does something like this. Consider his remarks regarding his disagreement with Popper, where he asks:

> How am I to persuade Sir Karl, who knows everything I know about scientific development and who has somewhere or other said it, that what he calls a duck can be *seen as* a rabbit? How am I to show him what it would be like to wear my spectacles when he has already learned to look at everything I can point to through his own?[44]

Kuhn can be read as saying that while he *sees* this, he also can see it *as* that, whereas Popper can only see that and cannot see it as this.

But all of this assumes, of course, that Kuhn's more general argument concerning paradigms and revolutionary change in science is correct. While I certainly believe that his views are a welcome alternative to the more formalistic, logical empiricism that has long dominated the history and philosophy of science, and currently dominates most sociology, it should be further criticised on two major accounts.

Paradigms as closed systems

In the first place, the notion of a 'paradigm', despite its usefulness and importance in sensitising us to the manner in which scientists learn and practise science, exaggerates the extent to which a paradigm represents a single, coherent, logical system. For Kuhn, entire scientific disciplines, or entire scientific communities, are treated as having the same logical coherence as, say, Newton's mechanics; everything fits together, constituting a kind of organic whole. He treats paradigms as if they were language-games existing in total isolation from other language-games which may have existed earlier or exist contemporaneously with the language-game (paradigm) to which the scientist is committed. Remember that, for Kuhn, paradigms include 'law, theory, applications, and instrumentation together', and they 'are the source of the methods, problem field, and standards of solution accepted by any mature scientific community at any time'.[45] In short, they provide scientists with a kind of map. Further, paradigms 'provide scientists not only with a map but also with the directions for map-making. In learning a paradigm the scientist acquires theory, methods, and standards together, usually in an inextricable mixture.'[46] Kuhn, then, views paradigms as of one piece, a consistent whole, which the scientist acquires as a result of his scientific training. This view that a paradigm constitutes a single, coherent, logical system is very similar to the functionalist view in sociology that a society forms a single functional 'social system'. Whereas the critics of functionalism in sociology argue that such a viewpoint does not allow for social change, Kuhn treats change within different scientific communities—dominated by paradigms—as coming about through revolutions involving gestalt changes and conversions.

Since Kuhn defines paradigms as closed logical systems, change can only be revolutionary—all at once. The entire paradigm must be totally accepted or totally rejected; there is no middle way. In other words, by formulating paradigms as coherent wholes, all of whose parts 'hold together', Kuhn has forced upon us a distinction between normal and revolutionary phases in science. Either the whole paradigm changes or nothing does, either we totally embrace or we totally reject a specific scientific paradigm. Once we accept Kuhn's notion of paradigm, the only way that we can preserve the possibility of scientific change is through sudden 'revolutionary' change. That is the only alternative to the continuous practice of normal science.

Whatever the considerable merits of Kuhn's work, it has the very severe consequence of viewing the individual scientist's behaviour as something that is 'determined' or 'caused'; one is simply swept along and limited by the paradigm in which one practises. Toulmin has been highly critical of Kuhn's standpoint as regards revolutionary change and paradigm shifts:

> It is a caricature, for instance, to depict the change-over from Newtonian to Einsteinian physics as a completely rational discontinuity. Even a cursory consideration of Einstein's influence on physics will show how little his achievement exemplifies a full-scale scientific revolution. In a highly organized science like physics, every proposed modification—however profoundly it threatens to change the conceptual structure of the subject—is discussed, argued over, reasoned about, and criticized at great length, before being accredited and incorporated into the established body of the discipline.[47]

The theory of paradigms has much to recommend it, so long as paradigms are not conceived of as totally coherent, closed systems. Although Kuhn discusses parallels between political and scientific revolutions, he fails to recognise the continuity involved in revolutions of a political nature. He states: 'Like the choice between competing political institutions, that between competing paradigms proves to be a choice between incompatible modes of community life.'[48] Yet no political revolution has ever led to the total and absolute break with the past that is central to Kuhn's views of scientific revolutions. Instead, certain continuities continue to survive; this is true of the American, French and Russian revolutions alike. Similarly with so-called revolutions in science; while there may be major discontinuities between, say, a fourteenth-century scholar and a twentieth-century physicist, this revolution has hardly occurred overnight. And while there are undoubtedly different world-views, observational languages, theoretical models, standards, and the like, within the general scientific discipline, it seems likely that they share enough disciplinary aims to be able to at least discuss, and understand one another when they do, two different theories which may, generally speaking, come from two different paradigms. This is not to deny, however, that two different scientific disciplines or two highly different 'schools' within a given discipline may find themselves almost totally unable to comprehend one another.

Incommensurability in Kuhn's work

This brings me to the second reason for criticising Kuhn's general position, a reason in some ways similar to the formulation presented above. Kuhn's history of science is intended to demonstrate that the 'historical record' shows something far different from what has usually been concluded from the standpoint of an older historiography of science. Whereas the older view emphasises progress and accumulation, Kuhn, as we know, argues against this view. Because of the incommensurability of old and new paradigms, there can be, Kuhn argues, no accumulation of scientific knowledge and no progress.

Kuhn sees his own work as providing a different perspective on science from that which has been dominant in the recent past:

History, if viewed as a repository for more than anecdote or chronology, could produce a decisive transformation in the image of science by which we are now possessed. That image has previously been drawn, even by scientists themselves, mainly from the study of finished scientific achievements as these are recorded in the classics and, more recently, in the textbooks from which each new generation learns to practise its trade. Inevitably, however, the aim of such books is persuasive and pedagogic; a concept of science drawn from

them is no more likely to fit the enterprise that produced them tha
an image of a national culture drawn from a tourist brochure or
language text. This essay attempts to show that we have been misle
by them in fundamental ways.[49]

Kuhn's conception of the history of science, then, is an attempt to 'se
the record straight' as to 'the way science has actually been practised'.[5]
His conception is a corrective to an older, mistaken view of science whic
has, in his words, 'misled' us. But this seems very similar to saying tha
whereas science has previously been seen from the perspective of on
dominant paradigm in historiography, Kuhn sees it from the perspectiv
of a new paradigm. In other words, Kuhn criticises the old 'textboo
history of science', as he terms it, from the vantage point of a new
paradigm of historical research into science. Of course, Kuhn himse
never refers to the existence of paradigms in the history or philosoph
of science, and instead restricts his focus to the natural sciences. Bu
he certainly does conceive of the 'new historiography' as being
different way of viewing history from that which was dominant i
recent historiography.[51] In fact his discussion of the old and new his
toriography appears highly similar to the picture he draws of differen
paradigms. What this means, therefore, is that Kuhn is in precisely th
same situation as the natural scientist who can only see the worl
through a particular scientific paradigm, and further that his new
historiography has no special status in relation to other historiog
raphies. His historiography and the earlier historiographies are, in hi
terms, incommensurable.

Kuhn is very much like Karl Mannheim's free intelligentsia
Apparently he can emancipate himself from the influence of hi
paradigm so that he has a clear and undisturbed view of the histor
and practice of science. He can see history as it 'really' was and the
compare this with the distorted accounts provided by the old traditio
in the history of science. For instance, Kuhn states that 'Far mor
historical evidence is available than I have had space to exploi
below'.[52] This seems to assume that the 'evidence' is just there, to b
discovered or reviewed, as if it represented what are usually referred t
as objective data. But is the evidence (as well as what is seen as *countin*
as evidence) not necessarily being viewed from the perspective of th
paradigm in which Kuhn's work is located? And how did Kuh
himself manage to escape from the paradigm in which he was traine
as a graduate student? He notes that fifteen years before writing *Th
Structure of Scientific Revolutions*, 'I was a graduate student in theoretica

physics already within sight of the end of my dissertation'.[53] Clearly, then, he had a rather long exposure to the dominant paradigm in theoretical physics. Kuhn goes on to say that his exposure to the history of science led 'to a drastic shift in my career plans, a shift from physics to history of science and then, gradually, from relatively straight-forward historical problems back to the more philosophical concerns that had initially led me to history'.[54] Kuhn's description is interesting for what it reveals about a scientist who had worked within a paradigm (theoretical physics) where he must have learned 'to force nature into the conceptual boxes supplied by professional education',[55] but is then able to view the world from a different perspective (the history of science). True, he speaks of a 'drastic shift', but was this a 'conversion' experience or gestalt switch, or is this not a necessary condition for moving from a natural science paradigm to a disciplinary view outside the natural sciences? In fact, Kuhn actually speaks of shifting 'gradually' from straightforward historical problems back to an earlier interest in philosophical concerns.

All of this is to say that Kuhn is totally lacking in reflexivity; he never applies his paradigm concept to himself and his own work. But, then, of course he really cannot. For, consistent with his own stand-point, he cannot stand both inside and outside the new paradigm of historiography. However, the very fact that he exempts himself and the new historiography from the mode of analysis which he applies to others, as well as ignoring his own switch from theoretical physics to the history of science, tends in my view to undermine the very position he has advanced and defends. Kuhn's arguments that 'the history of science shows . . .' or that 'the evidence reveals . . .' assume that there is one correct, transcendental viewpoint which can reveal what was hidden from earlier historians of science. This, I believe, is a further reason to doubt the completely closed and deterministic conception of paradigms described by Kuhn.

There is, moreover, an additional conclusion to be drawn from Kuhn's work. Recall that he emphasises the importance of paradigms for the practice of science, and also the general absence of paradigms in the social sciences, including presumably history. If indeed Kuhn would argue that the new historiography of science does not have a paradigm and, therefore, that my analysis above is incorrect, then we have an interesting situation. If the only way that someone can formulate the kind of analysis advanced by Kuhn, where different paradigms are compared, is from a position outside any paradigm, then the absence of a paradigm is a necessary condition for that kind of analysis and, hence, highly desirable. This conclusion is, of course, directly at odds with Kuhn's emphasis on the necessity and importance of paradigms.

In conclusion, there are several reasons for raising questions about paradigms, conversions and, most especially, the whole notion of incommensurability. I have tried here to suggest some of the problems raised by Kuhn's work. These problems are, I believe, different from those raised by Kuhn's critics. Further, I have attempted to indicate that, despite the alleged similarities betwen Kuhn and Wittgenstein, there are important differences as well. Finally, I have tried to argue that it is only because Kuhn formulates paradigms as totally closed systems that the problem of incommensurability arises, and that Kuhn himself is an exception to the general thesis which he advances.

6 The Social Nature of Mathematics

The mathematician is an inventor, not a discoverer.

LUDWIG WITTGENSTEIN[1]

As was noted in chapter 3, Mannheim and most other sociologists of knowledge hold that the natural sciences are immune from the influence of social factors. The natural sciences, logic and mathematics are, it is widely assumed, detachable from historical–social influences. Mannheim, for example, could not see how $2 \times 2 = 4$ could be thought about sociologically.[2] This has continued to be the view among sociologists of knowledge and science to the present day. Even C. Wright Mills, who did recognise that science and logic were subject to social influences, only partially grasped the extent to which they could be approached sociologically.[3] Ludwig Wittgenstein, on the other hand, provides us with a framework within which mathematics and logic can be viewed sociologically in a deeper sense than heretofore.

In this chapter, I will begin by considering very briefly the dominant realist view concerning mathematics and logic. I will then consider some evidence contrary to that view, and will suggest how the sociology of knowledge (informed by Wittgenstein) might be directly relevant. These concerns, however, are secondary to the main purpose at hand here. My principal aim, which will constitute the bulk of what follows, is to show how Wittgenstein has provided us with a way of seeing the practice of mathematics as a fully social activity. Furthermore, this examination of Wittgenstein's views of mathematics will clarify for us the interdependent relationship of sociology and philosophy.

For realists, our notions, as observed in the previous chapter, correspond to external essences which exist as self-evident truths to be discovered by use of our rational faculties. They hold that language is simply a copy of pre-established structures. The key to truth is provided by pure thought, of which logic and mathematics are the clearest examples. For instance Frege, who exercised a great influence on the early Wittgenstein, states: 'If everything were in continued flux, and nothing maintained itself fixed for all time, there would no longer be any possibility of getting to know about the world, and everything would be plunged into confusion.' True knowledge, then, must be based on changeless properties and principles. Further, Frege emphasises that 'Often it is only after immense intellectual effort, which may have continued over centuries, that humanity at last succeeds in achieving knowledge of a concept in its pure form, by stripping off the irrelevant accretions which veil it from the eye of the mind'.[4] On this view, mathematics and logic are reflections of the *a priori* structure of reality. The mathematician G. H. Hardy holds that 'mathematical reality lies outside us, that our function is to discover or to observe it, and that the theorems which we prove and which we decide grandiloquently as our "creation" are simply our notes of observation'.[5] Speaking of relations already existing 'out there', Morris Cohen asserts that 'the discovery of the proof that π is transcendental did not create any logical relations but showed us what the relation always has been'.[6] And perhaps surprisingly, the phenomenologist Alfred Schutz states that 'the expression $2 \times 2 = 4$ has an objective meaning regardless of what is in the minds of any or all of its users'.[7] For all of these men, mathematics is viewed as a realm of truths independent of knowing subjects. They believe that logic and mathematics live a rigorous existence independently of us. Formal concepts have a life of their own, with which we must fall in line.

Opposed to these viewpoints are those who hold that mathematical notions and conceptions of logic are cultural products. With regard to logic, De Gré notes:

> Certain rules are set up during the course of time by social groups as to how valid knowledge is to be acquired, and how propositions are to be logically operated with. The sociology of knowledge is interested in the social situations in which these rules were developed and the influence of those rules on social action.[8]

Currie and Toulmin have made the same point, documenting the sharp contrast between present-day and medieval logic.[9] Similarly with mathematics; the concepts and methods have undergone profound transformations since the time of Euclidean geometry. In Toulmin's words:

Such fundamental mathematical concepts as 'validity' and 'rigour', 'elegance', 'proof', and 'mathematical necessity', undergo the same sea-change as their scientific counterparts . . . Even the basic standards of 'mathematical proof' have themselves been re-appraised more than one since Euclid's time. The result is that the concepts, methods, and intellectual ideals of mathematics are no more exempt from 'the ravage of history'—as Descartes and Frege hoped and supposed—than those of any other intellectual discipline.[10]

Given the view that conceptions of logic and mathematics are very much cultural products, one might expect sociologists of knowledge to consider the social background and context in which these different concepts arose or are found. What were the cultural conditions, for example, that help account for the changes from medieval to modern logic? One might expect more studies like that by Granet, who considered the social–historical background of the number systems and mathematics of Chinese society.[11] This is one sense in which the sociology of knowledge or science is directly relevant to the study of logic and mathematics. There is, however, a more profound sense in which sociology can inform our conceptions of logic and mathematics.

Before moving on to discuss what might be termed a 'sociology of mathematics', it is first necessary to consider further the matter of realism.[12] If we are to examine the activity of doing mathematics, we must first look closely at the realist's conception of mathematical behaviour. Imagine that it is asked why someone concluded that $2 \times 2 = 4$. The realist's answer would be that 2×2 *does* equal 4; it has been observed to be true. That is to say, the truth of the proposition, the way that mathematical reality really is, *causes* one to reach this conclusion. It is as if ideas functioned independently of us, having a life of their own. In considering this example, David Bloor makes some useful observations.[13] The word 'cause' here, he notes, cannot possibly mean that cause constitutes the 'necessary and sufficient conditions' for reaching the conclusion that $2 \times 2 = 4$. If truth were to be a necessary and sufficient condition for reaching this conclusion, then there would be neither error nor ignorance. Bloor remarks on this problem as follows:

There is, however, another sense of the word 'cause' which fits with what has gone before and which would be consistent with the

idea that a proposition is believed because it is true. This is the teleo
logical, purposive, or goal-directed sense that is sometimes given to
the word. Suppose it were assumed that man has a natural tendency
to perceive the truth when presented with it, and that there is a
natural movement, as it were, towards the truth. In this case only
beliefs that are false would require explanation. Beliefs that are
true are natural and require no comment, for their truth is all the
explanation that is required. It might be said, on this view, that
truth is the cause of true beliefs, whilst a variety of other factor
cause the deviations into ignorance or error.[14]

The teleological view is in fact, Bloor argues, the account of knowledge
associated with most realists and with Mannheim's sociology of know
ledge. Mannheim observes that the process of knowing does not follow
only from the 'nature of things' or from 'pure logical possibilities', but
is often influenced by 'extra-theoretical' factors of diverse sorts.[15] In
other words, when people do what is logical or in the nature of things
no further explanation is required. Explanations—in this case, the
sociology of knowledge—are only required when people are not following what Mannheim called 'immanent laws', that is, proceeding
correctly towards the truth.[16] This sociology of knowledge is referred to
by Bloor as the 'sociology of error'.[17] In many ways, this approach is
similar to that of sociology more generally, where deviance and dis-
organisation are the focus of inquiry while everyday, ordinary behaviour
is taken for granted as unproblematic. Because of the viewpoint that
'extra-theoretical' factors are to be considered only with regard to
errors, ignorance, exceptions and deviations, sociologists of knowledge—
and sociologists more generally—have viewed the practice of mathematics as 'off-limits' as a topic for sociological inquiry. Since, however
teleology is built into the realist conception of mathematics, the
only way that we can get a foothold in considering mathematical
practice is to employ a different conception of mathematics. Wittgenstein provides the necessary alternative view.

Wittgenstein and Mathematics

Wittgenstein consistently opposes the idea that there exist standards
free of human practices, standards which can be invoked without the
possibility of contradiction and disagreement. This is as true in mathematics and science as elsewhere. Let us examine this in terms of the
example referred to earlier in the book: continuing the number

sequence 2, 4, 6, 8 in the same way. For realists, as Bloor notes, 'the correct continuation of the sequence, the true embodiment of the rule and its intended mode of application exists already. To obey the rule is to trace out what is already faintly there, existing "in advance" . . .'[18] But the realist conception of rule really does not take us very far—for even if the rule is already there, what rule does one use to decide whether one is applying the same rule on different occasions? That is, the realist assumption that there exists some logical or mathematical prototype which corresponds to the 'true' continuation of the number sequence still requires that there be a way (a rule) by which people can know that the supposed prototype is *really* the embodiment of the rule that is necessary for continuing the sequence. This poses the same problem all over again. What knowledge is required to know that *that* rule is the correct one? So, at each step there is the requirement of knowledge as to how the rule goes. At issue with realism, in Bloor's words, is 'the circular character of the epistemology. It presupposes precisely what it sets out to explain.'[19] It assumes that there is a 'natural movement' towards the truth at every step.

Since Wittgenstein rejects the realist approach with its teleological assumptions, how then does he account for someone correctly continuing the series 2, 4, 6, 8? And how is it that we generally reach agreement, that disputes in calculating are unusual? After all, Wittgenstein does emphasise that there is general agreement in doing mathematics:

> . . . there can be a dispute over the correct result of a calculation (say of a rather long addition). But such disputes are rare and of short duration. They can be decided, as we say, 'with certainty.' Mathematicians do not in general quarrel over the result of a calculation. (This is an important fact.)—If it were otherwise . . . then our concept of 'mathematical certainty' would not exist.[20]

The fact that we generally agree in our calculations is the result of how we *learn* mathematics, the way in which we are *trained*. As with any other language-game, the language-game of mathematics requires socialisation into the rules, standards, conventions and grammar that one must master in order to play the game correctly. Part of this requires learning that there are 'right' and 'wrong' ways of playing the game. In mathematics, we learn that one can be 'correct' and that one can also make 'mistakes'. As Wittgenstein notes: 'Our children are not only given practice in calculation but are also trained to adopt a particular attitude toward a mistake in calculating.'[21] And just as there are different systems of mathematics, so are there also different methods of training: 'It would also be possible to imagine such a training in a sort of arithmetic. Children could calculate, each in his own way—as long as they listened to their voice and obeyed it. Calculating in this way would be like a sort of composing.'[22] It would also result in the practice of an arithmetic very different from our own.

Returning now to the problem of following the number sequence, Wittgenstein deals with two questions:[23] (1) how is the application of a rule determined—that is, what makes *this* rather than *that* the correct application? and (2) when there are several applications of a rule, what constitutes *consistency* in the applications of that rule?

Regarding the first question, concerning the criterion for the way a rule or formula is intended, Wittgenstein poses the problem as follows:

> *How do I know* that in working out the series '+2' I must write '20004, 20006' and not '20004, 20008'? . . . 'But you surely know for example that you must always write the *same* sequence of numbers in the units: 2, 4, 6, 8, 0, 2, 4, etc.'—Quite true: the problem must always appear in this sequence, and even in this one: 2, 2, 2, 2, etc.—For how do I know that I am to write '2' after the five hundredth '2'?; i.e. that 'the same figure' in that place is '2'? And if I know *in advance*, what use is this knowledge to me later on? I mean: How do I know what to do with this earlier knowledge when the step actually has to be taken? (If intuition is needed to continue the series '+1', then it is also needed to continue the series '+0'.)
>
> 'But do you mean to say that the expression "+2" leaves you in doubt what you are to do e.g. after 2004?'—No; I answer '2006' without hesitation. But just for that reason it is superfluous to suppose that this was determined earlier on. My having no doubt in face of the question does *not* mean that it was answered in advance.[24]

Recall that Bloor describes the view which Wittgenstein opposes as being characterised by teleological assumption, that is, that the individual is being directed towards a definite end or result, that he is moved towards the result by some purpose in nature. While, to my knowledge, Wittgenstein says nothing explicitly about teleological explanations, he clearly rejects the influence of 'intuition'. He does this implicitly in the above quotation, and more directly elsewhere. Speaking of the same problem (continuing a number series) in the *Philosophical Investigations*, Wittgenstein rejects the idea that a new insight--intuition—is needed at every step to carry out the order '+n' correctly.[25] He states: 'If intuition is an inner voice—how do I know *how* to obey it? And how do I know that it doesn't mislead me? For if it can guide me right, it can also guide me wrong. (Intuition an unnecessary shuffle.)'[26] The question 'How am I to obey a rule?' is, then, a question neither about causes nor about intuitions. There are neither external (nature, the true number sequence) nor internal (intuition, instantaneous apprehension) forces involved here. The question, rather, is about the *justification* for my obeying the rule as I do.

The justification for using the formula is *the way we were taught to use it.* 'But,' asks Wittgenstein's imaginary interlocutor, 'then what does the peculiar inexorability of mathematics consist in?'

> Counting (and that means: counting like *this*) is a technique that is employed daily in the most various operations of our lives. And that is why we learn to count as we do: with endless practice, with merciless exactitude; that is why it is inexorably insisted that we shall all say 'two' after 'one', 'three' after 'two', and so on.—'But is this counting only a *use*, then; isn't there also some truth corresponding to this sequence?' The *truth* is that counting has proved to pay. 'Then do you want to say that "being true" means: being usable (or useful)?'—No, not that; but that it can't be said of the series of natural numbers—any more than of our language—that it is true, but: that it is usable, and, above all, it is *used*.[27]

Natural numbers, like our language, are neither true nor false; they are used. And the fact that numbers, like language, can be used in a great variety of different situations and can function without special preparation for every eventuality is due to *custom*. 'A person goes by a sign-post,' Wittgenstein says, 'only insofar as there exists a regular use of sign-posts, a custom.'[28] And, further: 'To obey a rule, to make a report, to give an order, to play a game of chess, are *customs* (uses, institutions).'[29] Mathematics, in short, is a human institution, a human product, a human invention. In so far as I continue the series '+n' correctly, then, it is made possible by the fact that I can play the language-game of mathematics.

Using a rule, applying a formula correctly, is to use or apply it the way it is generally applied in that language-game:

> I go through the proof and then accept its result.—I mean: this is simply what we *do*. This is use and custom among us, or a fact of our natural history.[30]

'The way the formula is meant determines which steps are to be taken.' What is the criterion for the way the formula is meant?

Presumably the way we always use it, the way we were taught to use it.[31]

The basic mathematical process of using a formula is shown by Wittgenstein to be embedded in social practices. The terms in the above, as Bloor point out, are sociological: 'what we *do*', 'the way we always use it' 'the way we were taught to use it'.[32] Mathematics is a social activity, a social practice. If human beings are trained *that* way, so that they calculate in *that* way, their results will generally agree. Every instance of the use of a formula is the culmination of a process of *socialisation*.

Given that the application of a formula is a social process, we must consider how it is that someone learns a language-game. The child, says Wittgenstein, learns not by explanations, but by training. Training differs from explanation in that—at least among children—it is largely non-verbal, and it is aimed at producing certain actions. 'The grammar of the word "knows",' Wittgenstein says, 'is evidently closely related to that of "can", "is able to". But also closely related to that of "understands". ("Mastery" of a technique.)'[33] And, further, 'It is only if someone *can do*, has learnt, is master of, such-and-such, that it makes sense to say that he has had this experience'.[34] One is trained in mathematics, then, in the same way as with any other language-game. This involves notions of right and wrong, errors and mistakes, rules and agreement. 'The words "right" and "wrong",' Wittgenstein emphasises, 'are used when giving instructions according to a rule. The word "right" makes the pupil go on, the word "wrong" holds him back.'[35] These 'rights and 'wrongs' lie in the language-game. Mathematics, Wittgenstein observes, is *normative*.[36] Therefore, 'logical inference is a transition that is justified if it follows a particular paradigm, and whose rightness is not dependent on anything else'.[37] The only truth involved here is that logical inference, like counting, has proved to pay— it is used by people like ourselves in our daily lives. There is no further necessity:

'But doesn't it follow with logical necessity that you get two when you add one and one, and three when you add one to two? And isn't this inexorability the same as that of logical inference?'—Yes, it is the same.—'But isn't there a truth corresponding to logical inference? Isn't it *true* that this follows from that?'—The proposition: 'Is it true that this follows from that?' means simply: this follows from that.[38]

What makes something a logical inference is the game we play with it, the attitude we take towards it. So, Wittgenstein remarks on the mathematical 'must' as follows: 'The mathematical Must is only another expression of the fact that mathematics forms concepts. And concepts help us to comprehend things. They correspond to a particular way of dealing with situations. Mathematics forms a network of norms.'[39] The answer to the first question—what justifies someone as applying a rule or formula correctly—is that *we use the formula in the way we were taught to use it.*

Let us now consider the second question. When there are several applications of a rule, what constitutes *consistent* application of that rule? Again, Wittgenstein lays heavy stress on the fact that people are trained to act in certain ways. Thus, when they encounter a new circumstance, they continue to act in a manner that they—and others —feel constitutes consistency. They continue to apply the rule 'naturally', that is, as a natural extension of their previous training. But there is no *external* guarantee that applying the rule will always follow previous training or practice. 'Consistency,' then, is defined in terms of what follows naturally, that is, as a result of previous training. Wittgenstein says:

> Isn't it like this: so long as one thinks it can't be otherwise, one draws logical conclusions. This presumably means: *so long as such-and-such is not brought into question at all.* The steps which are not brought into question are logical inferences.[40]

That is simply how we do it; there is no further justification. That is the practice of the group. There are no standards outside the practices of the group which serve to decide on the ultimate validity for the correctness of a practice. Wittgenstein writes:

> Is it now certain that people will never want to calculate differently? That people will never look at reality differently? But that is not at all the certainty that this order is supposed to give us. It is not the eternal correctness of the calculus that is supposed to be assured, but only, so to speak, the temporal.[41]

The consistency of applying a rule, we see, is not a matter of external correctness, it is not a matter of eternal and immutable laws. Wittgenstein says:

> Giving grounds, however, justifying the evidence, comes to an end; —but the end is not certain propositions striking us immediately as

true, i.e., it is not a kind of *seeing* on our part; it is our *acting*, which lies at the bottom of the language-game. If the true is what is grounded, then the ground is not *true*, nor yet false.[42]

Interpretation and Rules

It should be clear, however, that the above discussion is narrowly focused on mathematics as a particular language-game. As I noted in the previous chapter, we all learn to play a multitude of language-games. Thus, we learn to play the language-game of mathematics only through an appeal to and reliance upon earlier acquired linguistic abilities. Our original, everyday language constitutes a meta-language in use which underlies our learning and practising mathematics. It is Wittgenstein's recognition of this which distinguishes his views from the usual conventionalist accounts of rule-following. This is important in considering his observation that there is no guarantee that rules will always be interpreted as intended. The problem of continuing a series correctly (applying a formula) will again serve as an example. One person writes down a series, say 2, 4, 6 . . . , up to 1000. He asks a second person to continue the series '+2' beyond 1000, expecting him to write 1000, 1002, 1004, and so on. Instead, the second person writes 1000, 1004, 1008, 1012, and so on.

> We say to him: 'Look at what you've done!'—He doesn't understand. We say: 'You were meant to add *two*: look how you began the series!' —He answers: 'Yes, isn't it right? I thought that was how I was *meant* to do it.'—Or suppose he pointed to the series and said: 'But I went on in the same way.'—It would now be no use to say: 'But can't you see . . . ?'—and repeat the old examples and explanations.—In such a case we might say, perhaps: It comes natural to this person to understand our order with our explanations as *we* should understand the order: 'Add 2 up to 1000, 4 up to 2000, 6 up to 3000 and so on.'[43]

One thing shown by this example is that rules can be interpreted in more than one way; the rule-follower in the above example simply finds it 'natural' to interpret the rule '+2' in a different manner from that which is meant for correct rule-following. How can this be, how does it happen? The answer, I believe, is the fact that the natural (ordinary) language, which underlies the learning of mathematical (extraordinary) language, consists of a set of rules which can themselves be variously interpreted. But if this is true, there appears a tremendous problem. If all rules, including even those of the initially acquired language, are open to various interpretations, where do we stop? Do we not find ourselves in an infinite regress of rules, interpretations, rules, and so forth? Wittgenstein poses the question explicitly:

> This was our paradox: no course of action could be determined by a rule, because every course of action can be made out to accord with the rule. The answer was: if everything can be made out to accord with the rule, then it can also be made out to conflict with it. And so there would be neither accord nor conflict here.
>
> It can be seen that there is a misunderstanding here from the mere fact that in the course of our argument we gave one interpretation after another; as if each one contented us at least for a moment, until we thought of yet another behind it. What this shows is that there is a way of grasping a rule which is *not* an *interpretation*, but which is exhibited in what we call obeying the rule and going against it in actual cases.[44]

But what does it mean to speak of a way of grasping a rule which is not an interpretation? What Wittgenstein has in mind here, I believe, is some notion of a meta-language *in use* or, more specifically, the human activities which allow us to conduct and frame our investigations. This 'meta-language', however, is not only linguistic, for it includes a host of activities directed toward coping with the world around us. It consists of what we *do*, the ways we proceed, which allows us even to understand what it means to give an interpretation in the first place. In other words, the total activities and practices of human beings constitute a world-view. Various language-games are among the constituents making up a world-view. This meta-language in use is crucial in understanding Wittgenstein's remarks about exhibiting the rule in actual cases.

If someone already knows a language, he then can use that language and his understanding of it to explain to someone else how a specific rule is to be followed. Thus, we can explain a new rule or convention— say, in mathematics—by drawing upon the rules and conventions already *in use*. Once we have acquired an ordinary language, we can— and initially must—use the rules and conventions of that language to explain and teach an extraordinary language like mathematics. Those rules and conventions, those acquired in learning the language-game into which we are first trained, constitute the apparatus, as it were, by which we learn additional (extraordinary) languages. The rules and conventions *within* the already played language-game in the form of

life where we originally acquired language make it possible to learn
to play new language-games. They also make it possible, when 'going
on in the same way' when applying a mathematical formula, for someone to continue a series: 2004, 2008, 2012, etc. That is to say, he may
initially have been trained within a world-view different from that
into which most of the rest of us were trained.

While we can conceive of someone 'going on in the same way' as
above, it is generally unlikely. What I mean here is that there are
limitations to the actual language-games which it is possible to play.
There are, as I noted in the previous chapter, certain physiological
and psychological facts of nature which govern the possible alternatives
for people like ourselves. In training someone to play a language-game:
'I do it, he does it after me; and I influence him by expressions of
agreement, rejection, expectation, encouragement. I let him go his
way, or hold him back; and so on.'[45] The training involves gestures,
smiles, grunts, frowns, the raising and lowering of the teacher's voice,
and so on. But this is not to say that all language-games, as I observed
above, are playable. After all, I cannot teach my children to fly;
nor a mother cat her kittens to calculate sums. And certainly some
people are physically or mentally incapable of learning to play some
language-games played by others. Because of certain facts of nature
or certain individual limitations, not all language-games are playable.
The most general features of the world have conditioned the range of
language-games which it is physically possible for people like ourselves
to play. Wittgenstein writes: 'What would a society all of deaf men
be like? Or a society of the "feeble-minded"? *An important question*!
What then of a society that never played many of our customary
language-games?'[46] In a society of deaf men or the feeble-minded,
then, many of our customary language-games would not be played.
Here we see again that the language-games in use are limited by
certain facts of nature.

All of this seems to support my suggestion in chapter 4 that beneath
the wide variety of language-games there exists only *one* form of life.
At least if we conceive a form of life as including the general facts
of nature which, to some extent, govern the human possibilities for
learning to do this or that, we have to conclude that men everywhere
(so far as we know) share the same form of life. Of course, we can
conceive of alternative forms of life—as Wittgenstein often does, and
as did Calvino in chapter 2—but even these possibilities must be
formulated from within the form of life with which we are familiar.
Hence, an appeal to form of life as constituting a kind of meta-language

which allows us to stop the infinite regress of rule, interpretation, rule, and so on, is ultimately an appeal to necessary conditions or necessary truths. If so, then realists appear to be correct. But they are correct only in a limited sense, for they cannot demonstrate any *necessary* connection between certain facts of nature—which we can grant are everywhere the same—and the language-games we play. Even if we accept the realist doctrine that there exist ordinary, empirical truths about the world (for example, people whose heads are totally separated from their bodies will die, no one can walk on water, people do not disappear into thin air), these do not account for the conceptual truths reflected in various language-games.

None of this, it must be acknowledged, is dealt with explicitly by Wittgenstein. While the notion of 'form of life' has been widely used and variously interpreted, it has been generally left unexplored as to the precise role it plays in Wittgenstein's formulations. In my view, it is useful to conceive of form of life as coterminous with the general facts of nature. This is appropriate, I believe, because it helps us to see that Wittgenstein, while certainly not a realist, is not on the other hand a fully-fledged conventionalist. Wittgenstein stated that 'Our talk gets its meaning from the rest of our proceedings.'[47] What are those proceedings? Perhaps the following are examples:

'Strange coincidence, that every man whose skull has been opened had a brain!'[48]

I have a telephone conversation with New York. My friend tells me that his young trees have buds of such and such kind. I am now convinced that his tree is. . . . Am I also convinced that the earth exists?[49]

The existence of the earth is rather part of the whole *picture* which forms the starting-point of belief for me.[50]

Certainly talk about skulls containing brains, the existence of the earth, and the like, are part of our form of life. They help constitute the foundation which forms the basis for our *actions*. They underlie the ways in which we act and speak about the things in question. Concerning the assumption that the earth existed before our birth, Wittgenstein remarks: 'The assumption, one might say, forms the basis of action, and therefore, naturally, of thought.'[51]

Some Facts of Nature

If, as Wittgenstein argues, mathematics is a normative practice, what determines the standard practices of a group? Here, I return to the point made above: mathematics is an anthropological phenomenon. Again, this means there are certain facts of nature which make it possible for calculating, inferring, and so forth, to occur at all. Consider, for instance, the convention that twelve inches equal one foot. No one, Wittgenstein notes, will ordinarily see this as an empirical proposition. Instead, it is a convention. 'But,' he says, 'measuring would entirely lose its ordinary character if, for example, putting 12 bits each one inch long, end to end, didn't ordinarily yield a length which can in its turn be preserved in a special way.'[52] The conventional proposition that twelve inches equal one foot must be seen against the background of the constant shape or size of objects in nature; these objects do not suddenly expand or contract for no apparent reason. If they did, our whole idea of measuring would have to be revised. Not only is a proposition grounded in a technique, but also in the physical and psychological facts that make the technique possible. The convention about feet and inches is arbitrary. What is not arbitrary, however, is our notion of *measurement* which underlies the convention. For people like ourselves, who engage in what we call measuring, we obtain a certain consistency of results. Our normal language-games, including measuring, would lose their point if rule became exception and exception, rule. 'The procedure of putting a lump of cheese on a balance and fixing the price by the turn of the scale would lose its point,' Wittgenstein observes, 'if it frequently happened for such lumps to suddenly grow or shrink for no obvious reason'.[23]

In my view, the 'facts of nature' to which Wittgenstein refers have been given far too little attention by most commentators on Wittgenstein's work. Consider, for example, his remark about colours in *Zettel*:

'If humans were not in general agreed about the colors of things, if undetermined cases were not exceptional, then our concepts of color could not exist.' No:—our concept *would* not exist.[54]

Do I want to say, then, that certain facts are favourable to the formation of certain concepts; or again unfavourable? And does experience teach us this? It is a fact of experience that human beings alter their concepts, exchange them for others when they learn new facts; when in this way what was formerly important to them becomes unimportant, and *vice versa*.[55]

I want to say there is a geometrical gap, not a physical one, between green and red.[56]

But doesn't anything physical correspond to it? I do not deny that. (And suppose it were merely our habituation to *these* concepts, to these language games? But I am not saying that it is so.) If we teach a human being such-and-such technique by means of examples,—that he then proceeds like *this* and not like *that* in a particular case, or that in this case he gets stuck, and thus that this and not that is the 'natural' continuation for him: this of itself is an extremely important fact of nature.[57]

But if our concepts are in some way dependent on these facts of nature, should they not be our concern? Wittgenstein himself poses the question, and provides an answer:

If the formation of concepts can be explained by facts of nature, should we not be interested, not in grammar, but rather in that nature which is the basis of grammar?—Our interest certainly includes the correspondence between concepts and very general facts of nature. (Such facts as mostly do not strike us because of their generality.) But our interest does not fall back upon these possible causes of the formation of concepts; we are not doing a natural history—since we can also invent fictitious natural history for our purposes.[58]

Our concepts, our rules, our formulas, rest upon a certain background of physical and psychological facts. Without them, measuring, counting, calculating, and so on, would not be possible. Although these facts of nature constitute a necessary condition for our ways of doing things, they are not a sufficient condition. After all, wide variations in human behaviour are consistent with the facts of nature. Different logical systems, different mathematical systems, can exist against the wide background of physical and psychological facts of nature. So in the case of mathematical rule-following, and in the case of the particular mathematical system which we follow, we must account for it in terms of human institutions—not physical facts or realities.

Mathematics as a Social Convention

I have noted earlier in this chapter that mathematical notions may differ in different social–historical contexts and periods. Further evidence for this view is introduced by Bloor, who discusses the concept 'zero'.[59] He notes that while the Babylonians, for example, had a place-value notation, they had a somewhat different concept of zero. 'The nearest equivalent to zero,' Bloor reports, 'operated in the way that ours does when we use it to distinguish, say, 204 from 24. They had nothing corresponding to our use when we distinguish, say, 240 from 24.'[60] Apparently, context alone decides the absolute value in Babylonian mathematics.[61] If there are different notions of zero, then the concept is obviously not a dictate of logic or of our instincts. Clearly this conclusion is at odds with the views of Frege, Hardy and others who believe that concepts are independent of any particular language, independent of all human thought. While they assume that intuitions furnish a knowledge which will spontaneously build itself into propositions which are completely devoid of error, Wittgenstein's position allows us to recognise that the structure of a concept is dependent on the modes of calculation into which it enters. The concept of zero, like other numerical concepts, is, in short, part of the social institution of mathematics. And this institution is not everywhere the same.

Among all people, however, general agreement is required as to the correct results of calculating and inferring; not just any result is accepted as correct. 'If you draw different conclusions,' Wittgenstein says, 'you do indeed get into conflict, e.g. with society; and also with other practical consequences'.[62] But these shared agreements upon which our calculating, inferring, and so forth, rest are not the results of our having freely chosen from among a multitude of possibilities. Instead, 'thinking and inferring (like counting) is of course bounded for us, not by an arbitrary definition, but by natural limits corresponding to the body of what can be called the role of thinking and inferring in our life'.[63] The 'role of thinking and inferring', I believe, can be seen as referring to our customs and institutions. Mathematics— calculating, inferring, and so on—then, is dependent both on the facts of nature and on particular requirements or ideals that may differ for different peoples. Wittgenstein mentions in this regard the ideal of smoothness and calculating by machine. The interlocutor points out that 'experience has taught us that calculating by machine is more trustworthy than by memory. It has taught us that our life goes smoother when we calculate with machines.' 'But,' asks Wittgenstein, 'must smoothness necessarily be our ideal (must it be our ideal to have everything wrapped in cellophane) ?'[64] Mathematics is grounded, as it were, both in the biological and in the social. The rules of calculating, and so on, established by human beings like ourselves with certain biological capabilities and limitations, are appealed to in judging the correctness of particular calculations and inferences. These rules are used to decide whether what is in question is warranted or not; they always relate to human activities. There is no supreme authority beyond what we do; the ways in which we do, in fact, calculate, infer and do mathematics.

Still, the persistent critic may ask: but how do you know whether the agreed-upon rules *are* really the correct ones? Wittgenstein replies: 'The danger here, I believe, is one of giving a justification of our procedure when there is no such thing as a justification and we ought simply to have said: that's *how* we do it.'[65] There is no further justification, no ultimate foundation, for our procedures. This most assuredly does not mean that our procedures (for calculating, and so forth) are unreliable or untrustworthy, and that we can simply decide not to accept them. Wittgenstein writes:

> I mean: if a contradiction were now actually found in arithmetic that would only prove that an arithmetic with *such* a contradiction in it could render very good service; and it will be better for us to modify our concept of the certainty required, than to say that it would really not yet have been a proper arithmetic.
> 'But surely this isn't ideal certainty!'—Ideal for what purpose? The rules of logical inference are rules of the *language-game*.[66]

In fact, then, the question of whether we choose to accept or reject the rules of mathematics is never raised at all, any more than the question of whether or not we choose to be human beings rather than stones. Asking whether our human practices are correct or justified is to pose the question as to whether or not we are correct or justified in being the sorts of creatures we are.

The above discussion leads to an interesting conclusion: measuring, calculating, inferring, and so forth, are bounded by the facts of nature, but *particular* systems of measurement, calculation, and so on, are fully a matter of social convention. One or another type of mathematics is invented or created against the background of a certain consistency of objects in nature (they do not suddenly change size or shape, they do not suddenly disappear), the human capacity to remember numbers accurately, and the like, the various uses that counting and calculating have in our lives, and so forth. But while these facts of nature set certain limitations as to the possibilities of various language-games— including mathematics—they can account neither for the existence of particular language-games nor for the manner in which people learn to play those games.

In seeing that mathematics and logic are collections of norms, we see that they have the same ontological status as any other institutions. They are fully social in character. This means that the norms of mathematics and logic must be learned in the same manner as other norms of social life. Just as someone must learn the grammar of words like 'lose' (losing one's way, memory, composure) and 'living' (in sin, fear, a dormitory), one must learn the grammar of mathematics. A concern with grammar, as Wittgenstein emphasises, *is* a concern with the world, with *application*.[67] On this account, what Mannheim termed 'extra-theoretical' factors are very much involved in mathematics and logic. One cannot assume that mathematics and logic are fully governed by the 'nature of things' and by 'pure logic'.

The Interdependence of Philosophy and Sociology

There is, finally, a further consequence of our examination of Wittgenstein's conception of mathematics which needs to be considered: the relationship between philosophy and sociology. It has been a central theme of the present book that scientists must be aware of the extent to which their inquiries—whether they recognise it or not—rest upon certain assumptions. I have argued that sociology, especially, needs to be informed by philosophy. In addition, of course, I have tried to show the importance of a Wittgensteinian approach for understanding various social practices, including science and mathematics. One of my assumptions, which is shared by philosophically inclined writers like Winch and Louch, has been that philosophy is particularly illuminating for the discipline of sociology. But it is now important to point out that the argument can be reversed to show that sociology is required to illuminate philosophical problems.[68] Winch has argued that sociology is misbegotten philosophy, ignoring the question as to whether the relation might be reversed.[69] Let us, then, look at the issue more carefully. The question at hand concerns the nature of the relationship between sociology and philosophy, especially as it is revealed by Wittgenstein's analysis of rule-following. After all, Wittgenstein emphasises that philosophy, like other language-games, must base itself on concrete human existence, which includes agreement and socialisation as basic facts. The concept of 'agreement' is essentially a sociological concept.

Consider the general example used several times previously in this volume: continuing a series of numbers. One person writes down a mathematical series (2, 4, 6, 8) and someone else is supposed to continue the series in the same way. Evidence that the second person understands the rule is provided by his ability to continue the series correctly, that is, 10, 12, 14, 16, and so on. But whether the rule is employed correctly or not is dependent not only on the actions of the rule-follower himself, but also on the *reactions of other people* to what he does. Only in a situation where the rule has a public character can someone intelligibly be said to be following a rule at all. This is true of all language-games: mathematics, philosophy, logic, physics, and so on. Winch, of course, recognises this. He states, for example, that 'social relations really exist only in and through the ideas which are current in society'.[70] But at the same time, it seems to be that the 'ideas' which are current in society exist only in and through the existing 'social relations'. These social relations determine, for instance, what counts as an idea, as well as what counts as a good or bad idea. Winch himself emphasises this in pointing out that various categories of meaning, intelligibility, and so on, 'are logically dependent for their sense on social interaction between men'.[71] I am not denying that what is seen as this or that social relationship (helping, jealousy) is itself dependent upon societal ideas. Rather, the point here is that there is an interdependence between concepts and ideas on the one hand, and social relations on the other. To act 'logically', for instance, is to act in accordance with the rules that constitute logical reasoning. But the rules do not stand apart from the social relationships in which decisions about correct logical inferences are made. At the same time, the social relationships themselves are constituted by notions of rules and rule-following. To understand social relationships, we require an understanding of rules; while to understand rules, we require an understanding of social relations.

Time and again, Wittgenstein reminds us that language-games are based on agreement, that concepts and meanings are largely social creations. This means that they are *created by people in groups*. It is therefore not abstract logic or external entities existing 'out there' which are primary, but concrete human practices. Thus, language (and consequently science, art and religion) is pre-eminently a *social* phenomenon. Human actions and human agreement underlie all scientific and intellectual practices, including philosophy. If this is not directly relevant to sociology, what is? Thus it is a mistake to conclude, as Winch does, that philosophy occupies a privileged position in relation to sociology. His own work, in fact, reveals their mutual interdependence.

Furthermore, my consideration of the social nature of mathematics and my brief discussion of the relationship between sociology and philosophy again points to the social nature of science more generally. Winch fails to recognise that the truths of science are fully the product of human agreement within scientific communities, that *all* science is a human enterprise. He mistakenly exempts the natural sciences from his discussion of the problems characteristic of social scientific inquiry. To see this, let us briefly consider Winch's main argument in *The Idea of a Social Science*.

For the most part, Winch's book is an attempt to distinguish the problems and focus of the social sciences from those of the natural sciences. He emphasises that whereas the natural scientist has to deal with only one set of rules—those governing the investigation itself—for the social scientist, *what* he is studying, as well as his study of it, is a rule-ridden activity. Thus, for the social scientist there are two sets of rules: the procedural rules of his discipline and the rules involved among those whom he is studying. Winch's book is mainly concerned with the study of social phenomena in terms of grasping the rules of human activity, and he has little to say about the other set of rules involved in scientific investigations. He does make some passing comments, but then generally ignores the issues of rules as they pertain to the practice of science. However, concerning the individual scientific investigator's relations to his fellow scientists, Winch does note the following:

> The phenomena being investigated present themselves to the scientist as an object of study; he observes them and notices certain facts about them. But to say of a man that he does this presupposes that he already has a mode of communication in the use of which rules are already being observed.[72]

The investigator 'notices certain facts' about phenomena, then, only in terms of rules shared with other scientists. As Winch notes: 'What is important is that they have all *learned* in similar ways; that they are, therefore, *capable* of communicating with each other about what they are doing; that what any one of them is doing is in principle intelligible to the others.'[73]

Winch does not acknowledge that it is *these* rules which are involved in the settling of truth- and knowledge-claims in science. In fact he generally fails to recognise that the truths of science are fully the products of scientific communities. Not only does he fail to see this but, in the case of sociology, he seems to advance a thesis directly opposed to this viewpoint. He notes that Max Weber, whose genius it was to emphasise the importance of interpretative understanding—that is, grasping the point or meaning for the actors themselves of what is being done or said—believed that the ultimate test of the correctness of an explanation was the establishment of statistical regularities. Winch criticises this view, saying:

> Against this, I want to insist that if a proffered interpretation is wrong, statistics, although they may suggest that this is so, are not the decisive and ultimate court of appeal for the validity of sociological interpretations in the way Weber suggests. What is needed is a better interpretation, not something different in kind. The compatibility of an interpretation with the statistics does not prove its validity.[74]

In stressing the importance of rules and interpretative understanding, Winch is of course criticising the heavy emphasis on quantification in the social sciences. He is trying to show that the terms of an explanation must be familiar to the subjects of inquiry themselves as well as to the investigator. Instead of adopting the external point of the observer, the investigator must, says Winch, take full account of the subjectively intended sense of the behaviour.[75] In other words, Winch is arguing that the 'correctness' of an explanation is determined by the subjects of inquiry themselves rather than by the sociological investigator. If, for instance, a sociologist reports that people were engaged in 'warfare' and the people themselves report that they were 'playing a game', then, Winch holds, the latter is what they were 'really' doing. For Winch, the final court of authority as to the meaning of this or that, and the correctness of this or that interpretation, lies with the subjects of inquiry and not with the sociological investigator who frequently imposes the meanings and explanations from outside. In rejecting the idea of statistical correlations and predictions, he states: '"Understanding," in situations like this, is grasping the *point* or *meaning* of what is being said or done. This is a notion far removed from the world of statistics and causal laws. . . .'[76] But here we encounter a serious problem. For what is it to grasp the point or meaning? Is it to have a certain feeling or a certain image in one's mind? Here Winch departs from Wittgenstein—for what is involved is *showing* that one knows, that one understands.

The problem with Winch's line of reasoning is that it fails to see that it is one or another group of scientists—and not the individual investigator or the subjects of inquiry—that is the final arbiter as regards the correctness of various scientific explanations. So that when Winch says that if a proffered interpretation is 'wrong' and what is needed is a 'better' interpretation, he fails to recognise that what *counts* as a 'right' or 'wrong' explanation is decided by the scientific community. The individual scientist, then, 'explains' social phenomena by following procedures (rules) whose correctness is a communal matter. In other words, his explanatory achievements are fully dependent upon the judgements of the scientific community or the speciality area in which he works. The individual investigator shows that he *knows*, not because of some inner or mental processes or activities, but by performing the relevant activities of the collective. Whether one or another investigator's interpretation is correct is dependent on his publicly demonstrating that he has properly employed the relevant procedures of the discipline. In establishing the correctness of a proffered interpretation, the relevant scientific community does not consult the interpretation itself (for example, that 'there is an inverse relationship between crimes of violence and agricultural productivity because . . .'), but rather the *procedural rules* used to decide if what the interpretation proposes is correct.

If, in the case of Winch's example, these procedural rules in sociology were to include (as Winch says they should) the investigator's (1) having familiarised himself with the concepts and way of life in terms of which the people studied view their situation, and (2) having 'checked' his explanation with those studied and found it consistent with their subjectively intended sense, then—and only then—would these considerations (procedural rules) play a part in the establishment of the correctness of an interpretation based on 'interpretative understanding'. And even in that case, it is the sociological community which decides what *counts* as adequate familiarisation with a people or as having checked with them. But as it now stands, this close familiarity with the way of life of those studied is not a heavily emphasised procedural rule in sociology.

At issue with regard to Winch's formulation of a Wittgensteinian viewpoint as concerns the focus of sociology is his failure to recognise the full extent to which *all* science is a social activity. Moreover, to some extent he mistakenly exempts the natural sciences from his discussion of the relevance of some of Wittgenstein's ideas for the practice of science. He argues, for instance, that we must distinguish between physical' and 'conceptual' changes in the phenomena of interest, and provides the following example:

> By how many degrees does one need to reduce the temperature of a bucket of water for it to freeze?—The answer has to be settled experimentally. How many grains of what does one have to add together before one has a heap?—This cannot be settled by experiment because the criteria by which we distinguish a heap from a non-heap are vague in comparison with those by which we distinguish water from ice: there is no sharp dividing line.[77]

Winch's point here is that the change from water to ice is a physical change, whereas that from a non-heap to a heap is a conceptual one. But, in a sense, *they are both conceptual*. Shared standards among scientists allow for full agreement as to what counts as 'freezing' or 'ice'. Granted that there will be far less agreement within any group as to what is necessary for grains of wheat to *count* as a heap, and that, further, what counts as a heap in one group or culture may not count as such in another, nevertheless there are rules (sometimes explicit, often not) which determine what counts as this or that in the natural and social sciences alike. Thus with the natural sciences as with the social sciences, it is human agreement which underlies their practice.

I have tried to indicate in this chapter that mathematics, like science more generally, and in common with other human practices, is a fully social activity. Contrary to the views of Mannheim, there is no reason to exclude science and mathematics from sociological inquiry. It was perhaps because Mannheim was gripped by an implicit realism that he failed to see how mathematics and science were open to sociological consideration. Wittgenstein, with his rejection of realist accounts of rule-following, has provided us with a fully sociological account of what it is to follow a rule in doing mathematics. Mathematics, on this account, is an example of an extraordinary use of everyday (ordinary) language.

7 The Demarcation Problem in Science

In science it is usual to make phenomena that allow of exact measurement into defining criteria for an expression; and then one is inclined to think that now the proper meaning has been *found*. Innumerable confusions have arisen this way.

LUDWIG WITTGENSTEIN[1]

The problem of demarcating science from non- or pseudo-science has serious ethical and political implications for science itself and, indeed, for all societies in which science is practised. The conflicts and controversies surrounding the views of Copernicus, Galileo, Darwin or Lysenko make this abundantly clear. Sometimes these controversies involve what are generally regarded as non-scientific or political considerations. Examples of this are the banning of Copernicus's theory by the Catholic Church, and the support of Lysenko's position by the authorities in Russia in opposition to the neo-Darwinists. At other times, however, it is not the church, the state or the party that is involved in disputes about what is to be seen as science, but rather the scientific community itself. Much of the debate today concerning race and intelligence is regarded in some scientific circles as a debate concerning pseudo-scientific claims. The analyses and conclusions of those who claim a link between heredity and intelligence are viewed by some scientists as 'pseudo-scientific' and, consequently, these men are often defined as fakes, charlatans or pretenders by organised segments of the scientific community.

The issue of demarcation raises a number of difficult questions, among them the question as to what criteria distinguish science from non- or pseudo-science, and who should have the responsibility for establishing such criteria. These issues are at the very heart of recent controversies in the philosophy and history of science involving, among others, Popper, Kuhn, Polanyi, Feyerabend, Lakatos and Toulmin. Although these are the persons directly involved—in the sense that one can speak and read about the 'Popper–Kuhn' debate, for example—the problems raised go far beyond them to touch upon *all* scientific practice. Despite the enormous attention given these issues in the literature of philosophy today, they are given only scant attention in the sociological literature. In my view they are problems which are highly relevant to sociologists and which deserve their attention.

For the most part, I will have little to say about Wittgenstein in this chapter. Instead, I will begin by utilising a recent paper by Lakatos as a vehicle for introducing the demarcation problem.[2] Lakatos's paper is extremely useful because it sketches out the three major philosophical traditions with regard to the demarcation issue: scepticism, demarcationism and elitism. I will consider these *seriatim* and then, in the last part of the chapter, will consider the demarcation debate as it relates to the issue of 'power' in scientific practice.

Scepticism

This tradition has a long history and nowadays, says Lakatos, is best represented by the philosopher of science Paul Feyerabend. For sceptics, scientific theories occupy no privileged epistemological status as compared with other families of beliefs; no one belief-system is any more 'correct' or 'truer' than another. And while there is *change* from one theory to another or from one time to another in science, there is *no progress*. Feyerabend rejects not only the idea that there are permanent standards which remain in force throughout history (demarcation criteria) but also the idea that there are standards which are, and should be, binding upon the individual scientist. Whereas Lakatos and the demarcationists emphasise the importance of statute law and the elitists the importance of case law (as we shall soon see), Feyerabend is critical of both standpoints. That is to say, the demarcationists and elitists alike try to salvage 'rationality'—albeit in different ways—in science. For Feyerabend, however, 'The idea that science can and should be run according to some fixed rules, and that its rationality consists in agreement with such rules, is both unrealistic and vicious'.[3] For him, 'science' as a historical phenomenon contains elements which defy rational analysis. The choice between scientific theories, he asserts, is often a matter of *taste*.

Feyerabend asks for other possibilities, other cosmologies, other way of looking at and talking about the world. We must, he says, abandon 'normal' science and replace it with a science characterised by pro liferation. What we require, writes Feyerabend, is the 'revival o astrology, witchcraft, magic, alchemy, elaboration of Leibniz's *Mona dology*, and so on'.[4] In the chapter that follows, I will turn to a considera tion of proliferation, of other possible ways of looking at the world.

Since for a sceptic like Feyerabend there are no universal criteria (of anything), there is no possibility of producing any acceptable solution to the problem of appraising scientific theories. One theory cannot be appraised as better or superior to another. Lakatos has very little to say about scepticism, but does observe that: 'Sceptics make imaginative but unrealistic historians. For them history of science can only be a belief about beliefs. One reconstruction differs from another according to the irremediable bias of the historian: and one is no better than another.'[5]

Demarcationism

Lakatos uses this term not only to refer to the criteria for demarcating science from pseudo-science, but also in discussing the criteria for demarcating better from worse knowledge and for demarcating pro gress and degeneration in science. Demarcationists are concerned with applying *universal* criteria for appraising scientific progress. Many demarcationists assume the existence of 'third-world' criteria for logical truth and logically valid inferences. The 'first world' is for them the world of physical objects or of physical states; the 'second world' is the world of consciousness, of mental states, beliefs and dispositions to act and the 'third world' is what Popper, who originally formulated the existence of these three worlds, refers to as the world of *objective content of thought*.[6] Among the contents of Popper's third world are theoretical systems, problems, critical arguments and research programmes; but also the contents of journals, books and libraries. While the *producers o* knowledge live in the first and second worlds, the *products* (theories and so on) live and grow in the third world.

The third world, then, exists in an *objective* sense. In Popper's words

Knowledge in this objective sense is totally independent of any body's claims to know; also it is independent of anybody's belief or disposition to assent; or to assert, or to act. Knowledge in the objective sense is *knowledge without a knower*; it is *knowledge without a knowing subject.*[7]

Popper uses a standard argument for showing the independent existence of the third world, suggesting two thought experiments:

Experiment (1). All our machines and tools are destroyed, also all our subjective learning, including our subjective knowledge of machines and tools, and how to use them. But *libraries and our capacity to learn from them* survive. Clearly, after much suffering, our world may get going again.

Experiment (2). As before, machines and tools are destroyed, and our subjective learning, including our subjective knowledge of machines and tools, and how to use them. But this time, *all libraries are destroyed also*, so that our capacity to learn from books becomes useless.[8]

These libraries, then, contain what Popper regards as objective knowledge, and this is so whether or not anybody should ever read the libraries' books and their contents. Of course, as Popper points out, this objective knowledge may be true or false, useful or useless. Unfortunately he never tells us how to distinguish the true from the false, the useful from the useless. Nevertheless he is insistent as to the importance of the existence of this third world.

Popper stresses that 'a book, or even a library, need not even have been written by anybody: a series of books or logarithms, for example, may be produced and printed by a computer'.[9] What is important, he says, is the possibility of a book being understood or interpreted:

These books may be deciphered. They may be those logarithm tables never read before, for argument's sake. This makes it quite clear that neither its composition by thinking animals nor the fact that it has not actually been read or understood is essential for making a thing a book, and that it is sufficient that it might be deciphered. Thus I do admit that in order to belong to the third world of objective knowledge, a book should—in principle, or virtually—be capable of being grasped (or deciphered, or understood, or 'known') by somebody. But I do not admit more.[10]

It is not at all clear what is meant here, however. What does it mean to say that a book should 'in principle' be capable of being understood? After a nuclear holocaust, for example, should a book of logarithms be capable of being understood by future ages of 'mankind'? Should an African villager 'in principle' be able to grasp that book's contents?

Whatever the unclarity in the third-world notion, for demarcationists there exist *universal criteria* by which knowledge-claims can be
compared and appraised. Theories about these universal criteria also
constitute methodological knowledge, and are viewed as existing in
Popper's third world. While there are differences within the demarcationist school—so that Lakatos and Popper differ from one another to
some extent—all demarcationists agree that the question of whether a
theory is scientific or not is a question about the third world, as is the
question as to which of two theories is more progressive.

In addition to presupposing the existence of a third world, another
important way in which the demarcationists differ from the sceptics
and the elitists—as we shall see—is in their insistence on *full articulation*
in scientific knowledge and practice. Lakatos himself, a 'sophisticated'
as distinguished from a 'naive' falsificationist, states that the scientific
research programme which he advocates '*allows people do to their own
thing but only as long as they publicly admit what the score is between them and
their rivals*'.[11] This emphasis on full articulation, however, itself leads
to a number of crucial problems, as will be seen in the following pages.
Lakatos also distinguishes the views of the demarcationists from other
traditions in the philosophy of science by emphasising that they share
what he terms a 'democratic respect for the layman'. Although Lakatos
states this as if it were beyond dispute, I will return later to the question-
able content of that assertion. As will become clear in the following
discussion, there is in fact much in Lakatos's writings that needs to be
subjected to rather careful scrutiny.

Elitism

This, states Lakatos, is the most influential tradition among scientists.
Elitists share with the demarcationists—but not with the sceptics—
the view that good science *can* be distinguished from bad science;
theories *can* be compared and evaluated. But they share with the sceptics the view that there exist no formal, universal, explicit criteria by
which theories can be evaluated or science judged.

Whereas the demarcationists lay down *statute laws* of rational
appraisal, elitists hold that science can only be judged by *case law*.
Therefore, only scientists themselves are competent to make judgements
about questions of scientific practice. For those whom Lakatos calls
'elitists', there are no universal criteria of scientific judgement or progress, but instead much scientific knowledge—including some of that

involved in appraising scientific theories—is never fully articulated. It belongs to what Polanyi calls the 'tacit dimension.'[12] Because of the importance of this tacit knowledge, the layman cannot (or should not) appraise scientific theories. Lakatos, of course, uses the term 'elitism' perjoratively, as a way of negatively characterising those writers—Kuhn, Polanyi and Toulmin—who accept the impossibility of articulating universal scientific criteria, while at the same time making a distinction between good and bad scientific practice.

But Lakatos's criticisms do not stop there. He goes on to speak of what he describes as four 'abhorrent philosophical doctrines' characteristic of elitism: psychologism (or sociologism), the idea of an authoritarian closed society, historicism and pragmatism.[13] In discussing these four doctrines, I will use the same sub-headings employed by Lakatos in his discussion—although, as I will try to indicate, I believe that his charges and descriptions are unnecessarily harsh and one-sided.

'Elitists for psychologism and/or sociologism'

Because elitists reject the appraisal of such third-world products as propositions and research programmes—in that they reject correspondence theories and the existence of a third world—they focus instead on such second-world problems as what goes on in a scientific community, in the practice of science. Lakatos argues that elitists assess the *producers* rather than the *products* of scientific activity. Unfortunately, Lakatos makes far too much of this. While it may be true that elitists do sometimes pay more explicit attention than do demarcationists to the producers as opposed to the products, elitists and demarcationists alike consider *both* producers and products. Lakatos's simple-minded characterisation of the 'either/or' quality of the two traditions is mischievous and highly misleading. Therefore, a statement like the following should be taken with a grain of salt: 'As a consequence, while for the demarcationists the *philosophy of science* is the watchdog of scientific standards, for elitists this role is to be performed by the *psychology, social psychology, or sociology of science.*'[14]

On what does his accusation rest? Consider Lakatos's argument here. He points out that elitists claim that there are no universal criteria for appraising scientific achievements. That is indeed their position. But he adds to this observation the statement that elitists do 'admit the possibility of universal criteria for deciding whether *persons or communities* belong to the elite'.[15] In support of this statement, he quotes Polanyi as stating that 'To speak of science and its continued progress is to profess faith in its fundamental principles and in the integrity of scientists in applying these principles'.[16] Now what is the nature of Polanyi's 'sin' here? According to Lakatos, it is the heavy emphasis on *integrity*. Of course, he ignores that part of the quotation which concerns 'principles'. What, then, are we to make of Lakatos' own remarks elsewhere about 'a code of scientific honesty' or 'a code of scientific honor'? Furthermore, he speaks of answering colleagues' objections by 'separating rational and irrational (or honest and dishonest) adherence to a degenerating research programme'.[17] Are integrity and honesty really that different?

But, of course, Lakatos's charges rest on more than that. For instance he offers the following as an example of how elite scientists achieve what he terms 'quality control':

> If a scientist P proposes some theory T, in order to appraise the epistemological merit of T, the elitist has to decide whether the producer of T, say P, is a genuine scientist: he can only appraise the producer, *not* the product. His approval or acceptance of T follows from his approval of P. If he is faced with two rival theories T_1 and T_2 he investigates the rival producers P_1 and P_2 and concludes from 'P_1 is better than P_2' that 'T_1 is better than T_2'. This is psychologism. If the criteria are to apply to communities rather than individuals then we get sociologism.[18]

Contrary to what the reader might think, I did not invent the above quotation; it is entirely Lakatos's creation. Before considering the absurdities and misleading elements in his statement, let me first acknowledge that *sometimes* the producer rather than the product is appraised. In fact, Lakatos serves as an excellent example of such a tendency; he is so busy attacking the elitists that he pays no attention to what they are saying, to what their viewpoint is. *He* appraises the producers and not their products.

With regard to Lakatos's charges, one of the things that does characterise Kuhn, Polanyi, Toulmin and the other so-called elitists is their emphasis that the criteria by which scientific achievements are judged and evaluated *cannot be fully articulated*. There is, they argue, a tacit dimension, conventional wisdom, and the like, which are involved in evaluating the *products* of scientists' work. Polanyi states that: 'No rule can account for the way a good idea is produced for starting an enquiry and there are no rules either for the verification or the refutation of a proposed solution of a problem.'[19] But he also notes that precision and certainty are preferable to vagueness and conjecture, and adds: 'It is here, in the course of discovery and verification, that the premises of science exercise their guidance over the judgment of scientists.'[20] As much as possible, of course, these premises should be made explicit. Polanyi openly acknowledges, however, that 'no formulation of these premises ever proposed (or yet to be proposed) would have enabled a person lacking the special gifts and training of a scientist, competently to decide any of the serious uncertainties that have arisen in the various controversies or doubtful issues [in science]'.[21]

Polanyi makes a similar point regarding measurement and what he terms 'connoisseurship' which, he says, 'can be communicated only by example, not by precept'.[22] The point here is that Polanyi is most certainly not opposed to the formulation or existence of rules for verification or refutation, to rules for precise measurement or grading, or to objectivity. Indeed, he endorses the importance of making such rules, such criteria, explicit—*whenever this is possible*. But the thrust of his argument is that the practice of science is an 'art', that there are rules which cannot always be made explicit or articulated because they are not ('focally') known or recognised by the scientists who follow them.

Polanyi and the others whom Lakatos terms 'elitists' would agree, then, with his insistence that products rather than producers should be appraised. But, to repeat, they hold that not all criteria and standards involved in the appraisal can be fully articulated. In Polanyi's words:

> Things of which we are focally aware can be explicitly identified; but no knowledge can be made *wholly explicit*. For one thing, the meaning of language, when in use, lies in its tacit component; for another, to use language involves actions of our body of which we have only a subsidiary awareness.[23]

It is *not*, however, the position of Polanyi, or Kuhn, or Toulmin, that if scientist A is regarded as a better scientist than scientist B that A's theory is automatically better than B's. I do not deny that this kind of reasoning sometimes occurs. But it is not the elitists' policy, as Lakatos suggests.

What is correct in Lakatos's statement is his charge of 'sociologism'. But this is not, as he claims, because the 'in' group blithely decides that whatever its members or adherents produce is inevitably superior to what the 'out' group produces. No, there is 'sociologism' in the sense that scientific communities *do* distinguish between *their competence* to decide on scientific matters and the competence of laymen or, in some cases, other scientists from different disciplines. In this way, they are elitists.

Polanyi makes this very clear when he points out that no single scientist can be expected to be competent to judge more than a small portion of the total output of science. He goes on to say:

> Yet this group of persons—the scientists—administer jointly the advancement and dissemination of science. They do so through the control of university premises, academic appointments, research grants, scientific journals and the awarding of academic degrees which qualify their recipients as teachers, technical or medical practitioners, and opens to them the possibility of academic appointment.[24]

There is also, of course, elitism *within* scientific communities; some scientists are widely recognised as better scientists than others. Lakatos himself emphasises the importance of these elites when he notes, in another publication, that with a degenerating research programme:

> Editors of scientific journals should refuse to publish their papers which will, in general, contain either solemn reassertions of their position or absorption or counterevidence (or even of rival programmes) by *ad hoc*, linguistic adjustments. Research foundations, too, should refuse money.[25]

That statement is followed by an interesting footnote in which Lakatos states:

> I do, of course, *not* claim that such decisions are necessarily uncontroversial. On such decisions one has to use also one's *common sense*. Common sense (that is, judgment in *particular* cases which is not made according to mechanical rules but only follows general principles which leave some *Spielraum*) plays a role in all brands of non-mechanical methodologies.[26]

It does seem to me, then, that Lakatos recognises not only the existence of elites within science but also the employment of something akin to tacit knowledge or tacit understanding—what he calls 'common sense'.

Still, Lakatos strongly opposes the *case law* approach of the elitists and argues for the 'democratic' *statute law* of the demarcationists. He writes:

> The demarcationist lays down *statute* law of rational appraisal which can direct a lay jury in passing judgment. (One does not, for instance, need to be a scientist to understand the conditions under which one theory is more falsifiable than another.) Of course, no

statute law is either unequivocally interpretable or incorrigible. But a statute book—written by the 'demarcationist' philosopher of science—is there to guide the outsider's judgment.[27]

Now one might think that Lakatos's 'democratic respect for the layman' is betrayed by his statement that it is the demarcationist who lays down the law. And one wonders if Lakatos really believes that one does not need to be a scientist to understand and apply statute law. Can everyone do it, or just educated persons, or who? And even if everyone can apply statute law, it is after all *laid down* by the demarcationist philosopher of science. So to what extent is the demarcationist more democratic than the evil elitist?

Despite Lakatos's talk about his democratic respect for the layman, it seems to me that he shares with Kuhn, Polanyi, Toulmin and Popper the belief that experts (either philosophers of science or scientists) rather than laymen should and do decide as to what is to be regarded as science or pseudo-science, good or bad theories, and the like. Of course, Lakatos believes that the scientific community must utilise the demarcation criteria provided by the watchdogs of science: the philosophers of science. In fact, though, one might consider Lakatos and other demarcationists to be 'elitists' themselves in that they 'reconstruct universal criteria which great scientists have applied sub- or semi-consciously in appraising particular theories or research programmes'.[28] Are not 'great scientists' the elite of science?

Nevertheless, Lakatos is correct in pointing out some serious consequences of the elitist's position. He argues that since elitists claim that there are no explicit, universal criteria for determining progress or degeneration, this means that, once the criteria for membership in scientific communities are met, all changes within a scientific community must be regarded as *progress*. This, Lakatos observes, is historicism. He goes on to note that in 1970 he put the following problem to Kuhn, but never received an answer.

Let us imagine for instance that in spite of the objectively progressing astronomical research programmes, the astronomers are suddenly all gripped by a feeling of Kuhnian 'crisis'; and then they are all converted, by an irresistible *Gestalt*-switch to astrology. I would regard this catastrophe as a horrifying *problem*, to be accounted for by some empirical externalist explanation. But not a Kuhnian. All he sees is a 'crisis' followed by a mass conversion effect in the scientific community: an ordinary revolution. Nothing is left as problematic or unexplained.[29]

Such an occurrence might indeed be a 'horrifying *problem*'. But I wonder whether the fact that the elitists employ their own (internal) scientific standards really distinguishes them that clearly from the demarcationists. Lakatos notes: 'One may *obviously* even have perfect consensus and degeneration at the same time. But this means that we need (*and use*) criteria to judge scientific achievements rather than communities.'[30] Contrary to what Lakatos states, however, the elitists do have (and use) criteria for judging scientific achievements. Furthermore, who are the 'we' whom Lakatos refers to in his remarks above? They are not, it seems clear, laymen, but rather philosophers of science, who in Lakatos's own words act as the 'supreme watchdog'. And is this not a form of elitism as well?

'*Elitists for authoritarianism and historicism*'

Lakatos emphasises that elitists claim that only they are qualified to judge a scientific community's products. But, he properly asks, what if they should disagree among themselves? After all, they do distinguish between good and bad science, between real science and pseudo-science. One answer to the disagreement question is, Lakatos observes, that there are simply no disagreements, that *consensus* concerning scientific knowledge is achieved rather easily. If true, he says, this 'implies that scientists form a *totalitarian society without alternatives*'.[31]

Again, however, Lakatos is misleading. Polanyi is fully aware of the consensus problem, as can be seen from the following:

> Suppose for a moment that all scientists were charlatans, as some certainly are; or to make the assumption more plausible, that they are all self-deluded like Lysenko, or else dishonest or forced to conform to the views of people who are themselves either dishonest or self-deluded, as Lysenko's followers mostly were. Or suppose the standards of scientific reliability and significance were generally so debased as they are even now in some parts of the world; or going a step beyond this, that the natural sciences were replaced altogether by the occult sciences based on cabalistic methods. There might still exist a consensus between the various specialties acknowledging each other as scientists, and mutually acknowledging also the validity and significance of their respective domains of pseudo-science, and the public might be deluded by their joint assurances to accept what they call 'science' as science.[32]

s regards Polanyi, then, Lakatos is simply wrong. But his real targets
re Toulmin and the 'paradigm-monopology' thesis of Kuhn.³³ If
litists reject the idea of consensus—and the totalitarian scientific com-
1unity which Lakatos says it implies—they have two options, neither
f which Lakatos finds palatable. The elitists can either (1) acknow-
·dge (Lakatos says 'claim') that there is an authority structure within
:ience, or (2) argue that conflict within the elite will be resolved by
1e survival of the fittest.

Of course there is an authority structure within science. But while
akatos describes these authorities as supreme judges who are elected
>r 'emerge'), sitting in *camera*, and passing judgements according to
ise law,³⁴ I would describe this authority structure as consisting of
>urnal editors, scientists who advise research foundations, and the
ke. As I noted earlier, Lakatos himself speaks of the correctness of
·litors of scientific journals refusing to publish some kinds of papers
nd of funding agencies refusing money for certain types of projects.
'he difference between Lakatos and the elitists, then, is not the absence
f an authority structure or a scientific elite in the two traditions but,
1ther, that Lakatos's elite claim that they employ *statute law* (or de-
1arcation criteria) in making scientific decisions, while the elitists
mphasise that often *case law* is involved in such decisions. Lakatos asks
1e elitist: 'But what if the Supreme Court errs and leads the scientific
>mmunity into darkness?'³⁵ But, it seems to me, the same question
an be directed at Lakatos and the demarcationists. If they (that is,
1eir elite) disagree amongst themselves, how are such disagreements
> be settled? And if there are no disagreements (as to how demarcation
:riteria are to be employed, for instance), then is that not, in Lakatos's
·ords, 'a *totalitarian society without alternatives*'?

Elites for pragmatism'

. defining characteristic of pragmatism, according to Lakatos, is the
enial of the existence of the 'third world'. For pragmatists, knowledge
<ists not as a third-world phenomenon but as a state of mind. This
1ises the problem of how pragmatists compare theories, how they
ecide which of two or more theories is superior. In the pragmatists'
iew, one theory is superior to another if it is more 'pleasing', more
atisfactory', or 'works better'. For pragmatists, says Lakatos, there is
o product independent of the producers; truth is not predicated on
ropositions, but on human beliefs, activities, forms of life, paradigms,

and the like. Lakatos describes pragmatism as having as a central
element 'the idea that in the struggle of beliefs, activities, forms of life
the one which establishes *consensus* (or common happiness) by eradica
ting its rivals is the most progressive. And if it does it with irreversibl
success it is absolutely true.'[36] Truth, then, is established by the fac
that it 'works'. Lakatos notes this and observes: 'Pragmatism seems t
be separated from scepticism only by this stress on "absolute truth"
and on "progress" towards it. But this emphasis is nothing bu
rhetoric.'[37]

The power dimension

Up to this point, I have been discussing the three major philosophica
traditions with regard to the demarcation problem. I now want t
consider the demarcation controversy from a somewhat different per
spective, a perspective that introduces the concept of 'power' into th
discussion. It is my view that it is a concern with power—in its mos
naked form, violence—which is at the heart of Lakatos's vicious attac
on the non-demarcationists and behind Popper's criticism of the new
image of science introduced by Kuhn and others.

Let us begin to consider this issue by extending somewhat the gam
metaphor employed in earlier chapters where language-games wer
discussed, and by drawing on Mitroff's recent work.[38] Consistent wit
Wittgenstein, we can note first that, in common with most games, th
game of science is constituted by a variety of *rules*. These rules hel
determine what constitutes theorising, observing, testing, experimentin
and the like, as well as what counts as 'proper' or 'correct' theorising
experimenting, and the like. However, the game of science also include
individual *players* and groups of players (individual scientists, di
ciplines, 'schools'). The vast majority of these players give the bulk c
their time and attention to teaching and only a small portion to re
search and writing; most scientists publish little or nothing. Neve
theless, a sizeable minority of players are involved not only in teachin
but also in discovering nature's secrets (as they would put it) and
further, in communicating their findings to one or another scientifi
audience. Ziman, who emphasises the communal nature of science
notes that: 'The audience to which scientific publications are addresse
is not passive; by its cheering or booing, its bouquets or brickbats,
actively controls the substance of the communication that it receives.'
What Ziman is pointing to here is another feature of the game of science

the existence of *spectators*. These are the readers of scientific articles, books and monographs, that is, other players and non-players.

Thus far we have three elements in the game of science: rules, players and spectators. But like many other games, this game also involves individuals who have a special status as *referees* or *umpires*. These are people who have the responsibility for making judgements as to whether or not the rules are being followed correctly. Examples here would be the members of editorial boards of scientific journals, advisers to foundations and other agencies who award research funds, and perhaps certain senior professors in some universities; in short, the gatekeepers of science. Here too, of course, rules form a part. There are both the rules employed by the referees and umpires in making judgement and keeping score (here perhaps we have another category: scorekeepers), and the rules pertaining to what is necessary for some persons to become referees.

The game of science also includes rules (and rule-enforcers) concerning the appropriate *fields of play* (scientific journals, congresses, universities, laboratories), as well as the proper *equipment* for playing the game (microscopes, telescopes, mathematical models, statistics). As with many other games, there are also *awards* and *prizes* in the game of science: among them, tenure, professorships, high salaries, election to office, membership in certain honorary groups, positions at 'prestige' universities. Again, rules and referees are involved.

Finally in our far-from-complete list of features found in the game of science, there are the *rule-makers*, those who establish the rules by which the game is played. Here the parallel with other games is less obvious than with some of the other features mentioned. In the case of professional athletics, for example, it happens with some frequency that a designated group (say, the club-owners) can decide to change one or another rule. So in the United States, we find changes with regard to 'fair catches' in football, 'designated hitters' in baseball, and other similar alterations in the rules. With many other games, however, rule-changes are rare or almost unheard of; consider chess and bridge, for example.

Much of the discussion concerning demarcation criteria can, I suggest, be viewed profitably in the context of disagreement about how the game of science is to be played. Obviously this discussion centres on the whole issue of 'rules', but I am not certain whether the quarrels refer to questions about referees or about rule-makers, or whether both are involved in an inextricable mixture. But in any case I think that we can usefully examine Lakatos's and Popper's arguments in this context. The game metaphor helps us understand what underlies the epithets of 'sociologism', 'psychologism' and 'mob psychology' hurled by Lakatos and Popper at the advocates of the new image of science.

For Popper, the rules of the game of science are permanent and unchanging, that is, absolute; or, more specifically, it is the 'logic of scientific discovery' which is for Popper absolute. It is this which marks off science from other human activities (games). The logic of scientific discovery, as understood by Popper, allows only for gradual changes within the game of science. Every new discovery must be commensurable with previous science. 'Thus in science, as distinct from theology,' Popper writes, 'a critical comparison of the competing theories, of the competing frameworks, is always possible'.[40] Kuhn and Feyerabend, of course, deny this. For them, major changes are not gradual but, instead, are the result of 'scientific revolutions' where one generally accepted framework is replaced by another. This means that what were seen as the correct rules for playing the game of science before the revolution will no longer be seen as the correct rules after it. With a change of paradigms, we have a change in the rules of the game. This implication is regarded as horrendous by Popper and Lakatos. They are extremely critical of the idea that a theory's supporters can dictate scientific truth. That is, to continue our metaphor, they are unwilling to allow that the 'players' can, by consensus, decide to change the rules of the game.

Kuhn claims that he is explaining why an enterprise works, and that his explanation is sociological.

> Some of the principles deployed in my explanation of science are irreducibly sociological, at least at this time. In particular, confronted with the problem of theory-choice, the structure of my response runs roughly as follows: take a *group* of the ablest available people with the most appropriate motivation; train them in some science and in the specialties relevant to the choice at hand; imbue them with the value system, the ideology, current in the discipline (and to a great extent in other scientific fields as well); and, finally, *let them make the choice*. If that technique does not account for scientific development as we know it, then no other will. . . . Whatever scientific progress may be, we must account for it by examining the nature of the scientific group, discovering what it values, what it tolerates and what it disclaims.[41]

Popper, in contrast to Kuhn, has long opposed 'sociological' approaches to the explanation of science. Thirty years ago, he criticised the sociology of knowledge and the social determination of scientific knowledge.

> The sociology of knowledge argues that scientific thought, and especially thought on social and political matters, does not proceed in a vacuum, but in a socially conditioned atmosphere. . . . The social habitat of the thinker determines a whole system of opinions and theories which appear to him as unquestionably true or self-evident.[42]

These kinds of analyses, Popper argues, destroy the basis of rational discussion. More recently, he has expressed himself regarding the idea of turning to sociology or psychology for enlightenment.

> In fact, compared with physics, sociology and psychology are riddled with fashions, and with uncontrolled dogmas. The suggestion that we can find anything here like 'objective, pure description' is clearly mistaken. Besides, how can the regress to these often spurious sciences help us in this particular difficulty? It is not sociological (or psychological, or historical) *science* to which you want to appeal in order to decide what amounts to the question 'What is science?' or 'What is, in fact, normal in science?' For clearly you do not want to appeal to the sociological (or psychological or historical) lunatic fringe.[43]

Lakatos recognises the crucial importance of the debate between Kuhn and Popper, commenting:

> The clash between Popper and Kuhn is not about a mere technical point in epistemology. It concerns our central intellectual values, and has implications not only for theoretical physics but also for moral and political philosophy. If even in science there is no other way of assessing a theory but by assessing the number, faith and vocal energy of its supporters, then this must be even more so in the social sciences: *truth lies in power*. Thus Kuhn's position would vindicate, no doubt, unintentionally, the basic political *credo* of contemporary religious maniacs ('student revolutionaries').[44]

Popper and Kuhn, then, object strenuously to the Kuhnian viewpoint that science is governed by the collective wisdom of the scientific community. Thus Lakatos asserts that 'in Kuhn's view *scientific revolution is irrational, a matter of mob psychology*'.[45] The language used by Popper and Lakatos is indicative of the horror with which they regard the new image of science: 'fashions', 'uncontrolled dogmas', 'lunatic fringe', 'truth lies in power', 'mob psychology'. Their fear is that the new image of science leads first of all to relativism, and secondly to a relativism which can be grounded ultimately in the power of the collective or community, or in the power of certain individuals. It is as if Popper and Lakatos assume that the rules of the game of science are sacrosant and never-changing, or that if they change they do so very slowly—and under the guidance of certain rule-makers and referees (in this case philosophers of science, the 'watchdogs' to whom Lakatos refers). Let us consider this problem further.

The dominant image of science holds that there are certain rules of the game which are permanent and absolute. Whatever the players may think about these rules, they stand fast. As with chess, for example, players may decide not to follow these rules or to invent an entirely new and different set of rules. But then, according to the dominant image, the players are *no longer* playing chess or practising science. According to Kuhn, Toulmin and Feyerabend, however, the rules of the game are context-dependent, so that what constitutes chess or science in one time or place may not be the same as what counts as science or chess elsewhere. In fact the rules may suddenly change from one group or time to another. If the players come to invent or follow a new set of rules, they are still playing chess or the game of science. This in itself is bothersome enough to people like Popper and Lakatos.

The situation is made considerably more serious, however, by the possibility that a new set of rules may be imposed and enforced through the use of power or force. It is bad enough, according to Popper and Lakatos, that the rules can be changed as a result of fashions and changing majorities or consensuses, but the situation becomes really intolerable when force or power can be employed to change the rules. It is as if the rules of football were changed by the larger, more powerful players, and then changed again when a new group of players use their strength to gain ascendency. What we have here is the problem of relativism: the rules of the game of science are dependent on the social and historical location of particular groups of scientists. And since some groups and individuals are more powerful than other groups and individuals, we have a *relativism grounded in power*. This, I believe, is the (often implicit) conclusion which Popper and other critics draw from the work of Kuhn and others in the new image of science. This is their ultimate fear.

In my view, their fear is not totally unfounded; but at the same time it is a conclusion not very much different from what follows from their own position. Lakatos is quite explicit in his view that it is philosophers of science like himself who are, and should be, the watchdogs of science. It is they who provide the demarcation criteria which scientists should follow. In this sense they are rule-makers. Of course, Lakatos and Popper claim that they have not themselves made the rules, but have only reconstructed the universal criteria used by great scientists of the past (who presumably became 'great' only because their theories were 'truest'). In this sense they are perhaps referees, not rule-makers. But, whether they are rule-makers or referees, they too have and use power in enforcing their views. This is often lost sight of, most especially in those discussions where 'reason' (which they see themselves as representing) is contrasted with violence. At the core of the objections of Popper and Lakatos is their assumption that they rely on *reason*, while the views of Kuhn and Feyerabend allow for the possibility of *violence*.

Ideally, men's actions should be guided by reason. This has long been a cardinal point in Popper's writings. The alternative (Popper says the only alternative) to this is violence. When men or women disagree and a decision must be reached, Popper states that there are only two possible ways: argument and violence. One way is reasonable, the other is not. An individual who takes the attitude of reasonableness is described by Popper as a rationalist:

> A rationalist, as I use the word, is a man who attempts to reach decisions by argument and perhaps, in certain cases, by compromise, rather than by violence. He is a man who would rather be unsuccessful in convincing another man by argument than successful in crushing him by force, by intimidation and threats, or even by persuasive propaganda.[46]

Elsewhere he contrasts a rationalist attitude with what he terms irrationalism.[47] Those holding the irrationalist attitude insist 'that emotions and passions rather than reason are the mainsprings of human action. . . . It is my firm conviction that this irrational emphasis upon emotion and passion leads ultimately to what I can only describe as crime.'[48] This attitude, Popper says, 'must lead to an appeal to violence and brutal force as the ultimate arbiter in any dispute'.[49]

Further, Popper emphasises that the rationalist attitude considers the argument rather than the persons advancing it (the product rather than the producer).[50] This means that the persuasive force of an argument should be totally independent of the reputation, power or authority of the person doing the arguing. Popper, like other philosophers and logicians, conceives of an argument as a set of propositions which can be distinguished by (a) premises and (b) conclusions, between which holds (c) some logical relation. The truth of certain conclusions, then, follows logically from certain premises. Rationality, for Popper, is thought of as a function of the logical relations holding between the elements in an argument. Obviously, this is a rather restricted conception of argument and, consequently, of reason or rationality. In any case it is, Popper stresses, the argument itself which must be evaluated and considered—not the arguers. Or, in terms of our game metaphor, it is the *rules* and the players' abilities to follow them correctly that are important. These rules are what they are, as Popper would say, without knowing subjects.

Since Popper and Lakatos believe that there are permanent standards which govern scientific discourse and development throughout history (including the standards of correct argument), it is easy to see why they would be so opposed to certain conclusions of sociologists of knowledge and those advancing the new image of science. They think of reason as one and the same for all men at all times. Mills, on the other hand, states that: 'No individual can be logical unless there be agreement among the members of his universe of discourse as to the validity of some general conceptions of good reasoning.'[51] Since the criteria of logicality may differ among groups and over time, this means that not only what are accepted as valid arguments in the discourse *within a particular social group* but also what constitute the elements of reasoning and analysis *within a given individual* are the results of social conventions. In other words, reason and rationality are themselves relativised. If they are thoroughly relativised, then there exist no permanent, universal standards of reason. This is indeed a far-reaching conclusion. It is also more or less the conclusion reached by Kuhn. Feyerabend, rather than emphasising the relativity of rationality, advocates irrationality.[52] Whether one speaks of different standards of rationality or of irrationality, the conclusion here is the same. If there are no permanent, unchanging standards for rationality and scientific practice, then there is no reason why powerful groups may not compete to perpetuate *their* views of rationality, proper scientific standards, and the like. In other words, science becomes a political struggle with competing ideologies trying to gain dominance. Violence, rather than reason, may prevail. This, Popper and Lakatos agree, would be a disastrous conclusion.

In reaching this conclusion, however, they tend to overlook the elements of power and violence which already appear to exist in scientific practice. For them, not only are the rules of the game of science unchanging, but the players are all on an equal footing—with respect to both their access to equipment and their relationships to the referees. Of course they do recognise that some people are better players than others (and therefore garner more of the prizes and rewards), and assume this is because of their superior performances. But is there not violence in this everyday practice of science? I believe that there is.

Some persons occupy dominant positions in their particular scientific fields, that is, they are journal editors, professors at prestigious universities, and so on. They are in a position both to threaten and to use certain sanctions against those who are in subordinate relations to them. In short, some would argue, the dominants employ *symbolic violence* against their subordinates. Now Popper and Lakatos would deny this. After all, they might say, the dominants act 'rationally' in making their decisions; they merely apply their reason in determining whether or not other people's scientific work comes up to the proper standards (dictated entirely by the rules).[53] Obviously the dominants do not employ physical force or coercion, but this does not automatically imply that they therefore rely on value-free reason.

What is missing from the whole discussion of science involving Kuhn, Feyerabend, Popper and Lakatos is a full recognition of the *competitive* nature of science; it is not only theories that are in competition, but human beings as well. Instead of viewing scientists as being engaged in a struggle with nature to learn its secrets (which is an image frequently set forth by scientists), we can view scientists as being engaged in a struggle with one another for the ascendancy of the ideas of particular individuals and groups.[54] This means that those in dominant positions may not be willing to warrant the correctness or adequacy of the arguments and claims set forth by individuals in submissive positions, that is, they may define them as unreasonable or irrational. If there were *complete consensus* among all the players in the game of science and among the referees and scorekeepers as to how the game should be played, then, and only then, might it follow that those who win or come out on top have done so entirely because of their superior performances. Popper and Lakatos would like us to believe that this is presently the case in science. Kuhn, Feyerabend and Toulmin suggest that it is otherwise. They believe that one generally accepted view (or consensus) is replaced by another view which, if it is successful, involves a new consensus, and so on, throughout history. On their standpoint it would also seem to follow that superior performances win and are recognised (although only within a given paradigm). In other words they, too, play down the competitive element in science—even though, as Popper points out, the new image appears to allow for domination by powerful (or power-utilising) groups.

Although I do not entirely share their view, there are those who would argue that the situation of many scientists (such as those unable to secure tenure, to obtain research funds, to get their books and articles published) is the *result of (symbolic)* violence done to them by the dominant group within their discipline. This may not be the intentional policy of the dominant group, but is the inevitable result of widespread social conditions.

Those holding this view would argue that conceptions of reason, logic, and so on, are merely the reflection of deeper tendencies within society which lead to the exploitation of certain groups, that is, keep them in submission. If one adheres to this view, then one would conclude that the demands of people like Popper and Lakatos that scientists utilise reason and argument represent nothing other than a defence of their own privileged position. After all, it might be argued, they can resist change forever by continuing to go on talking and continuing to claim a willingness to listen to rational arguments from their opponents. But an argument which is based on someone else's terms can be seen as no argument at all. Those like Popper who modestly declare their fallibility are, on this reading, less than honest. For example, Popper characterises rationality as 'fundamentally an attitude of admitting that "*I may be wrong and you may be right, and by an effort, we may get nearer to the truth*"'.[55] Some of Popper's opponents (but not Kuhn) might answer by pointing out that it is useless to engage in such an 'effort' with Popper, in that there is virtually nothing that could bring Popper to admit that he is wrong. That is to say, the rules of the game are such that Popper and those sharing his position will not tolerate as reason or argument those 'utterances' (not, they say, reasons or arguments) put forth by their opponents. According to Popper's opponents in this (hypothetical) situation, *violence* (albeit of a symbolic nature) is being committed against them. The violence which Popper so dreads is, some might argue, already found in the practice of science and philosophy.

Popper himself acknowledges that he is not against the use of violence under all conditions. He writes that 'the use of violence is justified only under a tyranny which makes reforms without violence impossible, and it should have only one aim, that is, to bring about a state of affairs which makes reforms without violence possible'.[56] The use of violence may also be justified, he says, once democracy has been attained, in resisting 'any attack (whether from within or without the state) against the democratic constitution and the use of democratic methods'.[57] Thus violence is not always to be outlawed. In fact we might even want to argue that it represents rational or reasonable action under some circumstances. Popper would agree, I am sure, that waging war against Hitler was violent, but also reasonable under the circumstances. If one side in a dispute does not observe the method of reason and argument, then, we might want to say, violence is reasonable; or if the other side employs violence, we may be justified in using violence in return.

But even here there is a problem. What degree of violence, we must ask, is reasonable in redressing the injustices perpetrated against us? This is a question that surrounds a whole variety of actions: sit-ins, student occupations of buildings, strikes, the presence of foreign troops within our borders, and so on. Obviously this is an enormously difficult matter, and I will not even attempt to suggest an answer.

What I have been trying to show is that the 'either/or' nature of Popper's reason/violence dichotomy is not without problems; and that, further, there are groups of people (including scientists) who recognise, as Popper does not, that power rests within certain institutions in our society and that these power-holders regularly exercise violence against their opponents. In fact Popper himself has been the recipient of such violence, as he tells us in his autobiography where he speaks of the difficulties he had in getting his *The Open Society and its Enemies* published.

. . . university authorities not only were unhelpful, but tried actively to make difficulties for me. I was told that I should be well advised not to publish anything while in New Zealand, and that any time spent on research was a theft from the working time for which I was paid. The situation was such that without the moral support of my friends in New Zealand I could hardly have survived. Under these circumstances the reaction of those friends in the U.S. to whom I sent the manuscript was a terrible blow. They did not react at all for many months; and later, instead of submitting the manuscript to a publisher, they solicited an opinion from a famous authority, who decided that the book, because of its irreverence towards Aristotle (not Plato), was not fit to be submitted to a publisher. After almost a year, when I was at my wit's end and in terribly low spirits, I obtained, by chance, the English address of my friend Ernst Gombrich, with whom I had lost contact during the war. Together with Hayek, who most generously offered his help . . . he found a publisher. Both wrote most encouragingly about the book. The relief was immense. I felt that these two had saved my life, and I still feel so.[58]

Returning now to the controversy between Popper and Lakatos on the one side, and Kuhn, Polanyi and Toulmin on the other, we can see why the former pair are so insistent that there exist *universal* criteria for demarcating science from pseudo-science and for demarcating progress and degeneration in science. If, as Kuhn and the others say, these criteria are neither universal nor unchanging, then it seems to follow that the criteria are relative to, and dependent upon, the particular groups who happen to be dominant at a given time. If this is the case, then we can have people using violence to gain a position of dominance, and consequently there appear to be no safeguards against, for example, Nazi or Stalinist science. While Popper and Lakatos at least try to face up to this implication, Robert Merton avoids it entirely, stating that 'the criteria of validity to claims to scientific knowledge are not matters of national taste and culture. Sooner or later, competing claims to validity are settled by the universalistic facts of nature which are consonant with one and not another theory.'[59] Merton's view is, I believe, that held by most sociologists and philosophers of science. 'Universal facts of nature,' existing out there, will provide the ultimate source of evidence for the superiority of one theory over another, for distinguishing between science and pseudo-science. Merton simply takes it for granted that scientists constitute a legitimate part of the contemporary social structure.

Whatever Merton might claim, our consideration of what might be termed the Popper–Kuhn controversy leads inevitably to an awareness of the existence of the dimension of *power* in society and in the game of science. This does raise important questions, questions which are, as Lakatos stresses, highly relevant to the viability and health of the intellectual life of our time. While I have tried to sketch out some of the factors involved in the controversy and have suggested their possible consequences, I have had little to say about my own position on these matters.

Let me at least mention what might be relevant here. In so doing, I will return to the question which Lakatos put to Kuhn and which, he asserts, was never answered. What if 'the astronomers are suddenly all gripped by a feeling of Kuhnian "crisis"; and then they are all converted, by an irresistible *Gestalt*-switch to astrology'?[60] Or, I might add, what if the astronomers are all converted to astrology through the use of violence or coercion? If either of these occurred, would there be any reasons for preferring astronomy to astrology, any reasons for seeing one as science and the other as pseudo-science?

I believe that in the actual *practice* of science there are such reasons. While all sciences and all candidates for scientific status have the common characteristic of being constructed language-games (physics, sociology, astronomy), these different language-games differ as to their *utility*. Of course, philosophers of science are concerned with the 'world-picturing' function of various theories and not with their practical or technological consequences. Nonetheless, physics, chemistry, biology and astronomy are generally seen to 'work'. Thus, if there were a sudden switch from astronomy to astrology, there would arise the question of whether it worked, what could be done with it. Whether or not one thinks that it should be so, the utilitarian consequences of a particular world-view or paradigm do play a part in considerations of its status as 'true' or 'progressive' science. Further, as was emphasised in chapter 5, there are certain facts of nature which underlie various language-games and limit the directions they can take. Finally, as discussed earlier, just as the language-games of everyday life may over-lap, so may the language-games of science, so that a change from astronomy to astrology would not go unchallenged by persons in sister disciplines. A new science, or a new paradigm, say 'Xology', which holds that cars are run by little invisible men, can simply get no foothold with people like ourselves. Contrary to what Feyerabend says (and Lakatos fears), it is not the case that 'anything goes'.

Still, the problem of authority remains. That is, no easy answer has been forthcoming as to who should exercise responsibility for laying down demarcation criteria or other standards for scientific practice. Kuhn, Toulmin and Polanyi all claim that there are no formal, explicit criteria by which theories can be evaluated or science judged. Despite the absence of such criteria, they argue that only *practising scientists* themselves are competent to make judgements about questions of scientific practice. Lakatos and Popper, on the other hand, believe that the demarcationist *philosophers of science* should lay down the universal criteria for appraising scientific progress—although they note that these are the result of reconstructions of the standards followed by great scientists in the past. For Feyerabend, there apparently is no way of appraising one theory as better or superior to another—save, of course, personal preference and taste. Thus we have three different viewpoints as to the problem of authority in science.

But these three positions do not exhaust the alternatives. Authority for making judgements among competing theories and about science and pseudo-science could rest, as it once did, with the church, the state or the party. A variant of this would be the situation that Popper and Lakatos fear, where power or violence is exercised by one or another group to obtain a position of ascendancy. And it is conceivable that these judgements could be made more 'democratically', that is, a referendum could be held in which the public voted on the best or truest theory or on what was to be considered as constituting science.

While there appear to be several alternatives as to the question of where the authority for demarcation decisions should lie, none of those persons involved in the 'demarcation debate' would opt for having authority located in the state, church, party (or other powerful groups), or in the public at large. Feyerabend's position on this matter is far from clear, however, in that he does not directly confront the question of how appraisals of theories should be made (after all, he too has his preferences). But, of course, he claims that 'anything goes'.

Despite what Feyerabend says about scientific theories not occupying a privileged epistemological status as compared with other families of beliefs, and despite what Lakatos and Popper claim about demarcation criteria existing in the third world, they share a common characteristic with the elitists. All direct their arguments to an audience of scientists and philosophers and historians of science—not to the church, state, party, or to laymen. Further, I believe that Lakatos and Popper themselves are often inconsistent in their rejection of the autonomy of existing scientific communities. I have already noted Lakatos's recommendation that there are some papers which the editors of scientific journals should refuse to publish and that there are some projects which should not be funded. Popper, especially, is unclear in this regard. Consider the following statement from him.

> Every test of a theory, whether resulting in its corroboration or falsification, must stop at some basic statement or other which *we* decide to accept. If *we* do not come to any decision, and do not accept some basic statement or another, then the test will have led nowhere.[61]

Now, who are the 'we' whom Popper has in mind in writing these sentences? He also says that 'we are stopping at statements about whose acceptance or rejection the various investigators are likely to reach agreement'.[62] One wonders here whether the 'we' and the 'investigators' are identical groups. Popper goes on to assert:

If some day it should no longer be possible for scientific observers to reach agreement about basic statements this would amount to a failure of language as a means of universal communication. It would amount to a new 'Babel of tongues'; scientific discovery would be reduced to absurdity. In this New Babel, the soaring edifice of science would soon lie in ruins.[63]

Implicit in Popper's statements is the view that it is the disciplinary group of *linguistically connected* investigators, with their *shared* criteria in matters of scientific knowledge, that is indeed the proper legitising agency. Groups of scientists sharing the same extraordinary (scientific) language are what Kuhn and others refer to as 'scientific communities'. Whatever Popper's and Lakatos's attempts to escape the 'sociological' aspects of scientific knowledge, it appears that at bottom they, like the elitists, appeal to them as the court of last appeal.

The practice of science, then, is inescapably elitist. Whatever their particular standpoints in the controversy over demarcation, none of these men wants to leave decisions about scientific standards to the state or to laymen. All of them recognise the privileged place of scientific communities (if not of scientific knowledge) in contemporary society. Despite their differences, these men share an underlying attitude about science.

Our consideration of the various problems involved in the discussion about the location of authority in science should help clarify the nature of the scientific enterprise and, consequently, the relation of the individual scientific investigator to the scientific community in which he shares membership. That is to say, it helps us recognise that scientists have taken upon themselves the role of priests, attempting to seek out and suppress any deviation from the scientific world view. Rationality has come to be defined in terms of what is scientific, so that the words are often used interchangeably. This creates a kind of straitjacket in which the individual scientist is imprisoned or held captive. But recent discussions, involving Kuhn, Popper and the others considered in this chapter, have called the whole ideology of science into question, raising questions about what constitutes theories, rationality and science itself. They have helped underscore the extent to which science is a human construction, a human enterprise, so that we are better able to see that what constitutes 'rationality', for example, is not something fixed forever. What now constitutes rationality within one or another scientific discipline may come to be altered or revised, it may prove insufficient for a particular intellectual epoch. All of this means that the individual scientist may decide to stick to his guns when he finds himself in conflict with the reigning elite (the gatekeepers) in his discipline or subject area. By recognising that scientific standards are human constructions which may change, he may be better able himself to work towards bringing such changes about. Instead of conceiving of scientific standards as fixed and permanent, and accepting the judgement that his work has not met these 'sacred' standards, an awareness of the human character of science may help strengthen his resolve to cling to his views while, at the same time, trying to convince the wider scientific community to alter their standards or change their criteria.

In conclusion, the game of science is similar to, and yet different from, other games. It resembles other games in that it can be characterised by rules, players, referees, spectators, rule-makers, playing fields and equipment. But it differs from most other games in that it is a game whose rules appear to be frequently changing. (This is most especially the case in the social sciences.) All of this raises the question of the conditions under which the rules change, and also the question of who is to bear responsibility for such changes. These are questions which lie at the heart of the controversies involving the various philosophers and historians of science discussed in this chapter. Most sociologists seem totally unaware of these controversies, even though they are closely related to certain problems surrounding the sociology of knowledge, and are discussed by Kuhn and Popper in terms of their sociological aspects. I bring these disputes to their attention with the hope that some of them will give these vital questions the scrutiny which they deserve, and will perhaps formulate their eventual solution.

8 Possibilities and Persuasion

We feel as if we had to *penetrate* phenomena: our investigation, however, is directed not towards phenomena, but, as one might say:
towards the *'possibilities'* of phenomena.

LUDWIG WITTGENSTEIN[1]

What I'm doing is also persuasion. If someone says: 'There is not a
difference', and I say: 'There is a difference', I am persuading. I am
saying 'I don't want you to look at it like that'.

LUDWIG WITTGENSTEIN[2]

I noted in the previous chapter that Feyerabend emphasises the need
for new 'possibilities', new ways of looking at and talking about the
world. An anarchistic epistemology, he states, 'is not only a better
means for improving knowledge, or of understanding history. It is
also more appropriate for a free man to use than are its rigorous and
"scientific" alternatives.'[3] I assume that in the above, 'knowledge' refers
to scientific knowledge, and here lies the nub of the problem with Feyerabend's position. He fails to recognise the extent to which scientific
knowledge is the result of certain appraisals and judgements (warranting processes) within scientific communities. He fails to acknowledge
that science is a social enterprise, with an organised consensus of men
determining what is and is not science, and what is and is not to be
warranted as scientific knowledge. As Dolby points out: 'A scientist
does not establish his own results. There can only be scientific knowledge of what a group of people [scientists] can agree upon.'[4] Furthermore, Feyerabend's recommendation that 'anything goes', while
liberating (and therefore to be recommended) for the individual scientist, ignores the problem of how scientific knowledge is created. In this
chapter, I wish to begin by considering the notion of 'possibility' more
closely, following this with a brief discussion of the survival power of

169

possibilities, and then in the last portion of the chapter turning to persuasion and argumentation.

Possibilities

The major principle of Feyerabend's anarchistic methodology is that *anything goes*. Among other things, adherence to this principle leads him to reject the rule that agreement between theory and data should be regarded as favouring the theory while disagreement endangers the theory or causes it to be eliminated altogether. Instead, he suggests that scientists introduce and elaborate hypotheses which are inconsistent either with well-established theories or with well-established facts. This manoeuvre he terms proceeding 'counterinductively'.[5] Feyerabend also advocates a principle of 'proliferation', by which scientists invent and elaborate 'theories' which are inconsistent with accepted theories within the scientific community. He regards these two principles as essential parts of his anarchistic programme.

One wonders, however, whether the slogan 'anything goes' should be accepted without qualification, or whether on the contrary it needs to be considered more closely. I do believe that it is necessary to take a closer look at his position, and to do this with specific reference to the following question: can we say meaningfully that 'anything goes' in scientific practice, that anything is possible, or are there limits on what we can say and do as scientists? I will consider this question specifically in terms of 'possibilities' in science.

Let me begin by repeating the quotation standing at the head of this chapter:

> We feel as if we had to *penetrate* phenomena: our investigation, however, is directed not towards phenomena, but, as one might say, towards the '*possibilities*' of phenomena. We remind ourselves, that is to say, of the *kind* of statement that we make about phenomena.[6]

What Wittgenstein has in mind here is that certain phenomena only 'exist', as it were, because our *language* contains their possibility. There are language-games played which allow us to speak of certain phenomena. For example, the language-games of science more generally and of specific scientific disciplines (physics, sociology, psychology) create the 'possibility' of electrons, neutrons, electromagnetic waves, ids, egos, unconscious minds, roles, intentions, and so forth. It depends wholly on the grammar of one or another language-game what will be called possible and what not; it depends on what that grammar permits. Wittgenstein writes:

> But surely that is arbitrary!—Is it arbitrary? It is not every sentence-like formation that we know how to do something with, not every technique has an application in our life; and when we are tempted in philosophy to count some quite useless thing as a proposition, that is often because we have not considered its application sufficiently?[7]

What, for example, can we do with the following sentences: cars are not constructed, but result from sexual relations among adult male and female cars; contrary to what is widely believed, there are really only two chemical elements; many people have walked on water, but it has been kept a secret; despite what most people hold, our watches are run by little invisible men hidden inside; tables, chairs, in fact all so-called solid objects, alter their shape and colour when no one is observing them, and then when someone looks at them again they change back to their old condition. What application do these sentences have in our life? Could we say that they are in any way 'possible' for people like ourselves? I think not.

But why is this? Is it because they do not 'agree with reality'? Well, they are not part of *our* reality. More importantly, they do not 'tie in' with anything that constitutes our reality. There is nothing that gives them support. Of course, someone might ask: 'But who is going to believe such a thing anyway—that cars have parents, people walk on water, objects alter their shape and colour, and so on?' *We* do not believe such things; that is correct. It is important to remember, however, Wittgenstein's advice to 'imagine the facts otherwise than they are'. Consider, though, *how much* we would have to imagine otherwise for sentences like the above to constitute possibilities.

The lesson here is that all language-games consist of a plurality of beliefs and certainties which are interdependent and lend one another mutual support. In any natural ordinary language, then, most utterances must be 'true' (grounded) in terms of other *accepted* 'facts of nature', theories, propositions, assumptions, and the like. Similarly with science; at any given time in any given scientific (extraordinary) language, most propositions are taken as correct. This is not to say, however, that we are easily able to identify *which* are the correct statements, for that is always dependent on how they tie in or connect with other elements in a particular language-game. It would therefore appear that what is 'possible' in the way of new hypotheses, theories, new facts, is limited by what is established as certain or beyond doubt in a specific scientific community or speciality. The 'anything goes' slogan demands qualification.

Further, we should not forget that scientific languages represent an extension of ordinary languages, and that changes in the one can bring about reinterpretations and reinforcements in the concepts of the other. Thus the abandoning of a specific theory may have repercussions throughout the rest of the language-game in which it represents a part, in that it is linked to other elements in that particular language-game, but also in other language-games with which that language-game overlaps. And in all language-games there are some facts, theories, or whatever, that are obviously better entrenched than others and are difficult (impossible?) to conceive of as candidates for revision or rejection. Some things, that is, seem so firmly anchored to everything around them that their being called into question necessarily calls into question the whole system of which they form a part. They have been accepted (and, as we shall see in the following chapter, have been *used*) for so long that it is virtually impossible to conceive of the contrary.

In other words, certain possibilities are 'merely' possibilities in the sense that we can speak about or imagine them (imagine that blocks of flats grow out of the earth) but are unable to tie them in with other elements of our lives which seem firmly entrenched. It is difficult to see how they could ever acquire a foothold with us. There are other possibilities, however, which seem to occupy a different status: they are not only imaginable but seem capable of being tied into already existing certainties in our lives. Some possibilities are 'live', then (although perhaps only in a specific historical time), in the sense that they can be incorporated within an already accepted world-view, where they connect to more firmly anchored certainties and beliefs.

The most far-reaching possibilities are those which constitute radically different ways of looking at phenomena or, as Wittgenstein puts it, create the possibilities of phenomena. Here we can think of the contributions of such figures as Plato, Aristotle, Galileo, Newton, Einstein, Darwin, Machiavelli, Kant, Hegel, Marx, Freud, Wittgenstein. Some of these men were philosophers, some natural scientists, but all helped create new possibilities of world-views. They all provided mankind with something very much like Kuhn's 'paradigms', with new alternatives to the established ways of viewing (or constructing) the world. Although we often speak of the 'discoveries' of Einstein or Freud, for example, their world-views were human *inventions*. Their new ways of seeing, including those that broke with earlier cosmologies, were their own inventions. All of science consists of various inventions, including the idea that it *isn't* a human invention (and including also, of course, the idea that it *is*). The new alternatives set forth by Freud, Einstein, Marx and the other figures mentioned above contained some very general philosophical views, regulative ideals or world-pictures providing for new visions (or versions) of the world. In short, they provided for *new* worlds, as it were. Gailileo, for instance, helped to replace the Aristotelian world-view by a mechanistic one.[8] Similarly, Leibniz and Newton provided for different worlds (or world-views). The long controversy between them and their followers, Iltis observes, was fundamentally 'a clash of philosophical world views on the nature of God, matter and force'.[9] And the replacement of Newtonian mechanics by Einsteinian theory was a switch from one possible world-view to another.

Paradoxically, there are situations where it may be easier to entertain the possibility of a whole different system than that of an individual element within the system. Wittgenstein remarks:

> It would strike me as ridiculous to want to doubt the existence of Napoleon; but if someone doubted the existence of the earth 150 years ago, perhaps I would be more willing to listen, for now he is doubting our whole system of evidence. It does not strike me as if this system were more certain than a certainty within it.[10]

It is difficult to doubt the existence of Napoleon because so much evidence in our system connects up with it. But if our whole system of evidence is considered to be in some way mistaken, then perhaps we can be trained into another way of looking at the world—another way of creating the possibility of phenomena—wherein what *counts* as evidence will be radically different.

As regards possibilities, then, we have considered three types of situations. First, an element (proposition, theory, or whatever) is in no way a candidate for acceptance into the language-game because that which it calls into question is too firmly anchored within the language-game (that is, the 'new' element constitutes a virtual impossibility). In the second case, new elements may be introduced and older elements revised or replaced, either because they are not firmly entrenched within the language-game or because the revision (the new possibility) can be incorporated into the language-game as presently played. An example of the latter is the world-views of Newton and Einstein. While Newtonian and Einsteinian dynamics have radically different implications, nevertheless they share certain important elements in common: 'acceleration of falling bodies near the earth's surface', for instance. This is undoubtedly the case in much scientific practice where certain shared elements form the background against which new possibilities are evaluated and perhaps incorporated. Finally we have the situation where a whole new system (possibility) is created. Think here of Galileo, Freud, Darwin. Clearly it is not always easy to distinguish between the two situations where possibilities are able to obtain a hearing and gain a possible foothold. It seems doubtful, as argued in chapter 5, that those possibilities which constitute almost totally new systems (paradigms, in Kuhn's words) are fully incommensurable in the way that Kuhn suggests—undoubtedly this also depends on such things as the commitment and years of practice for particular individuals within a given world-view. With regard to my central interest in this chapter, however, the crucial distinction is between those possibilities which do become candidates for scientific status and those which are in some way, for us, impossible.

I hope it is clear that neither truth nor falsity enters into the picture here. The dominant views in the natural and social sciences alike, as we know, have assumed that science is cumulative and moves progressively closer to the truth. Kuhn and others have called that assumption into question. Kuhn's own new historiography of science itself provides us with a new way of looking at the practice of science historically. It constitutes a new possibility for viewing science, although it can claim no special status in regard to other historiographies. Because it constitutes a new possibility, it is to be welcomed. While neither true nor false, it may prove useful for those who wish to extend the conceptual schemes through which they view and explain the history of science.

The survival power of possibilities

I come now to the second point in this chapter, the issue as to how certain possibilities manage to survive and come to be viewed as viable alternatives, as new ways of seeing. It might seem that the wider the vision and the more minute the details offered (as to assumptions, definitions, prohibitions, and so on), the more a possibility stands as a viable candidate for acceptance by the scientific community. As sociologists, however, we must recognise that questions as to 'precision', 'specificity', and so on, are judged by scientific communities. No possibility is simply, on the face of it, 'better' or 'preferable' to another. Why, then, are some possibilities regarded as 'live options' and others not? Merely posing the question is to become aware of an enormous number of factors which must be considered if the question is to be dealt with in any detail. And it most certainly is not my intention in these few pages to try to frame an extended reply to this large question. On the other hand, I do not intend the question rhetorically, and must therefore at least touch on some of the elements which might be included in a more comprehensive reply to the 'survival' question. Later in the chapter, I will focus on one particular, and generally neglected, element involved in the survival of possibilities: persuasion and argumentation.

First of all, it seems apparent that the world-views formulated by some thinkers are more or less indistinguishable from the world-views set forth by other thinkers. Yet some world-views are given serious consideration, while others are ignored or forgotten. The enormous enthusiasm for Kuhn's work, in contrast to the response to some of the earlier ideas advanced by Mannheim and Mills, might be seen as an example of this. But in that case, at least, it appears that Kuhn has formulated a wider, more fully-developed *system* than was advanced by those earlier thinkers. What this appears to suggest is the greater survival power of possible systems as compared to possible ideas. Be that as it may, in order to simplify my discussion I will ignore the problem of the survival power of specific ideas or theories or hypotheses and will focus only on systems. Even this 'simplification', however, leaves us with a rather formidable problem of considering the following, which I will speak of roughly as the 'competition' between (1) similar systems (possibilities) under the 'same' social–historical conditions, (2) dissimilar systems under the same conditions, (3) similar systems under different social–historical conditions, and (4) dissimilar systems under different conditions.

Let us begin with the first of these possibilities. If two essentially similar systems, say A and A_1, are candidates for recognition under the same social–historical circumstances, why should A be given wide attention while the 'same' system (A_1) is met with total apathy or is widely ignored? Here it would seem that the following considerations are important. There are differences in the 'credibility' of the advocates of the two systems within the relevant scientific communities; here perhaps (as Lakatos argues) the producer rather than the product is evaluated. Similarly, there are differences in the credibility of the 'schools' or 'traditions' within which the advocates of the systems are located. There are differentials in access to various publication outlets among various system advocates, and certainly access to the gatekeepers of science is always crucial. The number of followers who may be expected to work on and spread an individual's system or world-view is another important consideration. A world-view advanced by a scientist in a large laboratory with many potential followers has a better chance for survival than the 'same' world-view advocated by a more isolated scholar or scientist. And, of course, there are what are generally regarded as more strictly 'scientific' considerations. Lemarck for example, was greeted with ridicule by the scientific community because of his failure to give careful attention to the process of verification. Mendel, on the other hand, delayed too long in publishing the results of his work. Hence Darwin received a positive response in the scientific community that these earlier scientists did not. This is not to say that Darwin's *Origin of Species* was immediately met with universal acceptance, for his theory conflicted both with certain contemporary principles in the philosophy of science and with the widespread belief in God as an underlying first cause.[11] Even though Darwin's earlier work concerning the voyage of the *Beagle*, living and fossil barnacles and coral reefs had met with a generally positive response within the scientific community and had helped to establish his reputation as a genuine inductive scientist, large segments of the scientific community ridiculed the *Origin*. One wonders whether the controversial *Origin* would have manifested the enormous survival power which it did, however, without these earlier works which served to establish Darwin's scientific credibility.

These are obviously only a few of the multitude of factors which may be seen as playing a part in the response of the members of a scientific community (or communities) to more or less similar world-views. Important here is the recognition that the survival chances of a given 'way of looking' or possibility are not dependent on some simple comparison of the systems with reality. Instead, there are a wide variety of factors—many of which Mannheim and others would regard as 'extra-theoretical'—which are involved in the competition between two essentially similar systems under the same social–historical circumstances.

What, then, of the second situation mentioned above, where two different systems—say A and B—are in competition under similar conditions? To begin with, all the factors listed for the first situation would operate here as well. But the situation here is somewhat more complicated than the first one, in that *different* world-views are being compared and evaluated (which Kuhn says is impossible). In this regard Johan Galtung, a methodologist of social science, lists ten 'dimensions' which he says can be used to evaluate competing theories. While my concern here is with systems, which are wider and more inclusive than theories, Galtung's list may be useful. According to Galtung, there are ten criteria which scientists use in evaluating theories: (1) generality, (2) range, (3) status of individual hypotheses, (4) formalisation, (5) axiomatisation, (6) relations to other theories, (7) predictability, (8) communicability, (9) reproducibility, and (10) fruitfulness.[12] Undoubtedly these criteria do play a part in the evaluation of competing theories. But these competing theories will score differently on the various rank-dimensions and different scores on the various dimensions may be weighted differentially. And this, of course, is a serious problem; for there are no firm guidelines as to how these criteria are to be employed. Beyond these considerations, there is the fact that during a particular historical period, the scientific community may be 'ready' for one system and not for another. Again, what Mannheim calls extra-theoretical factors are involved in the evaluation of different world-views or possibilities.

With regard to the third situation, concerning similar systems under different social–historical circumstances, it seems that all of the above-listed factors may be involved. Perhaps of paramount importance is the last-named: the extent to which a scientific community is ready for a new possibility. I have already suggested that this might have been the case with the positive reception to Kuhn's possible system (paradigms, and so on) in contemporary science and philosophy, while a similar conceptual system (Mannheim, Mills) met with far less positive acceptance at an earlier time and under different conditions. Matters are similar with the last of the four situations, where the survival power of dissimilar systems under varying historical conditions is to be considered. It again appears that most of the above factors are involved in the judgements made by scientific communities.

This discussion concerning the survival power of different possibilities is obviously rather cursory and limited in scope. One of the most obvious omissions is any mention of the political suppression of competing or unpopular viewpoints. Nor have I said anything about what the individual scientist (or more generally, the individual intellectual) can do to help ensure the success of his way of looking.[13]

In discussing the survival power of various possibilities, I am of course once again considering *competition* in science. I have mentioned some of the structural conditions involved in the struggle between competing world-views. The power dimension, which I discussed briefly in the previous chapter, is obviously of paramount importance here. Not only are there hierarchies *within* various disciplines, which create their own processes of submission and domination among various individuals and groups, but there are also hierarchies *among* the different scientific disciplines. Physics and mathematics, for example, are generally considered more prestigious, more important and more 'scientific' than sociology and psychology. This means that the 'tools' characteristic of the more dominant disciplines may come to be utilised in the less dominant or lower-status fields. The use of mathematics and statistics in sociology represents a clear instance of this phenomenon. At the same time, however, even the lowest disciplines in the pecking order of science are in a dominant position *vis-à-vis* certain everyday language-games. Thus the 'same' theoretical explanation advanced by a layman and a sociologist is generally given more credibility by the public if it is put forth by the latter than by the former. The point here is that there are a great variety of constraints—socio-economic, political, cultural, individual, as well as scientific—which play a part in the survival power of possibilities.

Persuasion

But what if all formulated possibilities were equally available or had maximum opportunity to be considered by the relevant scientific communities? That is, what if all 'other conditions' were equal? Is there nothing about the possibilities (world-views) *themselves* that is involved in their being accepted or rejected by various scientific communities? Often, of course, we are told that one system is preferable to another because it is truer or closer to the truth than another. That is, it is argued that the 'evidence' is such that every normal mind must yield to it. From this point of view, it is the *content* of the system or possibility itself, apart from anything else, that is definitive in the settling of knowledge- and truth-claims. This view, I have argued, is thoroughly unsociological, and I have attempted to broadly sketch out above some of the factors that might be involved in a more fully sociological explanation. For the most part, however, I have ignored the issue of how men come to be persuaded by the force of an explanation. By 'force' here, I do not mean the logical force, but something else. Let me illustrate this with the example of Freud and psychoanalysis.

An individual forgets to mail a letter, and insists that there was no reason for this. Even after reflection, he still holds that it was just forgetfulness, an oversight. A Freudian analyst insists that there must have been some unconscious reason for the man's having failed to mail the letter. Perhaps he unconsciously connected the mailing of the letter with some event or occurrence in his life which he finds painful and therefore must suppress. Or again, perhaps an analyst explains a patient's neurotic behaviour in terms of factors unknown to the patient himself. Painful events in the patient's childhood, let us say, are unconsciously suppressed. In the course of psychotherapy, a great variety of explanations may be offered as explaining the patient's behaviour. The question then arises: what is the correct or true explanation?

In my view, the correct explanation as regards the analyst–patient relationship is the one which the analyst gets the patient to accept. If none of the proffered explanations is accepted by the patient, then none of them is correct for him. How, then, does the analyst get the patient to accept an explanation? Granted that there are a variety of explanations which the analyst might set forth as the 'right' one, it is not my concern as to how he arrives at one rather than another. I am simply taking it for granted that the analyst himself will come to believe that a particular explanation is the correct one for *this* patient. My concern is with how he gets the patient to accept that explanation as the one which is indeed right or true. The analyst is capable of providing a number of 'possible' explanations for the patient's behaviour, but the 'right' one, I argue, is the one he gets the patient to accept. But what if the patient refuses to accept any of the proffered explanations? Is it then impossible to speak of the explanation that was really right? Of course not. But then the 'right' explanation is the one that is accepted by other analysts, other Freudians, or whatever; and once again, the question is how they came to accept his rather than another as the correct explanation. Someone might reply, 'But that is the right explanation, it is the one found in every single textbook or training manual on psychotherapy!' O.K.—but still the problem remains. At one time, there were most certainly competing candidates for the status of the right or best explanation. How did this one come to be the one that was chosen (emerged) as the right one? So I will continue to focus here on the analyst–patient relationship as a paradigm case of the 'persuasion problem'.

Wittgenstein discusses the problem as follows:

Suppose you were analyzed when you had a stammer. (1) You may say that that explanation . . . is correct which cures the stammer. (2) If the stammer is not cured the criterion may be the person analyzed saying: 'This explanation is correct,' or agreeing that the explanation given him is correct. (3) Another criterion is that according to certain rules of experience the explanation given is the

correct one, whether the person to whom it is given adopts it o
not.[14]

Wittgenstein goes on to remark that: 'Many of these explanations are
adopted because they have a peculiar charm. The picture of people
having sub-conscious thoughts has a charm. The idea of an under
world, a secret cellar. Something hidden, uncanny.'[15] This charm,
then, is one of the factors involved in patients' being persuaded of a
certain thing. Wittgenstein is quite explicit as regards the persuasive
power of psychoanalysis:

> If you are led by psycho-analysis to say that really you thought so
> and so or that really your motive was so and so, this is not a matter
> of discovery, but of persuasion. In a different way you could have
> been persuaded of something different. Of course, if psycho-analysis
> cures your stammer, it cures it, and that is an achievement. One
> thinks of certain results of psycho-analysis as a discovery Freud made
> as apart from something persuaded to you by a psycho-analyst
> and I wish to say this is not the case.[16]

The analyst's task, then, is to persuade the patient to give up one way
of thinking and to adopt another. What is involved in the interpreta
tion of dreams, Wittgenstein emphasises, is fitting the dream into a
context in which it ceases to be puzzling. This context, this scheme of
explanation, this possible system if we like, is provided by Freud and
employed by the Freudian analyst.

Speaking about Freud's *Interpretation of Dreams*, Wittgenstein argued
that, by use of free association, he could himself take any of Freud'
reports of his own dreams and arrive at exactly the same results a
Freud did—even though these were not Wittgenstein's dreams.[1]
'What Freud has done,' Wittgenstein says, 'is to propound a new
myth. The attractiveness of the suggestion, for instance, that al
anxiety is a repetition of the anxiety of the birth trauma, is just the
attractiveness of a mythology. "It is all the outcome of something tha
happened long ago." Almost like referring to a totem.'[18] Certain
mythologies are so compelling, so powerful, so attractive, that there i
an inducement to say, 'Yes, of course, it must be like that.'

Notice that in the above quotation Wittgenstein remarks tha
Freud's explanation is a 'myth' (that is, not scientific), and that it
being regarded as correct is dependent on its attractiveness and on per
suasion. He seems to believe that 'science' is in some way exempt from
the influence of compulsion and persuasion. Throughout much of hi

writing, in fact, there is a tendency to exempt science from the lines of inquiry followed in dealing with other topics. Here, I believe, he was profoundly mistaken. Had he had occasion to consider more directly the practice of science, he might have seen that persuasion is involved in the settling of truth- and knowledge-claims in all sciences. Wittgenstein did, however, show some awareness of this in speaking of what he termed 'the Darwin upheaval'.[19] While Wittgenstein for the most part exempted science from the influence of persuasion, I shall argue in the remainder of this chapter that the survival power of possibilities is very much dependent on their persuasiveness. And their persuasiveness, I shall contend, is itself partly a matter of rhetoric and argumentation.

Obviously, I assume that there is a parallel in the analyst–patient relationship and the relationship between the individual scientist and a particular scientific community (or the gatekeepers therein). Just as the analyst must persuade his patient of the correctness of his explanation, so must the scientist persuade the scientific community (or, at the very least, members of various sub-communities) of the correctness of his views. Further, in the case of new possibilities, he must try to get others to accept a new way of thinking about or conceptualising the world. He wants to get scientists who now see the world in one way to see it in another. Knowingly or not, the individual scientist has to persuade the scientific community (or certain segments thereof) to look at things his way.

Evidence for the existence of persuasion in science is found in Mitroff's study of Apollo moon scientists, forty-two eminent scientists who studied the moon rocks.[20] The group consisted of physicists, chemists, astronomers, geologists, geophysicists, geochemists and engineers. Included in their ranks were Nobel prize winners and members of the National Academy of Sciences. In short, they were a group of elite representatives of the scientific community. One of them is quoted as saying: 'I can't find any fundamental difference between the scientific method and the procedures for making progress in business and the arts. Where the evidence is not clear-cut, people reach out and grasp for straws. They are extremely subjective and intuitive. They invent elaborate analytic justifications to *convince* their colleagues.'[21] Another states: 'People want *to sell* their point of view, beat down the other guy because it means more glory, more ego satisfaction, more money. A scientist has the same internal wolves biting at him, his ego, his own work.'[22] Discussing the theoreticians and experimentalists in his field, the same scientist adds: 'The big people give the same talk at 6 or 8 different places, adding only enough data so it's publishable. They push very hard for an idea. That is more than just the theoreticians versus the experimentalists. Both have to *sell* a product . . . . You try to *sell* the possibility you think most likely.'[23]

Talk of 'selling' one's point of view and 'convincing' one's colleagues is very much akin to what I term persuasion.

Depending on the scientific community to which he belongs (physics, sociology, and so on) and the existing criteria for scientific practice within that community, the individual scientist has several tools for persuasion at his disposal: for example, mathematical deduction, logic and argumentation. But it is a mistake, I have argued earlier, to accept the usual picture of science drawn in science textbooks, where a heavy emphasis is laid on certain aspects of scientific practice. The following is a rather typical example drawn from a physics textbook:

> Through experimental science we have been able to learn all these facts about the natural world, triumphing over darkness and ignorance to classify the stars and to estimate their masses, composition, distances, and velocities; to classify living species and to unravel their genetic relations . . . . These great accomplishments of experimental science were achieved by men of many types . . . most of these men have in common only a few things: they were honest and actually made the observations they recorded, and they published the results of their work in a form permitting others to duplicate the experiment or observation.[24]

Similarly, the sociologist Daniel Bell emphasises that all students should learn the nature of hypothetico-deductive thought,[25] and goes on to stress the importance of 'the scientific method' which relies on 'devising alternative hypotheses, for any problem, devising crucial experiments, each of which would, as nearly as possible, exclude one or more hypotheses . . .'.[26] These ringing accounts of the dependence of scientists on observation, experiments, hypothetico-deductive thought and the scientific method, however, are called into question by accounts like Hall's of the battle between seventeenth-century geocentrists and heliocentrists:

> There was no proof for either side: there was only the choice between *this* way of regarding things which belonged to antiquity, and *that* which belonged to Galileo and modern science . . . the number of instances of his offering a precise piece of experiment in support of

his notions is small indeed. Even the positive assertions of experimental verification made by Galileo have been doubted.[27]

According to Hall, Galileo did not refute earlier views through experiment or by use of a hypothetico-deductive method at all. Kuhn, as we have seen earlier, also questions the usual versions of scientific practice.

Of course, scientists do employ observations, experiments and various elements of the scientific method in their work. But these are not sufficient to account for scientific change and for the acceptance by the scientific community of some possibilities rather than others. In fact the scientist may use a variety of devices in trying to persuade the scientific community to accept his way of looking at things. One of these, I claim, is *argumentation*, which the scientist uses to create or increase the adherence of other minds to the theses or world-views he presents. At the very least, he must create in his readers (or listeners) a willingness to pay attention to what he is saying. In short, he always has the task of gaining the adherence of the audience to whom he directs his claims. Most especially in the social sciences, where the use of logical reasoning and mathematical deduction is less prevalent than in the natural sciences, argumentation and rhetoric play a central role in the settling of truth- and knowledge-claims.

To repeat one of the central themes of this volume: ultimately it is the scientific community which must warrant the truth of our assertions, however we come to hold them. We must therefore always take an audience into account. Although Blum advocates ignoring the audience (community), I do not see how this is possible.[28] (After all, I am addressing these remarks to *you*. One can no more practise science alone than play tennis by oneself.) All of this leads to the question of how a scientist constructs an argument so as to elaborate a particular way of seeing the world and so as, at the same time, to persuade the scientific community of the usefulness of his way of seeing.

Argumentation and rhetoric: the importance of language

We can and must, I hold, consider the practice of science partially from the perspective of the individual scientist. To do so is most assuredly not to pursue the question of how the individual thinker can arrive single-handed at valid ideas or truths. That is more or less the route taken by thinkers as diverse as Locke, Descartes and Chomsky. Instead, following Wittgenstein, I am trying to consider the practice of science and the problem of scientific knowledge fully as to their *communal* aspects. Further, by giving *reasons* for this or that standpoint, I am acknowledging the authority of the scientific community whom I am addressing. Giving reasons—whether in the form of demonstration and procedural rules or in the form of argumentation—serves as evidence of the communal nature of science. Providing an argument, however, is different from showing that one has followed certain procedural rules correctly. If one has used procedural rules (methods, in the usual scientific sense, and deductive theories) in the correct manner, there is ideally no room for disagreement about the results. One investigator is considered to be fully interchangeable with another in the dominant scientific view (positivism). In that view, 'anyone' who follows the right procedures correctly will reach the same conclusions as would anyone else who also followed those rules. Thus the aim is to achieve a community-sanctioned certainty.

In this connection, it is useful to contrast *argumentation* with what I have referred to above as *demonstration*. Here I draw heavily on the formulation of Perelman, especially as set forth in *The New Rhetoric*:

> Every demonstration requires that the elements on which it is based should be univocal. They are supposed to be understood by everyone in the same way, by virtue of means of knowledge which are assumed to be intersubjective, and, if this is not the case, the object of reasoning is reduced artificially to those elements alone from which all ambiguity seems to be removed. Either the datum is presented immediately as something clear and significant, in a rationalistic conception of deduction, or attention is directed only to the form of the signs which is supposed to be perceived by all in the same way, such that handling of these signs does not lead to ambiguity; this is the conception of the modern formalists. In all these cases, interpretation does not raise any problems, or, at least, the problems it does raise are eliminated from the theory.[29]

Demonstrative proof, which is characteristic of positivistic science, is impersonal; it is binding on any normal mind, and its correctness is not dependent on the assent of any particular persons. In the practice of science, demonstration involves the application of rules enumerated beforehand. Demonstrations are intended to guarantee the truth of a science's affirmations. But demonstration, as Perelman observes, is based on a theory of knowledge which is not human, but divine; of knowledge as acquired by a unique and perfect Being.[30]

Argumentation, on the other hand, grants the status of knowledge to viewpoints (opinions, formulations) which have survived the criticisms and objections of the particular audience to whom they have been directed. Thus, knowledge—including scientific knowledge—is human and social. But there are no absolute criteria which can guarantee its infallability. Argument, Perelman emphasises, 'is never conclusive: by means of it the speaker tries to gain the adherence of a free being, employing reasons which that being should find better than those advanced on behalf of the competing theses'.[31] He says that a court-room judge 'who takes a decision after hearing both parties does not behave like a machine, but like a person whose power of evaluation, free but not arbitrary, is more often than not decisive for the outcome of the argument'.[32] Whether one addresses one's arguments to a judge or to one or another scientific community, the development of all arguments is a function of the *audience* to whom it is addressed. The aim is to produce a change or a commitment in the minds of the listeners or readers. And, of course, the use of argumentation implies that one has renounced resorting to force or violence (here it is consistent with the view of Popper and Lakatos), that one does not regard the audience as objects but as individuals whose free judgement can be appealed to; and, further, that one is willing to evidence a commitment and assume responsibility, that is, that one is willing to be 'seen' in his writing (or speaking). Argumentation, however, also has implications for the reader or listener. In the words of Perelman and Olbrechts-Tyteca:

> Since rhetorical proof is never a completely necessary proof, the thinking man who gives his adherence to the conclusions of an argument does so by an act that commits him and for which he is responsible. The fanatic accepts the commitment, but as one bowing to an absolute and irrefragable truth; the sceptic refuses the commitment under the pretext that he does not find it sufficiently definitive. He refuses adherence because his idea of adherence is similar to that of the fanatic: both fail to appreciate that argumentation aims at a choice among possible theses; by proposing and justifying the hierarchy of these theses, argumentation seeks to make the decision a rational one. This role of argumentation in decision-making is denied by the sceptic and the fanatic. In the absence of compelling reason, they both are inclined to give violence a free hand, rejecting personal commitment.[33]

Argumentation, I have tried to indicate, is very much different from demonstration (applying rules enumerated beforehand). With arguments one begins with two questions: (1) can you follow the argument? and (2) do you agree with it? In attempting as best he can to make his argument followable, the individual scientist acknowledges the existence and authority of the scientific community to whom his argument is directed. But because we (fortunately, I believe) do not have a completely clear idea (community agreement) as to what constitutes a 'compelling' or fully persuasive argument, it is not to be expected that arguments will ever secure complete agreement. But by choosing argumentation instead of demonstration, the individual scientist maintains his own personal responsibility for what he asserts. That is, readers may be able to follow the argument, but may *not agree* with it (may not be persuaded). With demonstration, however, agreement is supposed to be the outcome of having followed the rules in the right way. Like demonstration, argumentation is addressed to an audience, whom the individual tries to persuade. But arguments are non-compelling, while demonstration involves necessary truths, results or outcomes, and ideally mathematical certitude. Demonstration rests on the force of logical deduction, experimental evidence, the scientific method. Argumentation, however, is a persuasive device which men employ to bring about the adherence of other minds.

In science, as we know, certainty is supposed to result from demonstration, so that anyone who follows the proper procedural rules will reach exactly the same conclusions as would anyone else following the same rules. Thus argumentation, because it clearly involves the presence of the inquirer (his self), who is not simply a rule-follower, is viewed as inappropriate in science. At issue here, however, is not the question of whether argumentation should operate in science, but rather whether it does. Obviously I believe that argumentation is an element in communications between the individual scientist and the wider scientific community to which he belongs. As I suggested earlier, the persuasive element involved in the analyst–patient relationship is mirrored in the relationship between the individual scientist and the scientific audience to whom he directs his claims or to whom he directs his ways of looking at the world.

A concern with argumentation necessarily involves us with *rhetoric*. Among the ancients, rhetoric was the study of a technique to be used on the uneducated and illiterate. It was because of this that Plato in the *Gorgias* opposed rhetoric so strenuously. For example, addressing Gorgias, the famous teacher of rhetoric, Socrates shows his displeasure with rhetoric:

Socrates: You claim you can make a rhetorician of any man who wishes to learn from you?

Gorgias: Yes.

Socrates: With the result that he would be convincing about any subject before a crowd, not through instruction but by persuasion?

Gorgias: Certainly.

Socrates: Well, you said just now that a rhetorician will be more persuasive than a doctor regarding health.

Gorgias: Yes, I said so, before a crowd.

Socrates: And before a crowd means among the ignorant, for surely, among those who know, he will not be more convincing than the doctor.

Gorgias: That is quite true.

Socrates: Then if he is more persuasive than the doctor, he is more persuasive than the man who knows?

Gorgias: Certainly.

Socrates: Though not himself a doctor.

Gorgias: Yes.

Socrates: And he who is not a doctor is surely ignorant of what a doctor knows.

Gorgias: Obviously.

Socrates: Therefore when the rhetorician is more convincing than the doctor, the ignorant is more convincing among the ignorant than the expert. Is that our conclusion, or is something else?

Gorgias: That is the conclusion, in this instance.

Socrates: Is not the position of the rhetorician and of the rhetoric the same with respect to other arts also? It has no need to know the truth about things but merely to discover a technique of persuasion, so as to appear among the ignorant to have more knowledge than the expert?

Gorgias: But is not this a great comfort, Socrates, to be able without learning any other arts but this one to prove in no way inferior to the specialist?[34]

And elsewhere, Socrates remarks that rhetoric is not a reputable activity:

Gorgias: What is it, Socrates? Tell us and feel no scruples about me.

Socrates: Well, then, Gorgias, the activity as a whole, it seems to me, is not an art, but the occupation of a shrewd and enterprising spirit, and one naturally skilled in its dealings with men, and in sum and substance I call it 'flattery'.[35]

Despite Socrates' dismissal of rhetoric, it seems to me that he himself is using emotionally persuasive language for the purpose of undermining the position of those emphasising the power of rhetoric. Given the persuasiveness of Socrates' argument, it is no wonder that rhetoric has fallen into disrepute. But I see no compelling reason to accept a view of rhetoric as something involving a shrewd rhetorician and the common herd. While the rhetoric of the ancients was specifically the art of speaking persuasively in public, today argumentation (including, of course, rhetoric) involves the use of printed texts: books, monographs, articles, essays. What is common to the ancient and contemporary use of rhetoric is the idea of an *audience*, those to whom the argument is directed. Although this may sometimes involve an educated writer attempting to persuade the less-educated reader, this is certainly not always the case, especially in the practice of science. In scientific writings, the writer has the task of persuading his readers of the correctness or usefulness of this world-view. Needless to say, I am not suggesting that rhetoric is all that is involved in the acceptance by a scientific community of one or another possible version of the world. On the contrary, I have earlier in the chapter mentioned several other considerations which may be involved in the survival power of various possibilities.

My central point here is that *discursive means* for obtaining the adherence of other minds is a factor in the practice of science, even though it is totally ignored in most discussions of science. I do not see how scientists, most especially social scientists, can avoid using argumentation in their writings, most especially in their textbooks where they employ ordinary, everyday language as a means of getting the student or novice to accept the correctness of one or another extraordinary (scientific) language. Let us, then, consider the matter of discursive means in science.

I will begin, however, not with science, but with what is usually regarded as literature. John Fowles points to the importance of emotive language in the following:

> If he had been . . . a scientist, Shakespeare would have begun Hamlet's famous soliloquy with some properly applicable statement, such as 'The situation in which I find myself is one where I must carefully examine the arguments for and against suicide, never forgetting that the statements I shall make are merely emotional verbal statements about myself and my own present situation and must not be taken to constitute any statement about any other

person or situation or to constitute anything more than biographical data'.[36]

Clearly there is an enormous difference between the above and Hamlet's 'To be, or not to be' soliloquy. Any richness, depth of feeling or persuasiveness is missing. Instead, we have a dry, unemotional, unmoving statement. A wall is erected between the speaker and the listener (or between the writer and the reader), so that the utterances conform to the most deadly and 'objective' of scientific terminology. A language is used which is free of all kinds of expressions which might possibly sway or affect the listener's or reader's judgement. Much scientific language is equally dry and monotonous. However, this has not always been the case in science. To show this, Feyerabend quotes a report by Newton from the seventeenth century. Writing in 1666, Newton began his first page on colours as follows:

I procured me a triangular glass prisme, to try therewith the celebrated phenomena of colours. And in order thereto having darkened my chambers, and made a small hole in my window shuts, to let in a convenient quality of the sun's light, I placed my prisme at its entrance, that it might be thereby refracted to the opposite wall. It was at first a very pleasant divertisement, to view the vivid and intense colours produced thereby; but after a while applying myself to consider them more circumspectly, I became surprised to see them in an oblonge form. . . .[37]

Commenting on this quotation, Feyerabend asks us to remember that this report is about cold, objective, 'inhumane', *inanimate* nature, it is 'about stars, prisms, lenses, the moon, and yet these are described in a most lively and fascinating manner, communicating to the reader an interest and an excitement which the discoverer felt when first venturing into strange new worlds'.[38] Further evidence of a scientist communicating his interest and excitement is found in Darwin's *Origin of Species*, where the opening paragraph begins:

When on board H.M.S. 'Beagle', as naturalist, I was much struck with certain facts in the distribution of the inhabitants of South America, and in the geological relations of the present to the past inhabitants of that continent. These facts seemed to me to throw some light on the origin of species—that mystery of mysteries, as it has been called by one of our greatest philosophers. On my return home, it occurred to me, in 1837, that something might perhaps be made out on this question by patiently accumulating and reflecting on all sorts of facts which could possibly have any bearing on it. After five years' work, I allowed myself to speculate on the subject, and drew up some short notes; these I enlarged in 1844 into a sketch of the conclusions, which then seemed to me probable: from that period to the present day I have steadily pursued the same object.[39]

Newton and Darwin used language to set off resonances in the mind and spirit of the reader. Their language is the opposite of the linear, technical, non-emotive language of the technical specialist and of demonstration in general.

But we must not forget that demonstration and argumentation alike involve the medium of language in the communication between the individual scientist and the audience whom he addresses. Both have the task of forcing upon the audience a particular way of looking at the world. In cases where a new possibility is presented, which challenges and calls into question the established ways of looking (as did, for example, Freud and Marx), the individual has the task of getting the audience's attention and engaging them in dialogue. He must get them to look at phenomena from a different perspective. Argumentation, however, as opposed to demonstration, may be intensely personal. And it is certainly not precise or exact. Waismann speaks of what he terms a 'clarity neurosis', where men are

> haunted by fear, tongue-tied, asking themselves continually 'Oh dear, now does this make perfectly good sense?' Imagine that the pioneers of science—Kepler, Newton, the discoverers of non-Euclidean geometry, of field physics, the unconscious, matter waves or heaven knows what—imagine them asking themselves this question at every step—this would have been the surest means of sapping any creative power. No great discoverer has acted in accordance with the motto 'Everything that can be said can be said clearly'.[40]

Obviously this does not mean that scientists do not strive for clarity or precision, but these are not always the primary considerations in their arguments. With demonstration, on the other hand, clarity and precision are required as necessary conditions for scientists to reach agreement, to speak the same language, to meet the requirement of de-authorised speech where the writer is not to be seen in his (the) scientific assertions. With argumentation, the individual scientist tries to communicate what he 'knows/believes' in such a way as to get his way of seeing accepted, to get his views accepted by the scientific community in the discipline in which he practises his craft.

Taking Notice

The first task for the scientist is to get other scientists to 'take notice'. He may begin by communicating his way of seeing to a small circle of potential followers (students, colleagues, perhaps an 'invisible college' in which he shares membership). Because of his relationship with these persons, he may encounter little difficulty in getting their attention. But beyond his immediate circle of friends, students and colleagues, he may have more trouble in getting wider segments of the scientific community to take notice. Pareto considered this problem of drawing an audience's attention, stating: 'To argue about a thing with a person, in terms whether favourable or unfavourable, may arouse in him an inclination—if he hasn't it already—to interest himself in that thing; if he already has the inclination, it may whet it.'[41] And while not concerned specifically with scientific practice, Kierkegaard gives considerable attention to the problem of getting people to pay attention. He writes:

> In all eternity it is impossible for me to compel a person to accept an opinion, a conviction, a belief. But one thing I can do: I can compel him to take notice. In one sense this is the first thing; for it is the condition antecedent to the next thing, i.e., the acceptance of an opinion, a conviction, a belief. In another sense it is the last—if, that is, he will not take the next step.[42]

How does one do this? How do we compel someone to take notice? Kierkegaard says that one must be *indirect*, that one might have to use 'deception'. The reason for this, Kierkegaard argues, is that *direct* communication is often almost impossible. If the individual whom one wishes to have take notice is to be affected by our utterances, he must first be receptive to our communications. Often, however, his ability to receive is disturbed. In such cases, Kierkegaard states, we must resort to deception. What does he mean when he speaks of deception? 'It means that one does not begin *directly* with the matter one wants to communicate,' Kierkegaard tells us, 'but begins by accepting the other man's illusion as good money'.[43] If one is concerned with Christianity, 'one does not begin thus: It is Christianity I am proclaiming; and you are living in purely aesthetic categories. No, one begins thus: Let us talk about aesthetics. The deception consists in the fact that one talks thus merely to get to the religious theme.'[44] In a sense, much of Kierkegaard's own writing was concerned with a kind of 'psychological warfare' where he experimented with a variety of vehicles and modes of expression: direct and indirect communication, existential reflection, Christian sermons and dialectic lyric.

With regard specifically to Kierkegaard's emphasis on indirect communication and deception, one wonders whether such devices are used by scientists in trying to get the attention of the scientific audience. In this connection, Feyerabend in his controversial 'Against Method' speaks of the necessity of propaganda and psychological tricks.[45] Further, he endorses the importance of something very much akin to Kierkegaard's getting people to take notice. Feyerabend writes:

> Extreme positions are of extreme value. They induce the reader to think along different lines. They break his conformist habits. They are strong instruments for the criticism of what is established and well received. On the other hand, the current infatuation with 'syntheses' and 'dialogues' which are defended in the spirit of tolerance and of understanding can only lead to an end of all tolerance and of all understanding.[46]

Mitroff's Apollo moon study provides evidence of the operation of 'extreme positions' among scientists. His research found that, contrary to the norms of science as usually set forth, 'Every one of the scientists . . . indicated that they thought the notion of the objective emotionally disinterested scientist naive'.[47] Among the interview data which Mitroff reports are examples of scientists getting other scientists' to 'take notice'. One scientist is quoted as saying: 'If you make neutral statements, nobody really listens to you. You have to stick your neck out. The statements you make in public are actually stronger than you believe in. You have to get people to remember that you represent a point of view even if for you it's just a possibility.'[48] Another says that: 'In order to be heard you have to overcommit yourself,'[49] and a third states that 'there's so much stuff in the system that if one wants to be heard over the crowd, one must adopt a position more extreme than one believes in'.[50]

There are, in addition to direct communication, then, several other ways of getting the reader's (or the scientific community's) attention. One is by what Kierkegaard calls 'indirect' communication, where the writer initially introduces one topic or theme in order to get the reader's attention before moving on to the topic or theme of direct importance to him. Another is to adopt an extreme position in order to break the reader's usual habits of thought. This 'extreme' position might be formulated by use of extreme (polemical or highly emotive) speech, or by a highly unusual viewpoint (blue cheese is the basic element of the universe). Still another way of getting the reader to take notice is through the use of quotations.

Quotations appear to serve as a way of getting the scientific community's attention, or perhaps more properly of keeping their attention. By quoting the words of other writers or scientists one shows that the topic is legitimate, that is, it has been given attention by others. Of course, not all 'others' are equal when it comes to trying to get the reader to take notice (and treat seriously) the individual scientist's arguments. Thus, Newton, Galileo, Kierkegaard, Feyerabend and Kuhn, among others, are quoted here as writers who have considered the issues under consideration—even though other, lesser-known individuals may have expressed exactly the same viewpoints. Quoting shows that the writer and his audience share a similar background, similar values, a feeling of community, that is, it helps to link them within a tradition. Footnotes and references, as well as quotations, may serve to create the impression that a topic is important. The general significance of *whom* one quotes or cites is revealed in studies which show how various opinions are differentially evaluated, depending on the sources from whom they are described as coming.[51]

The above discussion is not intended to be an exhaustive treatment of the various discursive means by which a scientist attempts to convince the scientific community of the correctness of his position. The point is that *communication* between the individual and his audience is an important, though neglected, element in scientific practice. While positivistic science has tried to create a fully public, standardised way of speaking, I do not see how this is either possible or desirable. We may praise or criticise the importance of rhetoric and argumentation in science, but we cannot ignore them. Not only the *what* but also the *how* of a written (or spoken) argument needs to be recognised as a factor in the settling of truth- and knowledge-claims. The article, the essay, the monograph, the book, is a carrot on a string. And the reader/audience/scientific community's decision to eat the carrot involves a heavy dependence on rhetoric and argumentation.

Science involves more than just logical thinking and demonstration. More specifically, the context of justification, where truth-claims are settled, is not merely a matter of following correct rules and procedures, for the reader/audience is always involved. The individual scientist must convince the audience of the merit of his views, and for this he must rely on language. Generally we recognise the crucial place of language for the novelist, the poet, the playwright. Samuel Beckett, who was almost obsessed with the use and character of language, wrote: 'Among those whom we call great artists, I can think of none whose concern was not predominantly with his expressive possibilities, those of his vehicle, those of humanity.'[52] But the scientist, too, may often have to search for a means of communication or expressive possibilities for conveying 'world-views' or 'ways of seeing' that were not a subject for communication before. And, it seems obvious, it is not simply that words are to be employed. Of critical importance is *how* they are put together. The scientist, like the artist, must get the reader/audience to pay attention. And, again like the artist, he may enable us to experience situations and possibilities which we might not have experienced otherwise.

Language and writing

Let us consider this matter further by turning to two men who are directly concerned with language and writing: Roland Barthes and William Gass. In a recent article entitled 'Authors and Writers', Barthes states:

> The author performs a function, the writer an activity. Not that the author is a pure essence; he acts, but his action is immanent in its object, it is performed paradoxically on its own instrument: language. The author is a man who *labors*, who *works up* his utterance (even if he is inspired) and functionally absorbs himself in this labor, this work.[53]

Barthes goes on to stress that an author is a man who wants to be an author, while

> The writer, on the other hand, is a 'transitive' man: he posits a goal (to give evidence, to explain, to instruct) of which language is merely a means; for him language supports a *praxis*, it does not constitute one. Thus language is restored to the nature of an instrument of communication, a vehicle of thought.[54]

And, further,

> . . . the author's language is a merchandise offered through traditional channels, it is the unique object of an institution created only for literature; the writer's language, on the contrary, can be produced and consumed only in the shadow of institutions which have, originally, an entirely different function than to focus on language: the university, scientific and scholarly research, politics, etc.[55]

Barthes, it can be seen, lays heavy stress on the *differences* between the author (the novelist, the poet) and the writer (the scientist, the intellectual).

William Gass, on the other hand, points to some of the *similarities* between the use of language by the author and the writer, or more specifically between the author of fiction and the scientist. Gass speaks of the novelist constructing a world that is always a metaphorical model of our own. Gass writes:

> Hamlet, Horatio, and Marcellus walk upon the castle platform awaiting midnight and Hamlet's father's ghost. Hamlet says, 'The air bites shrewdly; it is very cold,' and Horatio answers, 'It is a nipping and an eager air'. Hamlet and Horatio do not think of it as cold, simply. The dog of air's around them, shrewd and eager, running at heels. The behavior of this dog is wittily precise in their minds. It nags—shrewishly, wifelike. . . . The nature of the weather is conveyed to us with marvelous exactitude and ease, in remarks made by the way, far from the center of action; so that we find ourselves with knowledge of it in just the off-hand way we would if, bent on meeting a king's ghost, we too went through the sharp wind. Yet Hamlet's second clause—'it is very cold'—is useless. 'The air bites shrewdly' is the clause that tells us everything. It is cold. The wind is out. The wind is alive, malevolent with wise jaws. The two clauses have a very clear relation. The first is metaphorical, the second literal. Both are about the weather; but one is art, the other not.[56]

Gass's point is that, through the use of metaphor, Shakespeare has communicated to us the nature of the weather. Of course, the nature of the weather can also be communicated more 'scientifically': the temperature was ten degrees and the wind-force five. But, Gass says, 'I think it will be obvious to anyone who fairly examines the meaning of Shakespeare's langauge that it renders the weather with a precision quite equal to the precision of the scientific, although the scientific precision is of a different kind'.[57]

The scientist works within an abstract, well-ordered, formal scheme, while the author has the task of forcing the reader to *infer* the same phenomenon reached by scientific language. But Gass emphasises that both the scientist and the artist view the transactions and phenomena of life through the lens of concepts. Just as the scientist constructs models, so, says Gass, does the author. Metaphors, he argues, represent a kind of model-making in terms of system, presentation and inference.[58] It would seem hard to deny that metaphors play an important part in the communication between a writer and his audience. Consider 'We must all hang together or we shall all hang separately', or the famous 'invisible hand' metaphor of Adam Smith: 'He intends only his own gain, and he is, in this, as in many other cases, led by an invisible hand to promote an end which was not part of his intention.'[59]

Metaphors, then, are one of the devices involved in argumentation, but there are many other devices which may also be found in the communication between an author or writer (including the scientist) and his audience. One of these, of course, is the technical language of the community in which one shares membership. But we should not forget that many technical terms are borrowed from everyday language (mass, force, role, status, and so on) and may therefore set off different resonances in different readers. In addition, there are arguments *ad hominem* and *ad personam*, the use of epithets, repetition, amplification and, as noted earlier, quotation. Further, there is humour, irony, riddles, silence, comparisons and contrasts, examples, illustrations and analogies.

I have tried to show that argumentation (including the use of metaphor, analogy, and so on) is an alternative to the heavy emphasis on demonstration, where definitive, unquestionable truths constitute the starting-point for scientific communication and intersubjectivity. But argumentation is more than an alternative, for it is difficult to conceive of communication among scientists which does not (often unknowingly) involve certain aspects of argumentation. Some of the consequences of argumentation are spelled out by Perelman and Olbrechts-Tyteca in the final passage of their book, *The New Rhetoric*:

> Only the existence of an argumentation that is neither compelling nor arbitrary can give meaning to human freedom, a state in which a reasonable choice can be exercised. If freedom was no more than necessary adherence to a previously given natural order, it would exclude all possibility of choice; and if the exercise of freedom were not based on reasons, every choice would be irrational and would be reduced to an arbitrary decision operating in an intellectual void. It is because of the possibility of argumentation which provides reasons, that it is possible to escape the dilemma: adherence to an objectivity and universally valid truth, or recourse to suggestion and violence to secure acceptance for our opinions and decisions.[60]

Argumentation rejects the positivist ideal of correct method and scientific certainty, and rehabilitates an emphasis on opinion and individual responsibility. The individual scientist who advances a new possibility, a new way of looking, a new world-view, has the task of finding the arguments that will enable him to gain their acceptance. Thus these arguments must not only meet the scientist's own self-constituted judgements but—to constitute scientific knowledge or truth—must also hold good for the scientific community whom he addresses.

Like the author, the scientist attempts to hand along to the reader/ audience a story, a mood, a vision, a way of looking. We are often told, of course, that art appeals primarily to the senses and science to the intellect, but both art and science are concerned with striking a responsive chord in the reader. Joseph Conrad's remarks about the novelist seem equally applicable to the communication between the scientist and the scientific audience to whom he addresses his arguments: 'My task which I am trying to achieve is, by the power of the written word, to make you hear, to make you feel—it is, before all, to make you *see*. That—and no more, and it is everything.'[61]

Implicit throughout these pages is my assumption that communication among scientists not only involves playing the language-game of one or another science or technical speciality but also involves a dependence on one or another everyday language. That is, there is not only the extraordinary (formal) language of the particular science but also ordinary language. Positivists often fail to recognise that the use of an extraordinary language in scientific communication rests upon ordinary language, and is therefore by itself not sufficient for intersubjective communication in the full sense of these words. They forget that an understanding of ordinary language has already to be presupposed in scientific discourse. There is a meta-language of understanding which is presupposed in all scientific language and communication. Furthermore, there is—most especially in the social sciences—a mixture of scientific and everyday language in scientific writings and utterances. In short, communication between scientists must involve not only the language-game of physics, biology or sociology, but other language-games as well. Wittgenstein teaches that one man cannot be said to be following a rule, and this is true in science as elsewhere. But he also teaches that men can and do follow a variety of rules in different language-games, and that language-games overlap. There is, he noted in his later work, *no universal language* which guarantees complete understanding and communication.

In this chapter I have considered possibilities and their survival power. Further I have argued that communication between the individual scientist and the scientific community to whom he directs his knowledge- and truth-claims involves a considerable degree of persuasion, and that ordinary language is a crucial element in the process of persuasion. If one accepts my general line of argumentation (if one is persuaded), this leads to an obvious question. Given competing possibilities—including the possible view of scientific communication sketched out above—how is the individual to choose, to locate certainties, to ground the ways in which he practises science and lives his life? This I consider in the following chapter.

9 Doubt and Certainty

The *truth* of certain empirical propositions belongs to our frame of reference.

LUDWIG WITTGENSTEIN[1]

If I have exhausted the justifications I have reached bedrock, and my spade is turned.

LUDWIG WITTGENSTEIN[2]

In the previous chapter I suggested that scientists can be seen as formulating alternative world-views or 'possibilities'. These possibilities constitute new ways of creating and looking at particular worlds: the worlds of social, psychological, biological, chemical or physical phenomena. Further, I have argued that for a world-view or possibility to constitute 'scientific' knowledge or truth, it is necessary that it be warranted as knowledge or truth by particular groups of people who form scientific communities. The process by which truth- and knowledge-claims are granted scientific status, I have emphasised, involves persuasion, which itself relies heavily on argumentation and rhetoric.

While my standpoint is obviously influenced by those contemporary writers who have pointed to the social character of scientific practice—Kuhn, Hanson, Feyerabend, Toulmin—my position differs from theirs in that I am more explicitly concerned with the *individual* scientist and his relationships with his scientific community. I acknowledge that what he 'knows/believes' may be at odds with, or unacceptable to, the scientific community. There are times, that is, when the individual practitioner is unable to secure the community-based agreement or certainty which will attach the 'knowledge' or 'truth' label to his claims. This means that what the individual scientist regards as firm or acceptable for himself may not have achieved the status of 'scientific'

199

knowledge or truth. But it also means that there may be community-warranted knowledge which the individual finds difficult to accept, although this obviously does not alter its status as scientific. In short, there may be conflicts between the individual scientist and the scientific community.

The conception of scientific practice sketched out in this volume, however, leads to two important problems. Prior to considering these problems, I will briefly review the general framework within which I have considered scientific practice. Following Wittgenstein, I have argued that we can only 'grasp reality' through the various descriptions and classificatory mechanisms afforded by language. Since there are differing cultural and scientific traditions, and therefore a variety of languages (and language-games), there are also differing accounts of reality. Consequently, the notion of 'objective, mind-independent reality' is called into question and rejected, in that we never encounter reality *an sich* (whatever that may be) but rather *our* reality. But 'our' reality, our world—including our scientific knowledge and truth—is a public and not a private or individual matter. As I indicated in my earlier discussion of 'seeing' (chapter 5), whatever we experience is always experienced from the perspective of one or another conceptual viewpoint (language-game). Our categorical frameworks constitute a social reality; they are publicly shared sets of concepts which are social creations. All of this, of course, is in direct opposition to those conceptions of objectivity and bias which concern themselves with the world and its contents as 'they really are'. If there is, as I have argued, no mind-independent reality to be known but only reality as viewed from the vantage-point of a particular perspective, then it is senseless to say, for example: 'I want to know about the world itself—actually and objectively—not just from this or that perspective, but as it *really* is.' For, in my view, the notion of the world as it 'really' is does not represent a viable idea; each and every description of the world must be offered or presented from one or another perspective. One simply cannot talk about what the world really is except from some framework of identification and description. What I have just said about the world, I have previously discussed in terms of the vocabularies and objectives of scientific inquiry. This is not to say that I am arguing that our knowledge of the world is in some way 'subjective' rather than 'objective'. Instead, I am rejecting the conception of objectivity as correspondence with some mind-independent, and therefore mind-inaccessible, reality in itself. Rather, I conceive of objectivity as that which meets public, intersubjective standards for warranting objectivity in particular scientific communities. In science, as elsewhere, language is the vehicle of interpersonal communication which determines what counts as objective, as truth, as reality, as constituting knowledge.

The conception of reality and science outlined in earlier chapters, however, leads to a pair of problems. First, what validates the view of reality and science set forth in this volume? After all, I cannot argue that my view corresponds to 'true' or 'authentic' reality, to the way things 'really' are. And, second, if there are indeed a variety of lan-gauge-games, with different standards for truth and knowledge, does this not call into question *all* conceptions of truth and knowledge? Does it not lead to a scepticism where absolutely nothing is certain, where nothing can be known? These two problems are not entirely independent of each other, and I will therefore consider the first only briefly, touching upon it again when I move to the second problem.

I have acknowledged that the conception of science and reality which I have put forward is a 'possibility'; it is one way of looking at and talking about the world. In this sense my position differs not only from the dominant view of sociological inquiry but also from the position of ethnomethodologists like Garfinkel and Sachs.[3] In common with most ethnomethodologists, they are concerned with the 'dis-covery' of underlying patterns, regularities, and the like. For example, Garfinkel says that his research is directed towards 'discovering the formal properties of commonplace, practical commonsense actions'.[4] And both Garfinkel and Wilson speak of the importance of documen-tary interpretation, which 'consists of identifying an underlying pat-tern behind a series of appearances such that each appearance is seen as referring to, an expression of, or a 'document' of, the underlying pattern'.[5] Ethnomethodologists assume that by becoming self-conscious about their own research procedures and language-use, and by utilising some sort of methodological reduction, they can gain objective know-ledge of the 'true' nature of social phenomena.[6] In short, they claim an epistemologically privileged position.

Consistent with the general argument of this volume, I refuse to claim that I have been providing a concrete description of scientific practice. Nonetheless, I have attempted to persuade you (my reader) of the desirability of viewing things my way. Is this because I wish to alert you to your 'false consciousness', to show you that you are 'mistaken' in your conception of the world and, more specifically, of scientific practice? No, of course not. For if I wish to avoid exempting myself from my own thesis, I cannot meaningfully speak of false consciousness or mistakes here—as if I had some privileged access to reality (as the ethnomethodologists claim) and could compare the way things 'really' are with your false and mistaken (earthly) views. No, I must in the final analysis rest content with my *commitment* to a conception which I find more comfortable, pleasing, liberating or useful *for me*. That is to say, I choose to live my life in terms of a framework which I can accept applying to myself and my own actions as well as to the actions of others. In short, I prefer the view of reality and science outlined in earlier chapters to the usual positivistic view where my actions—like those of other persons, if we are to be consistent—are completely subject to scientific laws, to deterministic (causal) influences which rob me of any freedom or responsibility. Still, it might be suggested that my response as to the desirability of this particular possibility as opposed to other possibilities is equivocal. For, it might be argued, there must be some solidity, certainty or firmly held beliefs which underlie my commitment to a whole variety of actions in my life. By rejecting the usual scientific assumption that rationality and science are totally governed by considerations of what is real, what can be explained, what can be predicted, I opt for the viewpoint that *praxis* is for me (and many others) the arbiter of theory. In much of my life it is what works, what allows me to find my way about in the world, that underlies my commitment to one rather than another possible way of viewing things. This means, then, a rejection not only of the view that there is *a* reality but also of the sceptical viewpoint that *nothing* is certain, that nothing stands fast for me.

Doubt and certainty

Here, as elsewhere in this volume, I draw heavily on Wittgenstein. Let us now consider his views on these matters. In his posthumously published *On Certainty*, Wittgenstein focuses on problems of epistemology or theory of knowledge.[7] He concerns himself with trying to explain how we know what we know and how we justify our beliefs. Throughout this work, Wittgenstein is involved in a three-cornered debate with two adversaries: Descartes and G. E. Moore, although the first is never mentioned by name. For Descartes, mathematical necessity was seen as the epitome of knowledge and certainty. True knowledge had to be backed either by fully incorrigible, self-authenticating data, or else by demonstrations as rigorous as those of mathematics. Descartes was concerned with the question of how an individual thinker could arrive at valid ideas or truths. Of course,

Descartes saw the task of the scientist as discovering the 'true structure' of the world. The fundamental maxim for Descartes was that of 'systematic doubt': distinguishing what is solid and reliable from what is lacking in these qualities. This was necessary, he emphasised, in order to establish a firm foundation on which science could be built. Descartes demanded certainty so that human knowledge could be reconstructed in such a manner that it should embody the certainty previously possessed only by mathematical knowledge. As part of this demand for certainty, he systematically undertook to doubt all those judgements which he had heretofore believed to be true. The goal was to see which of these judgements were beyond doubt. He began by doubting the existence of material things, like the earth, the sun, his own body and hands. He advanced three reasons for these doubts: he had been deceived by his senses in the past; he could never be certain that he was not dreaming; and, finally, perhaps he was being deceived by a cruel and evil spirit. Descartes concluded that two of his judgements were indeed beyond doubt: that there must exist a Perfect Being; and that in so far as a person thinks, he must exist. He felt that he had established the existence of a benevolent God. This was beyond doubt, as was his consciousness of his own mental states and processes.[8]

Descartes' sceptical doubts have given rise in succeeding generations to considerable philosophical discussion and controversy. One of those who expressed dissatisfaction with Descartes' arguments was Wittgenstein's Cambridge colleague, G. E. Moore.[9] It was Moore's claim that certain things were beyond doubt and were known with certainty. Among these were propositions like: 'Here is one hand and here is another,' 'The earth existed for a long time before my birth'. These kinds of propositions, Moore argued, proved the existence of the 'external world'. For him, such propositions had the same epistemological status as mathematical propositions. Although Moore felt that he had successfully refuted the sceptic's argument as formulated by Descartes, Wittgenstein tried to show that both Moore and the sceptic were mistaken about the nature of doubt, certainty and knowledge.

Among those few works where Wittgenstein's concern with epistemology is explored systematically, Kenny's recent volume is the best.[10] I will draw heavily on it in the next several pages. Kenny points to five theses regarding doubt in Wittgenstein's *On Certainty*: (1) doubt needs grounds; (2) doubt must amount to something more than just verbal utterances of doubt; (3) doubt presupposes the mastery of a language-game; (4) doubt ouside a language-game, or about a whole language-game, is impossible; and (5) doubt presupposes certainty.[11]

Doubt needs grounds. Here Wittgenstein partially agreed with Descartes, who invented the evil genius who might constantly mislead us. But whereas Descartes held that even an uncertain ground for doubting may create doubt, Wittgenstein felt that the mere imaginability of doubt is not sufficient. The grounds for doubt must also in some sense be reasonable. He writes: 'So rational suspicion must have grounds? We might also say: "the reasonable man believes this".'[12] Or consider the following:

> 'I know that I am a human being.' In order to see how unclear the sense of this proposition is, consider its negation. At most it might be taken to mean 'I know I have the organs of a human'. (E.g. a brain which, after all, no one has yet ever seen.) But what about such a proposition as 'I know I have a brain'? Can I doubt it? Grounds for *doubt* are lacking! Everything speaks in its favour, nothing against it. Nevertheless it is imaginable that my skull should turn out empty when it was operated on.[13]

In other words, while we can conceive of a person not having a brain, for instance, the existence of a brain connects up with so much else that grounds for doubt are lacking. If someone walks and talks and makes decisions, doubt about his having a brain can get no foothold with us.

Doubt must amount to something. Descartes' doubt was speculative, but Wittgenstein is concerned with its *practical* consequences as well. Speaking of the question as to whether or not the table is still there when no one sees it, he asks: 'But if anyone were to doubt it, how would his doubt come out in practice? And couldn't we peacefully leave him to doubt it, since it makes no difference at all?'[14] And later Wittgenstein says:

> For suppose a person of normal behaviour assured us that he only *believed* his name was such-and-such, he *believed* he recognized the people he regularly lived with, he believed that he had hands and feet when he didn't actually see them, and so on. Can we show him it is not so from the things he does (and says)?[15]

As we shall see later, Wittgenstein lays heavy stress on what man 'does and says' as important for the whole question of doubt and certainty.

Doubt presupposes the mastery of a language-game. This is one of the central themes running through Wittgenstein's later work. As he points out, even to doubt that *p*, one must first understand what is *meant* by saying that *p*. One must be certain of what the words mean. 'If you are not certain of any fact,' Wittgenstein notes, 'you cannot be certain of the meaning of your words either'.[16] Carried to its logical extreme, then, Cartesian doubt destroys itself; the words used to express doubt are themselves called into question. Wittgenstein pursues this line of thought further, saying:

> If I wanted to doubt whether this was my hand, how could I avoid doubting whether the word 'hand' has any meaning? So there is something I seem to *know* after all.[17]
>
> If, therefore, I doubt or am uncertain about this being my hand (in whatever sense), why not in that case about the meaning of these words as well?[18]

Doubt, Wittgenstein holds, presupposes that there is no doubt about the language-game in which the doubt is expressed. One can only express doubts from within the certainty residing in the nature of the language-game.[19] Further, the very nature of a language-game may exclude doubts about certain matters. There is simply nothing in the language-games which I play that will *count* as my doubting whether I exist or whether I was born.

Universal doubt is impossible. 'A doubt that doubted everything would not be a doubt,' Wittgenstein says.[20] Doubts always belong within particular language-games. Wittgenstein illustrates his point with the following example:

> A pupil and a teacher. The pupil will not let anything be explained to him, for he continually interrupts with doubts, for instance as to the existence of things, the meaning of words, etc. The teacher says 'Stop interrupting me and do as I tell you. So far your doubts don't make any sense at all.'
>
> Or imagine that the boy questioned the truth of history (and everything that connects up with it)—and even whether the earth has existed at all a hundred years before.
>
> Here it strikes me as if this doubt were hollow. But in that case— isn't *belief* in history hollow too? No; there is so much that connects up with it.[21]

The pupil has not learned how to ask questions, he has not learned the language-game which we are trying to teach him. Doubt depends on the existence of belief: 'The child learns by believing the adult. Doubt comes *after* belief.'[22]

Doubt presupposes certainty. Time and time again, Wittgenstein emphasises that doubt is parasitic upon certainty:

> If you tried to doubt everything you would not get as far as doubting anything. The game of doubting itself presupposes certainty.[23]

> Admittedly, if you are obeying the order 'Bring me a book', you may have to check whether the thing you see over there really is a book, but then you do at least know what people mean by 'book'; and if you don't you can look it up,—but then you must know what some other word means. And the fact that a word means such-and-such, is used in such-and-such a way, is in turn an empirical fact, like the fact that what you see over there is a book.
>
> Therefore, in order for you to be able to carry out an order there must be some empirical fact about which you are not in doubt. Doubt itself rests only on what is beyond doubt.
>
> But since a language-game is something that consists in the recurrent procedures of the game in time, it seems impossible to say in an *individual* case that such-and-such must be beyond doubt if there is to be a language-game—though it is right enough to say that *as a rule* some empirical judgment or other must be beyond doubt.[24]

Wittgenstein indicates that it is impossible to state definitively what particular elements must everywhere and for all time be beyond doubt. But there can be no language-games-unless *some* things are exempt from doubt. Only by being certain about some things can we raise doubts about others. That is, it is the grammar of the language-game, and not experience, which excludes doubt. It is not because I am acquainted with my own experiences from the 'inside', as it were, that I am certain about this or that. The criterion of certainty is laid down in the grammar of the language-game.

Mistakes

According to Wittgenstein, every language-game rules out certain doubts. To say that something cannot be doubted is not necessarily, however, to say that it is *known*. I will consider this shortly, but first we must examine Wittgenstein's treatment of 'mistakes' and other false beliefs. What is crucial about a mistake is that it is something that can be pointed out and, in principle, corrected:

> 'I cannot be making a mistake about the fact that I have just had lunch.'
>
> For if I say to someone 'I have just eaten' he may believe that I am lying or have momentarily lost my wits but he won't believe that I am making a mistake. Indeed, the assumption that I might be making a mistake has no meaning here.
>
> But that isn't true. I might, for example, have dropped off immediately after the meal without knowing it and have slept for an hour, and now believe I had just eaten.[25]

In the case of the above, then—where perhaps someone did fall asleep right after lunch—the mistake could be acknowledged and corrected. There are all kinds of things about which we are sure which nevertheless allow for mistakes: a friend's telephone number, the name of a hotel, the date of Wittgenstein's birth, the winner of the last World Series or World Cup. Mistakes, however, imply that there are recognised and accepted sources or authorities which allow us to correct them (telephone books, encyclopedias, World Almanacs, experts). I can make many mistakes, as can others, without there being a total loss of faith in my judgements. But there are other false beliefs besides mistakes. Wittgenstein considers mental disturbances:

> For months I have lived at Address A, I have read the name of the street and the number of the house countless times, have received countless letters here and given countless people the address. If I am wrong about it, the mistake is hardly less than if I were (wrongly) to believe that I was writing Chinese and not German.
>
> If my friend were to imagine one day that he had been living for a long time past in such and such a place, etc. etc., I should not call this a *mistake*, but rather a mental disturbance, perhaps a transient one.[26]

> If someone said to me that he doubted whether he had a body I should take him to be a half-wit. But I shouldn't know what it would mean to try to convince him that he had one. And if I had said something, and that had removed his doubt, I should not know how or why.[27]

There is a difference, Wittgenstein shows, between mistakes and madness. Whereas mistakes involve fasle judgements which can in

principle be corrected, madness involves judgements against which
nothing could serve as evidence to the contrary.

But the impossibility of mistakes does not necessarily imply madness.
Like Moore, Wittgenstein formulates several propositions where doubt
and mistakes are impossible. Speaking of Moore's propositions, Wittgenstein says:

> We don't for example, arrive at any of them as a result of investiga-
> tion.
>
>   There are e.g. historical investigations and investigations into the
> shape and also the age of the earth, but not into whether the earth
> has existed during the last hundred years. Of course many of us
> have information about this period from our parents and grand-
> parents; but mayn't they be wrong?—'Nonsense!' one will say.
> 'How should all these people be wrong?'—But is that an argument?
> Is it not simply the determination of a concept? For if I speak of
> a possible mistake here, this changes the role of 'mistake' and 'truth'
> in our lives.
>
>   I, L. W., believe, am sure, that my friend hasn't sawdust in his
> body or in his head, even though I have no direct evidence of my
> senses to the contrary. I am sure, by reason of what has been said
> to me, of what I have read, and of my experience. To have doubts
> about it would seem to me madness—of course, this is also in agree-
> ment with other people; but I agree with them.[28]

The point here is that there are propositions or convictions that constitute a system or structure, and individual propositions may not be
(are not) doubted because they are part of the system wherein a host
of propositions give one another mutual support.[29] Wittgenstein remarks:

> Might I not believe that once, without knowing it, perhaps in a
> state of unconsciousness, I was taken far away from the earth—that
> other people even know this, but do not mention it to me? But this
> would not fit into the rest of my convictions at all. Not that I could
> describe the system of these convictions. Yet my convictions do form
> a system, a structure.[30]

Mistakes and knowledge

I alluded briefly above to Wittgenstein's thesis that the absence of
doubt about something does not necessarily mean that we *know* it. It

is important to recall in the discussion that follows, however, that Wittgenstein is contrasting 'knowing' as it is used in our everyday language and as it is used in the language-game of philosophy. 'What I am aiming at,' he says, 'is also found in the difference between the casual observation "I know that that's a . . .", as it might be used in ordinary life and the same utterance when a philosopher makes it.'[31] Wittgenstein does not deny that in their everyday discourse people may claim 'to know' this or that, and that those claims are perfectly correct within those language-games. But in doing philosophy or science, one is playing a different language-game with different rules. If an individual says, for example, that he 'knows' that Blacks are innately inferior to whites or that Brand X gives him more energy than Brand Y, he is saying something different—playing a different language-game—from what would be the case if the same assertions were made by a geneticist or a chemist. Of course, as we have noted earlier, language-games do overlap, and it is not always clear what language-game is being played at a particular time. Or, perhaps more correctly, it is not always clear which of several language-games takes precedence for us at a given moment. The overlap of different language-games will be obvious in what follows.

In the *Philosophical Investigations*, Wittgenstein asserts: 'It can't be said of me at all (except perhaps as a joke) that I *know* I am in pain. What is it supposed to mean, except that I *am* in pain?'[32] For Wittgenstein, statements like 'I know I am in pain' and 'I know I have a toothache' are either nonsense or else mean exactly the same as 'I am in pain' and 'I have a toothache'. The reason they are nonsense is that it makes no sense to ask 'How do you know that you are in pain?' or 'How do you know that you have a toothache?' That is, it is senseless for someone to doubt whether he is having a given experience. If there is no room for doubt, there is no room for certainty. And without certainty, there is no sense of speaking of knowledge. Wittgenstein says: 'I know = I am familiar with it as a certainty.'[33]

Recall that I earlier stated that, for Wittgenstein, being certain does not mean that one cannot make a mistake. Similarly with knowledge; there must be some means of verification. It is not the *absence* of doubt that is crucial here, but the *senselessness* of doubt. Wittgenstein asserts: ' "I know" often means: I have the proper grounds for my statement. So if the other person is acquainted with the language-game, he would admit that I know. The other, if he is acquainted with the language-game, must be able to imagine *how* one may know something of the kind.' One can only use 'I know' for those sentences where one can also use 'I believe', 'I surmise' or 'I doubt'.[34] But, Wittgenstein says, it is nonsense for someone to say 'I believe that I am in pain', 'I surmise that I am in pain' or 'I doubt that I am in pain'. Therefore it follows that 'I know I am in pain' is also nonsense. *Knowledge*, in short, *is possible only when errors or mistakes are conceivable*, where doubt makes sense. Hence one cannot 'know' that one has a pain or a tooth-ache—although he can know that someone else has them. In Wittgenstein's words: 'Whether I *know* something depends on whether the evidence backs me up or contradicts me. For to say one knows one has a pain means nothing.'[35]

Let us now consider the Moore-type propositions which sup-posedly served to refute scepticism. Moore uses propositions where he knows things that presumably we all know as well: Moore 'knows' that the earth existed long before his birth, that he has two hands, that he has never been far from the earth's surface. Wittgenstein asks: 'Why doesn't Moore produce as one of the things that he knows, for example, that in such-and-such a part of England there is a village called so-and-so? In other words: why doesn't he mention a fact that is known to him and not to *every one* of us?'[36] When Moore says that 'I know' this or 'I know' that, he is mistaken in thinking that he is making a personal statement about himself. Wittgenstein examines the difference between 'I know . . .' and 'That is . . .':

> 'I know what kind of tree that is.—It is a chestnut.'
> 'I know what kind of tree that is.—I know it's a chestnut.'
>
> The first statement sounds more natural than the second. One will only say 'I know' a second time if one wants especially to emphasize certainty; perhaps to anticipate being contradicted. The first 'I know' means roughly: I can say.
>
> But in another case one might begin with the observation 'that's a . . .', and then, when this is contradicted, counter by saying: 'I know what sort of a tree that is,' and by this means lay emphasis on being sure.[37]

The point here is that 'I know' or, for that matter, 'We know' is meaningful only when stated by human beings (it would be meaning-less under ordinary circumstances, for example, to have an imper-sonal sign in a forest reading 'I know that this is a tree' or 'We know that this is a chestnut'). Under certain circumstances, it is a matter of indifference whether what is stated is 'I know' or 'that is'.[38] Witt-genstein asks 'What is the proof that I know something?' and answers 'Most certainly not my saying I know it'.[39]

Wittgenstein, then, raises questions both about the special place of 'I' in the assertion 'I know' and, as noted earlier, the general meaning of 'I know' itself. For, to repeat, 'I know' only makes sense when 'I am not sure', 'I doubt', 'I will test it', and so on, also make sense. Wittgenstein points out that: 'The propositions presenting what Moore *'knows'* are all of such a kind that it is difficult to imagine *why* anyone should believe the contrary.'[40] What Moore claims as 'knowledge' is not something that is subject to checking or verification:

> Moore says he *knows* that the earth existed long before his birth. And put like that it seems to be a personal statement about him, even if it is in addition a statement about the physical world. Now it is philosophically uninteresting whether Moore knows this or that, but it is interesting that, and how, it can be known. If Moore had informed us that he knew the distance separating certain states, we might conclude from that that he had made some special investigations, and we shall want to know what those were. But Moore chooses precisely a case in which we all seem to know the same as he, and without being able to say how. I believe e.g. that I know as much about this matter (the existence of the earth) as Moore does, and if he knows that it is as he says, then I know it too. For it isn't, either, as if he had arrived at his proposition by pursuing some line of thought which, while it is open to me, I have not in fact pursued.[41]

Without 'special investigations', checking, and the like, what Moore claims to 'know' (the existence of the earth or whatever) has no special status as philosophical or scientific knowledge. Moore does 'know' something in the everyday sense of knowing, but not as regards the language-game of philosophy.

'Standing fast'

Wittgenstein's unwillingness to grant the status of knowledge to the Moore-type propositions does not mean, however, that they do not have a rather special status. The kinds of propositions which Moore claimed to know, Wittgenstein prefers to speak of as 'standing fast' or as 'solid' for us:

> Instead of 'I know . . .', couldn't Moore have said: 'It stands fast for me that . . .'? And further: 'It stands fast for me and many others. . . .'[42]

'And isn't that what Moore wants to say, when he says he *knows* all these things?—But is his knowing it really what is in question, and not rather that some of those propositions must be solid for us?[43]

I should like to say: Moore does not *know* what he asserts he knows, but it stands fast for him, as also for me; regarding it as absolutely solid is part of our *method* of doubt and enquiry.[44]

Those propositions which stand fast are, says Wittgenstein, the foundation of the language-games which we play. They are not arrived at, however, by investigation or inquiry. Wittgenstein notes: 'I did not get my picture of the world by satisfying myself of its correctness; nor do I have it because I am satisfied of its correctness. No: it is the inherited background against which I distinguish between true and false.'[45] This inherited background, these foundations, form the basis for all our actions. But it would be wrong to say we 'know' them. What we have, then, is a world-view which constitutes the background against which truth and falsity are distinguished. The world-view itself, however, is not based on grounds, it is just there—like our life.[46]

Our inherited background, our world-view, includes a wide variety of firmly entrenched propositions which are usually unquestioned and taken for granted. They constitute the beginning point of our activities. They may be regarded, Wittgenstein observes, as a kind of mythology.[47] But this mythology is not something that we have been explicitly taught; no, we have learned it purely practically. Those propositions which form our world-view are seen by Wittgenstein as constituting the 'river-bed of thoughts':

The mythology may change back into a state of flux, the river-bed of thoughts may shift. But I distinguish between the movement of the waters of the river-bed and the shift of the bed itself; though there is not a sharp division of the one from the other.[48]

And the bank of that river consists partly of hard rock, subject to no alteration or only to an imperceptible one, partly of sand, which now in one place now in another gets washed away, or deposited.[49]

It seems to me that Wittgenstein is suggesting that the 'waters' in the above represent the language-game of testing, argument, mathematics, science, and so forth. The solid elements represented by the river-bed and the bank of the river are the foundations on which these language-games are built. This can be seen in the following passages:

To say of man, in Moore's sense, that he *knows* something; that what he says is therefore unconditionally the truth, seems wrong to me.— It is the truth only inasmuch as it is an unmoving foundation of his language-games.[50]

We say we know that water boils and does not freeze under such-and-such circumstances. Is it conceivable that we are wrong? Wouldn't a mistake topple all judgment with it? More: what could stand if that were to fall? Might someone discover something that made us say 'It was a mistake'?[51]

Vere we to relinquish our claim that certain things 'stand fast' for .s—that the earth existed before our births, that people die when their eads are cut off, that water boils under certain circumstances, and o on—our whole system of empirical knowledge would collapse. This is not to say, however, that what 'stands fast' for us today will ever change. After all, the flatness of the earth once constituted a oundation in an earlier language-game. Further, we do not acquire ur world-views one proposition at a time, but within a system. Wittenstein remarks:

All testing, all confirmation and disconfirmation of a hypothesis takes place already within a system. And this system is not a more or less arbitrary and doubtful point of departure for all our arguments; no, it belongs to the essence of what we call an argument. The system is not so much the point of departure, as the element in which arguments have their life.[52]

Our world-view, the way we construct and view reality, is an aspect f our history. It can change, but one cannot prove that one world-iew is more 'correct' than another. 'A reason can only be given *within* game,' Wittgenstein says. 'The chain of reasons comes to an end at he limits of the game.'[53] This is, of course, similar to the situation vhere different 'paradigms' (Kuhn) exist in science. The change from Newtonian mechanics to Einsteinian theory was a shift from one vorld-view to another. If two world-views confront one another, there s no external point from which the correctness of one or the other may e judged. Speaking of people who consult an oracle instead of a hysicist, Wittgenstein asks: 'Is it wrong for them to consult an oracle nd be guided by it?—If we call this "wrong" aren't we using our anguage-game as a base from which to *combat* theirs?'[54] We do not ret someone else to accept our world-view by 'proving' to him that ours is correct; rather, we convert him through persuasion.[55] Reason can be given, but 'At the end of reasons comes *persuasion*'.[56]

Now someone might ask: 'Is there, then, no objective truth? Isn' it true or false, for example, that someone has walked on water? Thinking within our system, it is correct to say that no one has eve walked on water. Perhaps investigations have been conducted which reveal that nothing counting as walking on water has ever been ob served. In fact our system of physics forbids it. How could such a thing be possible? Of course, someone else might answer: 'I don't know how it was possible, but I know that it has happened.' But as Wittgenstein says, 'We should feel ourselves intellectually very distant from someone who said this'.[57] Needless to say, if other people have walked on wate (as men have now been on the moon, which was not the case during Wittgenstein's time), then I could correctly say: 'I *know* that I have never walked on water.' I could give grounds for that knowledge But as things now stand, my not having walked on water is as sure a thing for me as any grounds I could give for it.[58] For a proposition to be capable of being true, Wittgenstein insisted, it must also be capable of being false.[59] However, certain propositions, as we have seen, are neither true nor false; instead they 'stand fast' for us. They are, as it were, fossilised empirical propositions which constitute the channels for ordinary, more fluid propositions. Wittgenstein writes:

> The propositions of mathematics might be said to be fossilized.— The proposition 'I am called . . .' is not. But it too is regarded a *incontrovertible* by those who, like myself, have overwhelming evidence for it. And this is not out of thoughtlessness. For, the evidence' being overwhelming consists precisely in the fact that we do not nee to give way before any contrary evidence. And so we have here a buttress similar to the one that makes the propositions of mathematics incontrovertible.
>
> The question 'But mightn't you be in the grip of a delusion now and later find this out?'—might also be raised as an objection to any proposition of the multiplication table.[60]

What would it mean for me later to 'find out' that my name was no really Derek Phillips, that 2×2 was not really 4, that water didn' boil or freeze at certain temperatures, that the earth didn't really exist before I was born? If none of those is capable of standing fast, i indeed I was said to be in the grip of a delusion, what sureness would I have in my own judgement as regards any 'new facts' which are intended to set me straight? If my name is *not* Derek Phillips, how can

I rely on what is meant by 'true' and 'false'? There are certain things which do stand fast, which constitute the inherited background and world-picture, against which I distinguish between true and false. They are fundamental. Someone might ask: 'What if you had to change your opinion on these most fundamental things?' Wittgenstein answers: 'You don't *have* to change it. That is just what their being "fundamental" is.'[61]

Learning and standing fast

Perhaps it is useful here to consider briefly the matter of learning and language-acquisition. How do we acquire those things which are fundamental and stand fast for us? To consider that, we must first face the question of how we acquire language more generally or, rather, how the child does.

Learning a language involves the child's initiation into some sort of framework or world-view about which there is wide agreement. Included in this world-view are what we regard as 'facts of nature' involving, among other things, basic needs (for food, shelter, comfort, and the like) and a certain cognitive apparatus (sense organs, physiological make-up, and the like). The child may have what we consider instincts—sucking, for example. But neither his instincts nor his cognitive apparatus are sufficient to satisfy his basic needs. Quite obviously, the child is dependent on others in his surroundings for his satisfactions and survival. Even so-called 'wolf children' depend on other living organisms for their survival.

In order for the child to encounter certain elements or aspects of his environment, he requires other social beings. Further, these things are not necessarily encountered in such a manner that first this, then that, and so on, are encountered and learned. That is, we need not accept that there must be something that is initially learned (or is programmed into the child as Chomsky believes) which constitutes the knowledge required to go on to the next step in learning.[62] There is not some first rule which he learns prior to and in order to learn further. Wittgenstein points out that the terms 'rules', 'agreement' and 'same' are internally related.[63] Men agree in the language they use, they share a common way of conceptualising experience. But their 'agreement' is not therefore a presupposition of agreement or disagreement in judgements, for agreement in concepts and agreement in judgements are not independent of each other. 'If language is to be a means of communication,' Wittgenstein says, 'there must be agreement not only in definitions but also (queer as this may sound) in judgments.'[64] In other words, it is not sufficient that there should be agreement in definitions and concepts, for this already involves agreement in judgements. They do not stand apart. The child's learning involves learning things together; he learns to connect (and separate) things in his environment. And in doing this he is fully dependent on other social beings. Before the child learns to understand or use language, there has already occurred a considerable amount of communication between the child and his parents. Thus he must first have learned to understand and respond to this non-verbal communication (smiles and frowns, for instance) before he is in a position to acquire language. And his learning to understand these non-verbal communications is not, I believe, due to his being programmed in a certain manner. With the aid of other persons, he learns to connect things. Eventually he comes to acquire language by utilising what he has already learned in the way of communication; he does not acquire linguistic competence by relying on linguistic information alone.

Learning language, like learning anything else, involves training. Wittgenstein emphasises: 'Any explanation has its foundations in training. (Educators ought to remember this.)'[65] In the case of language acquisition, children come to consciousness already, in a sense, united. Behind the child's learning language lies his parents' concern for him. Regarding the use of the word 'pain', Wittgenstein observes: 'Being sure that someone is in pain, doubting whether he is, and so on, are so many natural, instinctive, kinds of behaviour towards other human beings, and our language is merely an auxiliary to, and further extension of, this relation.'[66] A condition of brotherhood or shared human concern is thus prior to one's acquisition of language. Learning something involves, then, a process in which the incorporation of *public* judgements (an established pattern of physical gestures, a spoken language, or whatever) is linked with the thing itself. Rules and their employment are learned together. 'I cannot describe how (in general) to employ rules, except by *teaching* you, *training* you to employ rules.'[67] Wittgenstein continually emphasises that our talk gets its meaning from the rest of our proceedings. The child learns to communicate, to understand, to talk, from others in the environment. Thus, underlying the child's judgement that certain sentences are grammatical, for instance, is the fact that other competent speakers who train the child also judge them to be grammatical. That is, there is 'agreement in judgement' among speakers, allowing for the characterisation of these judgements as claims about language which can be publicly justified. We do not require, therefore, a theory of innate predispositions to account for why someone is able to make correct judgements about whether or not sentences are grammatical. The same holds for other usages and judgements regarding language.

Speaking more generally of those things which are fundamental and stand fast for us, we do not acquire beliefs in single propositions but in systems of propositions. Further, Wittgenstein stresses that: 'We do not learn the practice of making empirical judgments by learning rules: we are taught *judgments* and their connexion with other judgments. A *totality* of judgments is made possible for us.'[68] The child learns to believe a great variety of things. Slowly these things begin to form a system in which some things stand fast and are unshakable. They stand fast, not because they are intrinsically obvious or convincing, but because they are held fast by what lies around them. They give one another mutual support. We do not first learn rules for making judgements and then put them into practice. We often learn judgements along with definitions and concepts. First one learns. Doubt comes later. One must begin with non-doubting, that is part of judging. Wittgenstein writes:

> I am told, for example, that someone climbed this mountain many years ago. Do I always enquire into the reliability of the teller of the story, and whether the mountain did exist years ago? A child learns there are reliable and unreliable informants much later than it learns facts which are told it. It doesn't learn at all that that mountain has existed for a long time: that is, the question whether it is so doesn't arise at all. It swallows this consequence down, so to speak, together with *what* it learns.[69]

Just as when a child is told that someone climbed a certain mountain years ago there is no question of the mountain having existed for a long time, so there are other things that are simply taken for granted, even though they might not have been explicitly taught to us. No one ever taught me that my feet don't disappear when I am not paying attention to them, that I am not carried away to a distant planet during sleep and returned to my bed in the morning, that my great-great-grandparents had parents and lived on the earth. Not only was I never taught these things, but I have never even thought these particular thoughts before, Of course, I was taught many other things: that there are men and women, and that they differ from one another; that there exists a place called China; that dogs can't fly; that every human being has a brain. I learned these by believing my parents and other adults. Doubt, Wittgenstein stresses, comes *after* belief.[70] In this regard, he remarks: 'I learned an enormous amount and accepted it on human authority, and then I found some things confirmed or disconfirmed by my own experience.'[71]

We can and do, of course, test many of those things which we have learned. And sometimes we revise our beliefs, rejecting what we were taught earlier. But testing must always come to an end. Has anyone ever tested whether this typewriter remains in existence when no one is paying attention to it? I read about the life of Wittgenstein, and I may raise questions about certain accounts of it. But I do not ask whether *all* the reports about him are based on lies, forgeries, and the like. After all, in order to test anything I must already presuppose something that is not tested. Something has to be assumed, to stand fast. The difficulty, Wittgenstein points out, is to realise the groundlessness of our believing.[72] There are hypotheses—for instance, that the earth existed a long time before my birth—for which everything seems to speak; the opposite hypothesis has nothing on its side. Certain things stand fast:

> I believe that I have forebears, and that every human being has them. I believe that there are various cities, and, quite generally, in the main facts of geography and history. I believe that the earth is a body on whose surface we move and that it no more suddenly disappears or the like than any other solid body: this table, this house, this tree, etc. If I wanted to doubt the existence of the earth long before my birth, I should have to doubt all sorts of things that stand fast for me.
>
> And that something stands fast for me is not grounded in my stupidity or credulity.[73]

Now, someone may say: 'If everything speaks for certain things, if they stand fast, are they not certainly true?' One may, Wittgenstein says, designate them as such. 'But do they certainly agree with reality, with the facts?' With this question, Wittgenstein warns, you are already going around in a circle.[74] In his words: 'To be sure there is justification; but justification comes to an end.'[75]

Acting and showing

Time and time again, Wittgenstein repeats that giving grounds must come to and end some time. But the end is not an ungrounded proposition; it is an ungrounded way of *acting*.[76] That is, sure evidence is what we *accept* as sure; it is evidence that guides our actions. Acting, then, lies at the bottom of every langauge-game.[77]

Further, a language-game is only possible if one *trusts* something. Speaking of physics, Wittgenstein says:

> I am taught that under *such* circumstances *this* happens. It has been discovered by making the experiment a few times. Not that that would prove anything to us, if it weren't that this experience was surrounded by others which combine with it to form a system. Thus, people did not make experiments just about falling bodies but also about air resistance and all sorts of other things.
>
> But in the end I rely on these experiences, or on the reports of them, I feel no scruples about ordering my own activities in accordance with them.—But hasn't this trust proved itself? So far as I can judge—yes.[78]

This trust has proved itself for Wittgenstein because it *works* for him; the results of experiments in physics guide his actions. We, like Wittgenstein, get to know the nature of physics by employing its results, and we get to know the nature of calculating by learning to calculate. What is important for us is the *practical effects* of our 'belief' in calculation and in physics. It is not that we regard our belief in calculating or physics as sure because it is certainly true, but rather that we accept and act upon the evidence. Of course, there might be people who were never quite certain of those things, but their degree of certainty ('maybe', 'possibly', water will boil over a fire, for instance) is unimportant. What is important is what *difference* it makes in their actions, in their lives. What we know and what stands fast for us comes out in the way we act and speak about the things in question.[79]

Our lives *show* that we know or are certain about various things: that there is a chair over there, a table here, a typewriter in front of me. I tell someone, for example, 'move the chair', 'stand behind the table', 'get your hand off the typewriter', and so on. What I know and what stands fast for me are anchored in all my *questions* and *answers*, in all my actions. I show that I know, and what I know, by drawing its consequences—by showing it in what I say and do. Wittgenstein remarks:

> But how can we *show* someone that we *know* truths, not only about sense-data but also about things? For after all it can't be enough for someone to assure us that *he* knows this.
>
> Well, what must our starting point be if we are to shew it?

We need to shew that even if he never uses the words 'I know . . .', his conduct exhibits the thing we are concerned with.[80]

Imagine the following proposition: 'I know that water placed in a pan on a hot stove will boil.' I have never heard my wife utter these words, although I could imagine a case where she might. But her actions, day in and day out, show this knowledge. They show that she is sure of her ground. From the fact that for many years she has boiled water (always on the stove, never in the refrigerator) shows that she knows. Her actions speak louder than her words, for, as Wittgenstein points out: 'The utterance "I know . . ." can only have its meaning in connection with the other evidence of my "knowing".'[81]

Consider the following. Someone has learned that plants and flowers, like human beings, have feelings, desires and preferences. His commitment to looking at the world in this way is shown by speaking lovingly to his plants, playing soft music for them, or whatever. All serve as evidence of his commitment. Someone else says that he believes in the Last Judgement. He shows his commitment by regulating his life in terms of it. Perhaps he is ill and tells us: 'This is a punishment for my evil ways; God is punishing me.' He accounts for his illness, then, in terms of what he knows to be true. Another person is ill, he has frequent headaches. He tells us that they are due to unresolved sexual conflicts, that he must therefore act to resolve them or see a psychiatrist or change his ways. Someone else—a Marxist social scientist— knows that working-class people suffer from 'false consciousness', and he is striving to awaken their consciousness. Each of these persons shows, in a different way, his or her commitment to one or another belief-system. Often, as Wittgenstein notes, an individual shows the firmness of his beliefs (that is, what stands fast for him) by the *risks* he is willing to take.[82] Dare one offend God, Freud, Marx, one's parents, Weber, Durkheim, one's colleagues, the scientific community? The accompanying feeling of knowing this or that is a matter of indifference. What is important is whether it makes a difference in people's lives— in their commitments and actions, and in the risks they take.

Here we return finally to the individual scientist, standing not alone but as part of a tradition with a history, with a collective set of practices, with a language-game in which certain things stand fast and others are known. He is (we are) committed to a particular set of ideas, a particular possibility or world-view. Thus with our consideration of Lakatos, Feyerabend, Kuhn and Popper in chapter 7, where we encountered 'relativism', 'absolute demarcation criteria', 'third worlds', 'anarchistic epistemology', and the like, we have seen that each of these men is committed to a particular view of scientific practice. And while some of their ideas are grounded in other ideas, eventually the grounding comes to a halt. The difficulty, as Wittgenstein says, is to realise the groundlessness of our believing. We, including those philosophers and historians of science mentioned above and in earlier chapters, justify this idea with that idea, and that with another, and so on. But eventually justifications come to an end. 'If I have exhausted the justifications I have reached bedrock, and my spade is turned. Then I am inclined to say: "This is simply what I do".'[83] The difficulty is to stop.

Of course, it belongs to the logic of all scientific investigations and practices that certain things are not doubted. The writings of Kuhn, Polanyi and Feyerabend, as well as much found in the pages of this volume, exhibit an acceptance of certain things that are beyond doubt for each of us. At the same time, our arguments have the aim of *raising doubts* about much that usually stands beyond doubt in science: that science is cumulative, that scientific observations are theory-neutral, that metaphysical and normative judgements are absent from science, that there are laws and regularities to be discovered 'out there', that theories are in some simple manner tested against observations and data, that all knowledge can be quantified and made explicit, that verification and falsification are explicit scientific processes, and so forth. But many elements of our (Kuhn, Feyerabend, and so on) investigations are themselves not doubted. Not everything can be investigated, and we are each forced to rest content with assumptions. 'If I want the door to turn,' Wittgenstein remarks, 'the hinges must stay put'.[84]

The conceptual scheme developed here is simply one alternative among others. Accordingly its legitimation is not *a priori* and absolute, but rather *a posteriori*. Its merit can only be determined by an open and democratic competition with rival schemes which also have the goal of organising our experiences into a systematised view of science and scientific practice. Will others find it a useful way of conceptualising science? Will it serve to help other persons in the practice of science and in finding their way about in the world? These are the kinds of questions that need to be asked of any conceptual scheme. *Practice*, as I have emphasised, is the arbiter of theory.

Each of us is committed to certain ideas because ultimately these ideas are rooted in how we choose to live our lives. In terms of how I live my life, practise science and write about it, I must make various commitments as to what stands fast and what is certain for me. Some things that others might doubt are 'idle' for me because they do not tie in with anything else in my life. Thus certainty arises because I cannot see where doubt would get a foothold. This certainty, as Wittgenstein would say, is not based on agreement concerning opinions but on agreement in form of life. My certainty, my commitment, is shown in what I have written throughout this volume. My writing shows not what science 'really' is (whatever that would mean); instead, it shows my own mode of speaking, my discourse. My writing exemplifies my version of good speech. Nothing I have said is intended to be a concrete description of scientific practice; my discussions and classifications do not picture anything. No, they are features of my commitment—of my theorising. This does not mean, of course, that I have produced this volume from the position of the solitary inquirer. My text shows my commitment to a particular version of authoritative speech and theorising, to a particular mode of existence, to a way of living my life.

My concern in this volume is not with the reality of objects, say scientific practice, but with ways of seeing that provide for such a reality. To theorise, as I have throughout this volume, is to show the world in a form in which it has meaning *for me*. Theorising always represents a moral and political commitment. I choose not to play a language-game where demonstration, correct procedure, scientific method, and the like, guarantee that 'anyone' who follows the rules of 'good' scientific practice will reach the same conclusions, that is, will convey nature's message in an identical manner. To the contrary, I elect to show my commitment, my self, my authorship, my responsibility. Through my theorising, I display a possible version of science and scientific practice that has meaning for me. Wittgenstein writes: 'My life consists in my being content to accept many things.'[85] So it is with the contents of this book. Somewhere justification comes to an end. Let it end here. My spade is turned.

Notes

Preface

1. Robert K. Merton, 'Paradigm for the Sociology of Knowledge', in James E. Curtis and John W. Petras (eds), *The Sociology of Knowledge* (New York: Praeger, 1970) pp. 342–73.
2. John Schaar, 'Legitimacy in the Modern State', in Philip Green and Sanford Levinson (eds), *Power and Community* (New York: Random House, 1970) p. 279.
3. Ibid., p. 292.
4. Alvin W. Gouldner, *The Coming Crisis of Western Sociology* (New York: Basic Books, 1970).
5. Hannah Pitkin, *Wittgenstein and Justice* (Berkeley and Los Angeles: University of California Press, 1972).
6. Peter Winch, *The Idea of a Social Science* (New York: Humanities Press, 1958).

1 Wittgenstein the Man

1. Quoted in M. O'C. Drury, *The Danger of Words* (London: Routledge & Kegan Paul, 1973) p. xiv.
2. Alvin W. Gouldner, *The Coming Crisis of Western Sociology* (New York: Basic Books, 1970).
3. Ibid.; Jürgen Habermas, *Knowledge and Human Interests* (Boston: Beacon Press, 1971); Aaron V. Cicourel, *Method and Measurement in Sociology* (New York: Free Press, 1964).
4. Thomas S. Kuhn, *The Structure of Scientific Revolutions*, second edition (Chicago: University of Chicago Press, 1972); Michael Polanyi, *Personal Knowledge* (New York: Harper & Row, 1964); Paul K. Feyerabend, 'Against Method: Outline of an Anarchistic Theory of Knowledge', *Minnesota Studies in the Philosophy of Science*, Vol. 4 (Minneapolis: University of Minnesota Press, 1970) pp. 17–130; Stephen Toulmin, *Human Understanding*, vol. 1 (Oxford: Oxford University Press, 1972).
5. There is very little available concerning Wittgenstein's personal life. Among the few books that have him as their central focus, the best are: Paul Engelmann, *Letters from Ludwig Wittgenstein with a Memoir* (Oxford: Basil Blackwell, 1967); Norman Malcolm, *Ludwig Wittgenstein: A Memoir* (Oxford: Oxford University Press, 1967); Allan Janik and Stephen Toulmin, *Wittgenstein's Vienna* (New York: Simon and Schuster, 1973); Georg Henrik von Wright, 'A Biographical Sketch', in Malcom, op. cit.;

William Warren Bartley III, *Wittgenstein* (Philadelphia: J. B. Lippincott, 1973); and Bernhard Leitner, *The Architecture of Ludwig Wittgenstein* (Halifax, Nova Scotia: The Press of the Nova Scotia College of Art and Design, 1973). I draw heavily on these books throughout this chapter.

6. von Wright, op. cit., p. 6.

7. Quoted in Leitner, op. cit., p. 18.

8. Janik and Toulmin, op. cit.

9. Quoted in Leitner, op. cit., p. 18.

10. Quoted in Ved Mehta, *The Fly and the Fly-Bottle* (London: Weidenfeld and Nicolson, 1963). See also Bertrand Russell, *The Autobiography of Bertrand Russell* (London George Allen and Unwin Ltd., 1968) p. 99.

11. Russell, op. cit., p. 99.

12. Henry David Thoreau, *Walden* (New York: New American Library, 1960) pp. 14–15.

13. Quoted in Mehta, op. cit., p. 41.

14. Malcolm, op. cit., p. 39.

15. Bartley, op. cit.

16. Leitner, op. cit., p. 19.

17. Bartley, op. cit., p. 117.

18. Ibid., p. 126.

19. Ibid.

20. Engelmann, op. cit., letters 21 and 41. It also seems likely that another source of Wittgenstein's anguish was his apparent homosexuality, about which he was extremely fearful and ashamed. Several years earlier he had written to Engelmann (op. cit., p. 32) 'Things have gone utterly miserably for me lately. Of course, only because of my own baseness and rottenness. I have continually thought about taking my own life, and now too this thought still haunts me. *I have sunk to the bottom.* May you never be in that position!' Bartley, op. cit., reports that throughout these years Wittgenstein would seek out situations where he was removed from the temptations of easy and casual relationships with street youths. This may of course have been a factor in his decision to become a schoolteacher in isolated Austrian villages.

21. Leo Tolstoy, *A Confession* (London: Oxford University Press, 1967) p. 24.

22. Ibid., pp. 17–18.

23. Ibid., p. 18.

24. Bartley, op. cit., p. 133.

25. Quoted in Leitner, op. cit., p. 20. See also Bernhard Leitner, 'Wittgenstein's Architecture', *Art Form* (February 1970) p. 61.

26. P. A. Schilpp (ed.), *The Philosophy of Rudolf Carnap*, vol. 11 of the Library of Living Philosophers (La Salle, Ill.: The Open Court Publishing Company, 1963) pp. 25–6.

27. Quoted in Janik and Toulmin, op. cit., p. 20.

28. Malcolm, op. cit., pp. 24–5.

29. Janik and Toulmin, op. cit., p. 205.

30. Malcom, op. cit., p. 36.

31. F. R. Leavis, 'Memories of Wittgenstein', *The Human World* 10 (1973) p. 66.

32. Ibid., pp. 66, 70.
33. Engelmann, op. cit., p. 109.
34. Malcom, op. cit., p. 36.
35. Janik and Toulmin, op. cit., p. 27.
36. Ibid., p. 16.
37. Erich Heller, *The Disinherited Mind* (London: Bowes and Bowes, 1971) p. 242.
38. Janik and Toulmin, op. cit., p. 65.
39. Quoted in ibid., p. 89.
40. Heller, op. cit., p. 89.
41. Quoted in Janik and Toulmin, op. cit., p. 79.
42. Ibid., p. 117.
43. Especially influential here was the work of the journalist Fritz Mauthner. See Janik and Toulmin, op. cit., p. 128.
44. Ibid., p. 168.
45. Ludwig Wittgenstein, *Philosophical Investigations* (New York: Macmillan, 1953) paragraph 255.
46. Ludwig Wittgenstein, *Remarks on the Foundation of Mathematics* (Cambridge, Mass.: MIT Press, 1967) section II paragraph 4.
47. Ibid., section IV paragraph 53.
48. Quoted in Janik and Toulmin, op. cit., p. 192.
49. Malcolm, op. cit., p. 41.

2   The 'Early' and 'Later' Wittgenstein

1. Quoted in M. O'C. Drury, *The Danger of Words* (London: Routledge & Kegan Paul, 1973) pp. ix–x.
2. Ludwig Wittgenstein, *Notebooks 1914–1916* (Oxford: Basil Blackwell, 1961) p. 62. Throughout this volume I will refer to Wittgenstein's works in the following manner: *Notebooks 1914–1916* as NB, followed by page number; *The Blue and Brown Books* (New York: Harper Torchbook, 1958), BB, followed by page number; *Lectures and Conversations* (Berkeley and Los Angeles: University of California Press, 1972), LC, followed by page number; *On Certainty* (Oxford: Basil Blackwell, 1969), OC, followed by paragraph number; *Philosophical Grammar* (Oxford: Basil Blackwell, 1974), PG, followed by page number; *Philosophical Investigations* (New York: Macmillan, 1953), PI, Part I, followed by paragraph number; Part II, followed by page number; *Remarks on the Foundations of Mathematics* (Cambridge, Mass.: MIT Press, 1967), RFM, followed by section and paragraph numbers; *Tractatus Logico-Philosophicus* (New York: Humanities Press, 1961), TLP, followed by sentence number; *Zettel* (Berkeley and Los Angeles: University of California Press, 1967) Z, followed by paragraph number.
3. NB, p. 53.
4. TLP, 1.
5. Ibid., 2.
6. Ibid., 2.06.
7. Ibid., 2.1, 2.12.

8. Ibid., 3.141.
9. Ibid., 3.202, 3.21.
10. Ibid., 3.203, 3.22.
11. Ibid., 4.0311.
12. Ibid., 2.18, 2.161, 2.15.
13. Ibid., 2.14.
14. Georg Henrik von Wright, 'A Biographical Sketch', in Norman Malcom, *Ludwi*
Wittgenstein: A Memoir (Oxford: Oxford University Press, 1967) pp. 7–8.
15. TLP, 4.011.
16. Ibid., 4.014.
17. Ibid., 4.021.
18. Ibid., 2.223, 2.224, 2.225.
19. Ibid., 4.31–4.45, 5.101.
20. Ibid., 4.31.
21. Quoted in G. E. M. Anscombe, *An Introduction to Wittgenstein's Tractatus* (London
Hutchinson University Library, 1959) p. 161.
22. TLP, 4.022.
23. Ibid., 4.12.
24. Ibid., 4.121.
25. Ibid., 4.1212.
26. Ibid., 5.6.
27. PI, p. x.
28. Malcom, op. cit., p. 69.
29. PI, p. ix.
30. Ibid., 1.
31. Quoted in ibid., 1.
32. Ibid., 1.
33. Ibid., 3.
34. Ibid., 27.
35. Ibid., 43.
36. Ibid., 23.
37. Ibid., 138.
38. Ibid., 116.
39. Ibid., 19.
40. Ibid., p. 251.
41. Ibid., p. 226.
42. Ibid., 23.
43. Ibid., 27.
44. Ibid., 288.
45. Ibid., p. 180.
46. Ibid., 654.
47. Ibid., 249.
48. Ibid., p. 224.
49. Z, 332.
50. BB, p. 81.

51. Quoted in Harold Morick (ed.), *Wittgenstein and the Problem of Other Minds* (New York: McGraw-Hill, 1967) p. 177.
52. BB, p. 17.
53. PI, 7.
54. Ibid., 66.
55. Ibid., 66–7.
56. Ibid., 7.
57. Ibid., 208.
58. LC, pp. 1–2.
59. PI, 208.
60. LC, p. 3.
61. NB, p. 181.
62. BB, p. 103.
63. LC, p. 2.
64. PI, 284.
65. Ibid., 250.
66. Ibid., 23.
67. Ibid., 25.
68. Ibid., 415.
69. Allan Janik and Stephen Toulmin, *Wittgenstein's Vienna* (New York: Simon and Schuster, 1973) p. 228.
70. PI, 251.
71. Ibid.
72. Ibid., 230; italics added.
73. Ibid., 432.
74. Ibid., 53.
75. Ibid., 225.
76. RFM, V: 32.
77. PI, 185.
78. Ibid., 145.
79. Stanley Cavell, *Must We Mean What We Say?* (New York: Charles Scribner's Sons, 1969) p. 52.
80. Ibid.
81. BB, p. 90.
82. Stanley Cavell, 'Existentialism and Analytic Philosophy', *Daedalus*, 93 (1964) p. 964.
83. PI, 371.
84. Ibid., 372.
85. BB, p. 25.
86. Hannah Fenichel Pitkin, *Wittgenstein and Justice* (Berkeley and Los Angeles: University of California Press, 1972) p. 120.
87. Eugene A. Nida, 'Principles of Translation as Exemplified by Bible Translations', in Reuben A. Brower (ed.), *On Translation* (Cambridge: Harvard University Press, 1959) p. 13.
88. PI, p. 212.

89. Ibid., 90.
90. BB, p. 16.
91. PI, 23.
92. Ibid., 345.
93. Ibid., 351.
94. Ibid., 354; italics added.
95. Ibid., 355.
96. BB, p. 24.
97. PI, 454.
98. Pitkin, op. cit., p. 123.
99. Italo Calvino, *Cosmicomics* (New York: Collier Books, 1970) p. 60.
100. Ibid., pp. 59–60.
101. Ibid., p. 100.
102. Ibid., p. 52.
103. An especially useful discussion of the private language problem can be found in Esa Itkonen, *Linguistics and Metascience* (Kokemäki, Finland: Societas Philosophica et Phaenomenologica, 1974).
104. PI, 258.
105. Ibid., 261.
106. Ibid., 202.
107. PG, pp. 44–5.
108. Ibid., p. 62.
109. Ibid., p. 46.
110. Ibid., p. 64.
111. PI, 153.
112. Ibid., 180.
113. Ibid., 34.
114. Ibid., 59.
115. Ibid., p. x.
116. Ibid., 133.
117. Ibid., 2, 48.
118. Ibid., 122.
119. Ibid., p. 230.
120. Cavell (1969), op. cit., p. 179.
121. LC, p. 33.
122. Ibid., pp. 37, 41.
123. Cavell (1969), op. cit., pp. 182–4.

3 Two Images of Science

1. Useful discussions of positivism can be found in the following books: John Passmore, *A Hundred Years of Philosophy* (Harmondsworth: Penguin Books, 1970); A. J. Ayer (ed.), *Logical Positivism* (New York: Free Press, 1966); E. A. Burtt, *In Search of Philosophical Understanding* (New York: Mentor Books, 1967); Leszak Kolakowski, *Positivist Philo-*

sophy (Harmondsworth: Penguin Books, 1972); Jürgen Habermas, *Knowledge and Human Interests* (Boston: Beacon Press, 1971); R. Harré, *The Philosophies of Science* (Oxford: Oxford University Press, 1972).

2. Auguste Comte, *The Positivist Philosophy of Auguste Comte*, freely translated and condensed by Harriett Martineau (London: George Bell & Sons, 1896) pp. 28, 30, 38.

3. Robert A. Nisbet, 'The French Revolution and the Rise of Sociology', *American Journal of Sociology* 69 (1943) p. 327.

4. Emile Durkheim, *The Rules of Sociological Method* (New York: Free Press, 1938) p. 27.

5. Carl G. Hempel, *Philosophy of Natural Science* (Englewood Cliffs, N.J.: Prentice-Hall, 1966) p. 1.

6. Whitney Pope, 'Classic on Classic: Parsons' Interpretation of Durkheim', *American Sociological Review* 38 (1973) p. 413.

7. Durkheim, op. cit., p. 27.

8. Ibid., pp. 31, 35.

9. Ibid., p. 94.

10. Carl G. Hempel, 'Studies in the Logic of Explanation', in Carl G. Hempel (ed.), *Aspects of Scientific Explanation and Other Essays in the Philosophy of Science* (New York: Free Press, 1965) p. 253.

11. Hans Reichenbach, *The Rise of Scientific Discovery* (Berkeley: University of California Press, 1951) p. 158.

12. Sanford Labovitz and Robert Hagedorn, *Introduction to Social Research* (New York: McGraw-Hill, 1970) p. 3.

13. Robert K. Leik, *Methods, Logic, and Research in Sociology* (Indianapolis, Ind.: Bobbs-Merrill, 1972) p. 29.

14. Ernest Nagel, *The Structure of Science* (New York: Harcourt, Brace & World, 1963) p. 4.

15. Hans Reichenbach, *Experience and Prediction* (Chicago: University of Chicago Press, 1938).

16. Matilda White Riley, *Sociological Research* (New York: Harcourt, Brace & World, 1963) p. 4.

17. Labovitz and Hagedorn, op. cit., p. 1.

18. Neil J. Smelser, *Essays in Sociological Explanation* (Englewood Cliffs, N.J.: Prentice-Hall, 1968) p. 43.

19. Emile Durkheim, *Suicide* (Glencoe, Ill.: Free Press, 1951) p. 325.

20. Durkheim (1938), op. cit., of course, emphasised the necessity of explaining social facts in terms of other social facts: '*The determining cause of a social fact should be sought among the social facts preceding it . . .* ' (p. 1).

21. Joseph Ben-David, *The Scientist's Role in Society* (Englewood Cliffs, N.J.: Prentice-Hall, 1971) p. 1.

22. John Ziman, *Public Knowledge* (Cambridge: Cambridge University Press, 1968) p. 135.

23. Rolf Klima, 'Scientific Knowledge and Social Control in Science,' in Richard Whitley (ed.), *Social Processes of Scientific Development* (London: Routledge & Kegan Paul, 1974) p. 97.

24. Ben-David, op. cit.; Bernard Barber, 'The Sociology of Science,' in David L. Sills (ed.), *International Encyclopedia of the Social Sciences*, vol. 14 (New York: Macmillan, 1968) pp. 92–101.

25. Joseph Ben-David, 'Reflections on the State of Sociological Theory and the Sociological Community', paper read at Conference of the Research Committee of the Sociology of Science of the International Sociological Association, London (1972) p. 4.

26. Robert K. Merton, *The Sociology of Science* (Chicago: University of Chicago Press, 1973) p. 270; italics added.

27. Norwood Russell Hanson, *Patterns of Discovery* (Cambridge University Press, 1958) p. 98. Clearly there is a similarity here to some of Wittgenstein's ideas in the *Philosophical Investigations*.

28. Thomas S. Kuhn, *The Structure of Scientific Revolutions* (Chicago: University of Chicago Press, 1962) p. x.

29. Ibid., p. 10.

30. Ibid.

31. Ibid., p. 108.

32. Ibid., p. 102.

33. Thomas S. Kuhn, *The Structure of Scientific Revolutions*, second edition (Chicago: University of Chicago Press, 1970) p. 192.

34. Paul K. Feyerabend, 'Explanation, Reduction, and Empiricism', in H. Feigl and G. Maxwell (eds), *Minnesota Studies in the Philosophy of Science*, vol. 3 (Minneapolis: University of Minnesota Press, 1962) p. 29.

35. Ibid., pp. 50–1.

36. Kuhn (1962), op. cit., p. 110.

37. Ibid., pp. 17–18.

38. Ibid., p. 120.

39. Thomas S. Kuhn 'Reflections on my Critics', in Imre Lakatos and Alan Musgrave (eds), *Criticism and the Growth of Knowledge* (Cambridge: Cambridge University Press, 1970) p. 240.

40. Kuhn (1962), op. cit., p. 147.

41. Ibid., p. 150.

42. Ibid., p. 119.

43. Kuhn (1970), op. cit., p. 264.

44. Ibid., p. 253.

45. Ibid., p. 254.

46. Karl Mannheim, *Ideology and Utopia* (London: Routledge & Kegan Paul, 1972) p. 243.

47. Kuhn (1962), op. cit., p. 121.

48. Mannheim, op. cit., p. 77.

49. Ibid., p. 250.

50. C. Wright Mills, *Power, Politics, and People* (ed. Irving Louis Horowitz) (New York: Ballantine Books, 1963) p. 247.

51. Ibid., p. 433.

52. Ibid., p. 434.

53. Ibid., p. 455.
54. Ibid., pp. 459–60.
55. Karl R. Popper, 'Normal Science and its Dangers', in Lakatos and Musgrave, op. cit., p. 56.
56. Kuhn (1970), op. cit., p. 265.
57. TLP, 342.

4 Relativism and Wittgenstein

1. Karl Mannheim, *Essays on the Sociology of Knowledge* (London: Routledge & Kegan Paul, 1952) p. 184.
2. Ibid., p. 186.
3. Karl Mannheim, *Ideology and Utopia* (London: Routledge & Kegan Paul, 1972) p. 86.
4. Mannheim (1952), op. cit., p. 190.
5. Mannheim (1972), op. cit., p. 77.
6. Ibid., p. 250.
7. Ibid., p. 80.
8. Ibid., p. 262.
9. Alexander von Schelting, 'Review of *Ideology and Utopia*', *American Sociological Review* 1 (1936) pp. 664–74; Howard Becker, 'Review of *Ideology and Utopia*', *American Sociological Review* 3 (1938) pp. 260–2.
10. Robert K. Merton, *The Sociology of Science* (Chicago: University of Chicago Press, 1973) p. 503.
11. Ibid.
12. Vergil G. Hinshaw, 'Epistemological Relativism and the Sociology of Knowledge', *Philosophy of Science* 15 (1948) p. 4.
13. C. Wright Mills, *Power, Politics, and People* (ed. Irving Louis Horowitz) (New York: Ballantine Books, 1963) p. 455.
14. Peter L. Berger and Thomas Luckmann, *The Social Construction of Reality* (Garden City, N.Y.: Doubleday, 1967) pp. 14–15.
15. Ibid., p. 13.
16. Karl R. Popper, *The Open Society and Its Enemies*, vol. 2 (New York: Harper Torchbooks, 1963) pp. 216–17.
17. Ibid., p. 217.
18. Robert K. Merton, *Science, Technology and Society in Seventeenth Century England* (New York: Harper Torchbooks, 1970) (originally published in 1938).
19. Thomas S. Kuhn, *The Structure of Scientific Revolutions* (Chicago: University of Chicago Press, 1962) p. 108.
20. Ibid., p. 170.
21. Israel Scheffler, *Science and Subjectivity* (Indianapolis, Ind.: Bobbs-Merrill, 1967) p. 17.
22. Ibid., p. 19.
23. Roger Trigg, *Reason and Commitment* (Cambridge: Cambridge University Press, 1973).

24. PI, 24.
25. Ibid., 466.
26. Ibid., 467.
27. Ibid., 25.
28. Ibid., 174.
29. Z, 532–4.
30. Ibid., 540–1.
31. PI, 174.
32. Ibid., p. 230.
33. Z, 383.
34. Ibid., 384.
35. Ibid., 388.
36. Thomas S. Kuhn, 'Reflections on my Critics', in Lakatos and Musgrave, op. cit., p. 273.
37. Z, 350.
38. OC, 204.
39. Z, 352.
40. Ibid., 357.
41. Ibid., 358.
42. Ibid., 364.
43. PI, 68–9.
44. RFM, 4.
45. PI, p. 200.
46. Ibid., 494.
47. Ibid., 120.
48. Alfred Schutz, *Phenomenology of the Social World* (London: Heinemann Educational Books, 1972) p. 32.
49. Kuhn (1962), op. cit., pp. 44–5.
50. Ibid., p. 45.
51. Ibid., pp. 45–6.
52. PI, 65.
53. John Ziman, *Public Knowledge* (Cambridge: Cambridge University Press, 1968) p. 9.
54. OC, 191–2.

5   Paradigms and Incommensurability

1. Thomas S. Kuhn, *The Structure of Scientific Revolutions*, second edition (Chicago: University of Chicago Press, 1970) p. 267.
2. Paul K. Feyerabend, 'Consolations for the Specialist', in Imre Lakatos and Alan Musgrave (eds), *Criticism and the Growth of Knowledge* (Cambridge: Cambridge University Press, 1970) p. 219.
3. Ibid., p. 227.
4. Thomas S. Kuhn, *The Structure of Scientific Revolutions* (Chicago: University of Chicago Press, 1962) p. 10.

5. Ibid.
6. Derek L. Phillips, *Abandoning Method* (San Francisco and London: Jossey-Bass, 1973).
7. Kuhn (1962), op. cit., p. 102.
8. Ibid., p. 149.
9. Ibid.
10. Ibid.
11. Ibid., p. 79.
12. Ibid., p. 85.
13. Ibid., p. 117.
14. Michael Dummett, 'Wittgenstein's Philosophy of Mathematics', *The Philosophical Review* 68 (1959) p. 331.
15. Ibid., p. 333.
16. RFM, I: 116.
17. Ibid., I: 152.
18. Ibid., I: 141.
19. Ibid., V: 26.
20. Ibid., I: 64.
21. Ibid., V: 15.
22. Ibid., V: 18.
23. PI, 23.
24. RFM, V: 15.
25. PI, II: 230.
26. Kuhn (1962), op. cit., p. 110.
27. PI, II: 200.
28. Ibid., II: 212.
29. C. Wright Mills, *Power, Politics, and People* (ed. Irving Louis Horowitz) (New York: Ballantine Books, 1963) p. 460.
30. Kuhn (1962), op. cit., p. 120.
31. Norwood Russell Hanson, *Patterns of Discovery* (Cambridge: Cambridge University Press, 1958) p. 5.
32. Ibid., pp. 15–16.
33. Ibid., p. 17.
34. Kuhn (1962) op. cit., p. 121.
35. Ibid., p. 149.
36. Popper, in Lakatos and Musgrave, op. cit., p. 56.
37. Kuhn (1962), op. cit., pp. 121–2.
38. Jerome S. Bruner and A. L. Minturn, 'Perceptual Identification and Perceptual Organization', *Journal of General Psychology* 53 (1955) pp. 21–8.
39. Jerome S. Bruner and Cecile C. Goodman, 'Value and Need as Organizing Factors in Perception', *Journal of Abnormal and Social Psychology* 42 (1947) pp. 33–44. See also Jerome S. Bruner, *Beyond the Information Given* (New York: Norton, 1973).
40. Kuhn (1962), op. cit., p. 110; italics added.
41. Ibid., p. 111.
42. See, for example, Bruner (1973), op. cit.; U. Neisser, *Cognitive Psychology* (New

York: Appleton-Century-Crofts, 1967); Jean Piaget, *On the Development of Memory and Identity*, Heinz Warner Lecture Series, vol. 2 (Worcester, Mass.: Clark University Press, 1967).
43. Kuhn (1962), op. cit., p. 114.
44. Kuhn (1970), op. cit., p. 3; italics added.
45. Kuhn (1962), op. cit., p. 10.
46. Ibid., p. 108.
47. Stephen Toulmin, *Human Understanding*, vol. 1 (Oxford: Oxford University Press, 1972) p. 103.
48. Kuhn (1962), op. cit., pp. 92–3.
49. Ibid., p. 1.
50. Kuhn (1970), op. cit., p. 4.
51. Kuhn (1962), op. cit., p. 3.
52. Ibid., p. xi.
53. Ibid., p. vii.
54. Ibid.
55. Ibid., p. 5.

6   The Social Nature of Mathematics

1. RFM, I: 167.
2. Karl Mannheim, *Ideology and Utopia* (London: Routledge & Kegan Paul, 1972) p. 263.
3. C. Wright Mills, *Power, Politics and People* (ed. Irving Louis Horowitz) (New York: Ballantine Books, 1963).
4. Gottlob Frege, *The Foundations of Arithmetic* (trans. J. L. Austin), second edition (Oxford: Basil Blackwell, 1953) p. vii.
5. G. H. Hardy, *A Mathematician's Apology* (Cambridge: Cambridge University Press, 1941) pp. 63–4.
6. Morris Cohen, *Reason and Nature* (Glencoe, Ill.: Free Press, 1953) p. 193.
7. Alfred Schutz, 'Subjective and Objective Meaning', in Anthony Giddens (ed.), *Positivism and Sociology* (London: Heinemann Educational Books, 1974) pp. 42–3.
8. Gerard De Gré, 'The Sociology of Knowledge and the Problem of Truth', in James E. Curtis and John W. Petras (eds), *The Sociology of Knowledge* (New York: Praeger, 1970) pp. 664–5.
9. Ian D. Currie, 'The Sapir–Whorf Hypothesis', ibid., pp. 403–21; Stephen Toulmin, *The Uses of Argument* (Cambridge: Cambridge University Press, 1958).
10. Stephen Toulmin, *Human Understanding*, vol. 1 (Oxford: Oxford University Press, 1972) pp. 251–2.
11. Marcel Granet, *La Pensée Chinoise* (Paris: La Renaissance du Livre, 1934).
12. David Bloor, 'Wittgenstein and Mannheim on the Sociology of Mathematics', *Studies in History and Philosophy of Science* 2 (1973) pp. 173–91. I draw heavily on this excellent paper throughout the chapter.
13. Ibid., p. 178.
14. Ibid.

15. Mannheim, op. cit., pp. 239–40.
16. Ibid.
17. Bloor, op. cit., p. 180.
18. Ibid., p. 181.
19. Ibid., p. 182.
20. PI, p. 225.
21. RFM, V: 40.
22. PI, 233.
23. Bloor, op. cit., p. 184.
24. RFM, I: 2.
25. PI, 186.
26. Ibid., 213.
27. RFM, I: 4.
28. PI, 198.
29. Ibid., 199.
30. RFM, I: 63.
31. Ibid., I: 2.
32. Bloor, op. cit., p. 184.
33. PI, 150.
34. Ibid., p. 209.
35. RFM, V: 33.
36. Ibid., V: 45.
37. Ibid.
38. Ibid., I: 5.
39. Ibid., V: 48.
40. Ibid., I: 155.
41. Ibid., II: 84.
42. OC, 204.
43. PI, 185.
44. Ibid., 201.
45. Ibid., 208.
46. Z, 371.
47. OC, 229.
48. Ibid., 207.
49. Ibid., 208.
50. Ibid., 209.
51. Ibid., 411.
52. RFM, V: I.
53. PI, 142.
54. Z, 351.
55. Ibid., 352.
56. Ibid., 354.
57. Ibid., 355.
58. PI, 230.
59. Bloor, op. cit.

60. Ibid., p. 186.
61. O. Neugebauer, *The Exact Sciences in Antiquity* (Princeton, N.J.: Princeton University Press, 1952).
62. RFM, I: 116.
63. Ibid.
64. Ibid., II: 81.
65. Ibid., II: 74.
66. Ibid., V: 28.
67. PI, 370–4.
68. This idea is set forth by Bloor, op. cit., in a footnote. I am trying here to expand on his observation.
69. Peter Winch, *The Idea of a Social Science* (New York: Humanities Press, 1958) p. 43.
70. Ibid., p. 133.
71. Ibid., p. 44.
72. Ibid., p. 85.
73. Ibid., p. 86.
74. Ibid., p. 113.
75. Ibid., p. 117.
76. Ibid., p. 115.
77. Ibid., p. 73.

7 The Demarcation Problem in Science

1. Z, 438.
2. Imre Lakatos, untitled paper, read at seminar on 'Programmes of Knowledge and Growth in Science', Europäisches Forum, Albach, Austria (1973).
3. Paul K. Feyerabend, 'Against Method: Outline of an Anarchistic Theory of Knowledge', *Minnesota Studies in the Philosophy of Science*, vol. 4 (Minneapolis: University of Minnesota Press, 1970) pp. 17–130.
4. Ibid., p. 106.
5. Lakatos, op. cit., p. 4.
6. Karl R. Popper, *Objective Knowledge* (Oxford: Oxford University Press, 1973) p. 106.
7. Ibid., p. 109.
8. Ibid., pp. 108–9.
9. Ibid., p. 115.
10. Ibid., p. 116.
11. Lakatos, op. cit., p. 8.
12. Michael Polanyi, *Personal Knowledge* (New York: Harper & Row, 1964).
13. Lakatos, op. cit., p. 11.
14. Ibid., p. 12.
15. Ibid.
16. Polanyi, op. cit., p. 16.
17. Imre Lakatos, 'History of Science and its Rational Reconstructions', *Boston Studies in the Philosophy of Science* 8 (1971) p. 92.

18. Lakatos (1973), op. cit., pp. 12–13.
19. Polanyi, op. cit., p. ix.
20. Ibid., p. 165.
21. Ibid.
22. Ibid., p. 54.
23. Ibid., p. x.
24. Ibid., p. 216.
25. Lakatos (1971), op. cit., p. 105.
26. Ibid., p. 126.
27. Lakatos (1973), op. cit., p. 7.
28. Ibid.
29. Ibid., p. 17.
30. Ibid., p. 16.
31. Ibid., pp. 17–18.
32. Polanyi, op. cit., p. 218.
33. Thomas S. Kuhn, *The Structure of Scientific Revolutions* (Chicago: University of Chicago Press, 1972); Stephen Toulmin, *Human Understanding*, vol. 1 (Oxford: Oxford University Press, 1972).
34. Lakatos (1973), op. cit., p. 18.
35. Ibid.
36. Ibid., p. 22.
37. Ibid.
38. Ian Mitroff, *The Subjective Side of Science* (New York: Elsevier, 1974).
39. John Ziman, *Public Knowledge* (Cambridge: Cambridge University Press, 1968) p. 9.
40. Karl R. Popper, *Conjectures and Refutations* (London: Routledge & Kegan Paul, 1963) p. 57.
41. Thomas S. Kuhn 'Reflections on my Critics', in Imre Lakatos and Alan Musgrave (eds), *Criticism and the Growth of Knowledge* (Cambridge: Cambridge University Press, 1970) pp. 237–8.
42. Karl R. Popper, *The Open Society and Its Enemies*, vol. 2 (New York: Harper Torchbooks, 1963) p. 212.
43. Karl R. Popper, 'Normal Science and its Dangers', in Lakatos and Musgrave, op. cit., pp. 57–8.
44. Imre Lakatos, 'Falsification and the Methodology of Scientific Research Programmes', in Lakatos and Musgrave, op. cit., p. 93; first set of italics added.
45. Ibid., p. 178; italics in original.
46. Popper, *Conjectures and Refutations*, op. cit., p. 356.
47. Popper, *The Open Society and its Enemies*, op. cit., p. 227.
48. Ibid., pp. 233–4.
49. Ibid., p. 234.
50. Ibid., p. 225.
51. C. Wright Mills, *Power, Politics, and People* (ed. Irving Louis Horowitz) (New York: Ballantine Books, 1963) p. 427.
52. Feyerabend, op. cit.

238   WITTGENSTEIN AND SCIENTIFIC KNOWLEDGE

53. Popper himself has experienced this, as we shall see later.
54. Of course, nature does set limits here, as mentioned in earlier chapters.
55. Popper, *The Open Society and its Enemies*, op. cit., p. 225.
56. Ibid., p. 151.
57. Ibid.
58. Karl R. Popper, 'Autobiography', in Paul A. Schilpp (ed.), *The Philosophy of Karl Popper* (La Salle, Ill.: The Library of Living Philosophers, 1974) p. 95.
59. Robert K. Merton, *Social Theory and Social Structure* (Glencoe, Ill.: Free Press, 1963) p. 554.
60. Lakatos (1973), op. cit., p. 17.
61. Karl R. Popper, *The Logic of Scientific Discovery* (New York: Harper & Row, 1965) p. 104.
62. Ibid.
63. Ibid.

8   Possibilities and Persuasion

1. PI, 90.
2. LC, p. 27.
3. Paul K. Feyerabend, 'Against Method: Outline of an Anarchistic Theory of Knowledge', *Minnesota Studies in the Philosophy of Science*, vol. 4 (Minneapolis: University of Minnesota Press, 1970) p. 21.
4. R. G. A. Dolby, 'The Sociology of Knowledge in Natural Science', in Barry Barnes (ed.), *Sociology of Science* (Harmondsworth: Penguin Books, 1972) p. 316.
5. Feyerabend, op. cit., p. 26.
6. PI, 90.
7. Ibid., 520.
8. See G. Holton, *Introduction to Concepts and Theories in Physical Science* (Reading, Mass.: Addison-Wesley, 1952).
9. C. Itlis, 'The Leibnitzian–Newtonian Debates: Natural Philosophy and Social Psychology', *The British Journal for the History of Science* 4 (1973) p. 343.
10. OC, p. 185.
11. David L. Hull, *Darwin and his Critics* (Cambridge, Mass.: Harvard University Press, 1973).
12. Johan Galtung, *Theories and Methods of Social Research* (New York: Columbia University Press, 1968) p. 459.
13. With regard to the survival of political theories, see Sheldon S. Wolin, 'Paradigms and Political Theories', in Preston King and B. C. Parekh (eds), *Politics and Experience* (Cambridge: Cambridge University Press, 1968) pp. 125–52.
14. LC, p. 25.
15. Ibid.
16. Ibid., p. 27.
17. Ibid., pp. 50–1.
18. Ibid.

19. Ibid., p. 26.
20. Ian L. Mitroff, *The Subjective Side of Science* (Amsterdam and New York: Elsevier Publishing Company, 1974).
21. Ibid., p. 65.
22. Ibid., p. 70.
23. Ibid., p. 68.
24. C. Kittel, W. D. Knight and M. A. Ruderman, *The Berkeley Physics Course*, vol. 1, *Mechanics* (New York: McGraw-Hill, 1962) p. 4.
25. Daniel Bell, *The Reforming of General Education* (New York: Doubleday Anchor, 1968) p. 243.
26. Ibid., p. 245.
27. A. R. Hall, quoted in E. McMullin (ed.), *Galileo: Man of Science* (New York: Basic Books, 1967) p. 70.
28. Alan F. Blum, 'The Right Conduct of Sociology', unpublished paper (1970).
29. Ch. Perelman and L. Olbrechts-Tyteca, *The New Rhetoric* (Notre Dame, Ind.: University of Notre Dame Press, 1971) p. 120.
30. Ch. Perelman, *The Idea of Justice and the Problem of Argument* (London: Routledge & Kegan Paul, 1963).
31. Ibid., p. 101.
32. Ibid.
33. Perelman and Olbrechts-Tyteca, op. cit., p. 62.
34. Plato, *The Collected Dialogues* (ed. E. Hamilton and H. Cairns) (Princeton: University Press, 1969) *Georgias* 458e–459c.
35. Ibid., 463a–c.
36. John Fowles, *The Aristos* (London: Pan Books, 1968) p. 206.
37. Feyerabend, op. cit., pp. 96–7.
38. Ibid., p. 97.
39. Charles Darwin, *On the Origin of Species*, facsimile of first edition, with introduction by E. Mayr (Cambridge, Mass.: Harvard University Press, 1966) p. 1.
40. Quoted in A. J. Ayer (ed.), *Logical Positivism* (New York: Free Press, 1966) pp. 359–60.
41. Vilfredo Pareto, *The Mind and Society* (New York: Harcourt, Brace & Co., 1935) p. 1205.
42. Søren Kierkegaard, *The Point of View for My Work as An Author* (New York: Harper Torchbooks, 1962) p. 35.
43. Ibid., p. 40.
44. Ibid., p. 41.
45. Feyerabend, op. cit., p. 23.
46. Ibid., p. 111.
47. Ian L. Mitroff, 'Norms and Counter-Norms in a Select Group of the Apollo Moon Scientists: a Case Study of the Ambivalence of Scientists', *American Sociological Review* 39 (1974) p. 587.
48. Ibid., p. 588.
49. Ibid., pp. 588–9.
50. Ibid., p. 589.

51. See for example S. E. Asch, 'The Doctrine of Suggestion, Prestige and Imitation in Social Psychology', *Psychological Review* 55 (1948) pp. 250–76.

52. Samuel Beckett, *Three Novels* (New York: Grove Press, 1948) p. 19.

53. Roland Barthes, 'Authors and Writers', *New American Review* 13 (1971) p. 136.

54. Ibid., p. 139.

55. Ibid., pp. 139–40.

56. William H. Gass, 'In Terms of the Toenail: Fiction and Figures of Life', *New American Review* 10 (1970) pp. 55–6.

57. Ibid., p. 56.

58. Ibid., pp. 59–60.

59. Adam Smith, *An Inquiry into the Nature and Causes of the Wealth of Nations* (New York: Random House, 1937) p. 194.

60. Perelman and Olbrechts-Tyteca, op. cit., p. 514.

61. Quoted in John Hersey (ed.), *The Writer's Craft* (New York: Alfred A. Knopf, 1974) p. 16, from Joseph Conrad, *The Nigger of the Narcissus* (London: J. M. Dent & Sons, Ltd., 1897).

9 Doubt and Certainty

1. OC, 83.

2. PI, 217.

3. Harold Garfinkel, *Studies in Ethnomethodology* (Englewood Cliffs, N.J.: Prentice-Hall, 1967); Harvey Sachs, mimeographed lectures, University of California, Irvine (n.d.).

4. Garfinkel, op. cit., p. viii.

5. Ibid.; Thomas P. Wilson, 'Conceptions of Interaction and Forms of Sociological Explanation', *American Sociological Review* 35 (1970) p. 700.

6. I have discussed this at greater length elsewhere. Derek L. Phillips, *Abandoning Method* (San Francisco and London: Jossey-Bass, 1973). See also Paul Attewell, 'Ethno-methodology since Garfinkel', *Theory and Society* 1 (1974) pp. 179–210.

7. OC.

8. R. Descartes, *Philosophical Works of Descartes* (trans. E. S. Haldane and G. R. T. Ross), Dover edition, 2 volumes (London: Constable, 1955).

9. G. E. Moore, 'A Defence of Common Sense', reprinted in *Philosophical Papers* (London: Allen & Unwin, 1959) pp. 32–59.

10. Anthony Kenny, *Wittgenstein* (London: Allen Lane, 1973).

11. Ibid., p. 205.

12. OC, 323.

13. Ibid., 4.

14. Ibid., 120.

15. Ibid., 428.

16. Ibid., 114.

17. Ibid., 369.

18. Ibid., 456.

19. Ibid., 457.

20. Ibid., 450.
21. Ibid., 310–12.
22. Ibid., 160.
23. Ibid., 115.
24. Ibid., 519.
25. Ibid., 659.
26. Ibid., 70–1.
27. Ibid., 257.
28. Ibid., 138, 281.
29. Ibid., 102.
30. Ibid., 185.
31. Ibid., 406.
32. PI, 246.
33. OC, 272.
34. Ibid., 21.
35. Ibid., 504.
36. Ibid., 462.
37. Ibid., 591.
38. Ibid., 588.
39. Ibid., 487.
40. Ibid., 93.
41. Ibid., 84.
42. Ibid., 116.
43. Ibid., 112.
44. Ibid., 151.
45. Ibid., 94.
46. Ibid., 559.
47. Ibid., 95.
48. Ibid., 97.
49. Ibid., 99.
50. Ibid., 403.
51. Ibid., 558.
52. Ibid., 105.
53. PG, p. 55.
54. OC, 609.
55. Ibid., 262.
56. Ibid., 612.
57. Ibid., 108.
58. Ibid., 111.
59. NB, p. 55.
60. OC, 657.
61. Ibid., 512.
62. Noam Chomsky, *Aspects of the Theory of Syntax* (Cambridge: Mass.: MIT Press, 1965).
63. PI, 224–5.

64. Ibid., 242.
65. Z, 419.
66. Ibid., 545.
67. Ibid., 318.
68. OC, 140.
69. Ibid., 143.
70. Ibid., 160.
71. Ibid., 161.
72. Ibid., 166.
73. Ibid., 234.
74. Ibid., 191.
75. Ibid., 192.
76. Ibid., 110.
77. Ibid., 204.
78. Ibid., 603.
79. Ibid., 395.
80. Ibid., 426–7.
81. Ibid., 432.
82. Ibid., 54. Wittgenstein himself showed what he believed, what was important to him, by refusing to don the official costume prescribed for all candidates for a degree at Cambridge, and by refusing to dine at 'High Table' (because of the symbolic fact that the High Table itself was placed on a raised platform higher than the main floor of the dining hall where the undergraduates ate). This is reported in Allan Janik and Stephen Toulmin, *Wittgenstein's Vienna* (New York: Simon and Schuster, 1973) p. 205. More importantly, Wittgenstein showed what he felt about academic philosophy by giving it up altogether for several years.
83. PI, 217.
84. OC, 343.
85. Ibid., 344.

Index